Additional Praise for *Never Enough*

"Written with a reporter's eye, a parent's heart, and insights gleaned from leading experts in psychology and neuroscience, as well as heartbreaking and heartwarming wisdom from the parenting trenches, *Never Enough* is the book for our times. Journalist Jennifer Wallace offers a fresh and refreshing framework (with loads of practical advice) to help parents raise children in ways where healthy, happy, and successful aren't tradeoffs. Buy this book: Help your kids get what really matters."

—Ned Johnson, bestselling coauthor of *The Self-Driven Child*

"We are in the midst of a mental health crisis. *Never Enough* is a must-read wake-up call to society to reexamine our values and priorities. More than a book, this is the start of a movement we desperately need."

—Eve Rodsky, *New York Times* bestselling author of *Fair Play*

"I valued every page of this smart and urgent book. Jennifer Wallace is someone to be listened to, carefully, with highlighter handy. The next generation deserves it."   —Kelly Corrigan, bestselling author and host of the *Kelly Corrigan Wonders* podcast and *Tell Me More* on PBS

"Thoughtfully, expertly, and without judgment, Wallace guides readers through the stressful terrain of our achievement culture and offers a more emotionally intelligent route forward. *Never Enough* is a book for parents, schools, and communities, but it's more than that: it's a primer for living a rich, meaningful life."   —Robin Stern, PhD, cofounder and associate director of the Yale Center for Emotional Intelligence

"A humane and clear-eyed guide that deserves to be one of our new north stars for parenting."   —Richard Weissbourd, senior lecturer and director of the Making Caring Common Project at the Harvard Graduate School of Education

"In *Never Enough*, Jennifer Wallace takes on the challenge of translating important research meticulously and provides actionable ways to support our children's mental health with the critical construct of mattering. Mattering is one of the few constructs that is actually in our parental control and doing so is a light lift that has a major impact."
—Aliza Pressman, host of the *Raising Good Humans* podcast and cofounder of The Mount Sinai Parenting Center

"Toxic achievement culture gets in the way of parents offering unconditional and unwavering love and weakens our family relationships and harms our children. Jennifer Wallace has digested hundreds of studies and personal stories and distilled them into a powerful book that shares the ultimate truth: what young people need, what we all need, is to know we matter, unrelated to our resumes or trophies—to know we are enough as we are." —Kenneth R. Ginsburg, cofounder and director of the Center for Parent and Teen Communication at Children's Hospital of Philadelphia and author of *Building Resilience in Children and Teens*

"In this profound yet accessible book, Wallace has earned her place as one of the most important voices of her generation. A deep thinker on the critical issues facing modern parents, Wallace offers the antidote to the toxic achievement pressure that is facing kids, teens, young adults, and parents alike. *Never Enough* speaks to new parents straight through to empty nesters." —Lisa Heffernan, cofounder of Grown & Flown and *New York Times* bestselling author

"With impressive research, compassion, and clarity, Jennifer Wallace shows us how our current equation of raising kids to take our love and return it as achievement is a recipe for sorrow on both sides, and shows us how to readjust that equation so that joy and growth can begin."
—Lenore Skenazy, founder of the Free-Range Kids movement

"*Never Enough* has landed on my top-five list of most meaningful books for parents and caregivers of teens to read! Wallace offers practical antidotes to the toxic achievement culture that does serious harm to our youth. This book will help you see and activate your role in this work to help you show up for your teens." —Hina Talib, pediatrician and adolescent medicine specialist at the Atria Institute

Never Enough

Never Enough

When Achievement Culture
Becomes Toxic—
and What We Can Do About It

JENNIFER BREHENY WALLACE

PORTFOLIO ▪ PENGUIN

Portfolio / Penguin
An imprint of Penguin Random House LLC
penguinrandomhouse.com

Most Portfolio books are available at a discount when purchased in quantity
for sales promotions or corporate use. Special editions, which include personalized
covers, excerpts, and corporate imprints, can be created when purchased in
large quantities. For more information, please call (212) 572-2232 or e-mail
specialmarkets@penguinrandomhouse.com. Your local bookstore can also assist
with discounted bulk purchases using the Penguin Random House corporate
Business-to-Business program. For assistance in locating a participating retailer,
e-mail B2B@penguinrandomhouse.com.

Grateful acknowledgment is made for permission to reprint a modified version of the
table by Marty Rossmann under the new title "Age-Appropriate Chores" on page 188.

LIBRARY OF CONGRESS CATALOGING-IN-PUBLICATION DATA
Names: Wallace, Jennifer Breheny, author.
Title: Never enough : when achievement culture becomes toxic—
and what we can do about it / Jennifer Breheny Wallace.
Description: New York : Portfolio/Penguin, [2023] |
Includes bibliographical references and index.
Identifiers: LCCN 2022059938 (print) | LCCN 2022059939 (ebook) |
ISBN 9780593191866 (hardcover) | ISBN 9780593191873 (ebook)
Subjects: LCSH: Academic achievement—Psychological aspects. |
Achievement motivation in adolescence. | Performance in children. | Overachievement.
Classification: LCC LB1062.6 .W35 2023 (print) | LCC LB1062.6 (ebook) |
DDC 370.15—dc23/eng/20230313
LC record available at https://lccn.loc.gov/2022059938
LC ebook record available at https://lccn.loc.gov/2022059939

Printed in the United States of America
6th Printing

Book design by Alissa Rose Theodor

To my children, William, Caroline, and James—

and young people everywhere

Contents

Author's Note

Due to the sensitive nature of these conversations, some names and identifying details have been changed. In those cases, I included only a first name. Everyone identified with a full name explicitly chose to be.

INTRODUCTION

Running with Their
Eyes Closed

I n one of my early interviews for this book, I met Molly, a high
school junior living in Washington State. She began by telling me
that many of her classmates on the Advanced Placement track
either went to bed or woke up at 3:00 a.m. to cram in all their studying. Molly confessed sheepishly that she "wasn't a night person," and
told me that she went to bed "around midnight" most nights and
sometimes woke up early, around 5:00 a.m., to study before tests
or to put the finishing touches on a paper. When I asked her how,
as a varsity athlete, she maintained her stamina on only five hours
of sleep, Molly tightened her high ponytail and answered me without any irony: "Those days, I run the laps in practice with my eyes
closed."

Three years later, that conversation has stuck with me. That
image—a generation running in circles with their eyes shut—is an

apt, if devastating, metaphor for the new normal in the classrooms, on the playing fields, and in the late-night bedrooms of many of today's teens. In communities like Molly's, the past several decades have given rise to a professionalized childhood, in which seemingly every minute of a child's life is managed to maximize their potential. Academics, athletics, and extracurricular activities have become increasingly competitive, adult-led, and high-stakes. These kids are running a course marked out for them, without enough rest or a chance to decide if it's even a race they want to run.

This trend has not come without a cost. For decades now, researchers have been studying how adverse childhood experiences, such as living in poverty or amid community violence, increase risks to a child's health and well-being. In 2019, a national report published by some of the country's top developmental scientists added a surprising new group of children to our country's most "at-risk" youth. Students attending what researchers call "high-achieving schools"—generally speaking, competitive public or private schools with high standardized test scores—are found to have "relatively high levels of adjustment problems, likely linked with long-standing ubiquitous pressures to excel at academics and extracurriculars," the report noted. One expert estimated that one in three American students may be impacted by this excessive pressure to achieve.

For the past ten years I've been reporting on modern family life. When I wrote about the growing research around achievement pressure and this newly identified "at-risk" group for *The Washington Post*, the article quickly made its way around. Strangers tracked me down through my website to find out more, and friends emailed me about seeing the article hanging in their school lobbies or linked in their school newsletters. Parents sent it to each other, as did teachers, principals, and coaches. Suddenly, I found myself in the middle of an urgent discussion, one that had started years ago with the psychologist Madeline Levine's groundbreaking 2006 book, *The Price of Privilege*, in which she wrote about the emptiness, anxiety, and depression among the high-performing adolescents she treated in her practice. Now there was data to back up Levine's experiences. The profound, unsettling paradox was undeniable: students who are afforded every opportunity were statistically more likely to experience worse outcomes than their middle-class peers according to tangible measures of well-being.

Worrying about the well-being of high-performing students can feel awkward, even absurd. After all, most of them come from families who don't have to worry about housing or healthcare and can afford to spend money to alleviate their problems. Do these families really need our attention? With so much suffering in the world, do the hardships of the children of the top 20 percent of Americans matter? Without a doubt, youth who live in poverty and face hunger, violence, and discrimination are significantly more likely to experience adversity than their peers in high-achieving schools. There is no question about that. But as the researcher Suniya Luthar put it when I raised those very questions, "No one is putting pain on a scale: a child in pain is a child in pain, and neither chooses their circumstance."

Changes in what it means for a child to succeed are taking place against—and directly contributing to—a backdrop of intense childhood suffering. We find ourselves in a true national crisis, collectively facing a devastating epidemic of stress, anxiety, and depression among our youth—so much so that in 2021, U.S. Surgeon General Dr. Vivek Murthy issued a rare public health advisory on the topic: "Recent national surveys of young people have shown alarming increases in the prevalence of certain mental health challenges—in 2019, one in three high school students and half of female students reported persistent feelings of sadness or hopelessness, an overall increase of 40 percent from 2009." The mental health of young people is shaped by many factors, noted Murthy, from their genes to their relationships to larger social forces, like messages in media and popular culture that can "erode their sense of self-worth—telling them they are not good-looking enough, popular enough, smart enough, or rich enough." But the takeaway is clear: living with toxic stress is harming a large portion of our youth, and as the adults in the room, it is our job to do something about it.

As both a journalist and a mom of three adolescents, I felt compelled to find out more. In early 2020, I conducted a first-of-its-kind national parenting survey with help from a researcher at the Harvard Graduate School of Education. I wanted to understand the pressure kids and parents were feeling and why they felt it. The survey struck a nerve. Conversations about it popped up on parenting websites and on Facebook feeds. In just a few days, over six thousand parents around the country had filled it out.

Achievement pressure wasn't just an issue of a few isolated communities—it was affecting families from coast to coast. Parents were eager to share their experiences and thanked me for the opportunity to talk openly about what everybody was feeling but nobody was saying. The survey asked parents how much they agreed with statements like:

"Parents in my community generally agree that getting into a selective college is one of the most important ingredients to later-life happiness." (73 percent of parents agreed.)

"Others think that my children's academic success is a reflection of my parenting." (83 percent of parents agreed.)

"I wish today's childhood was less stressful for my kids." (87 percent of parents agreed.)

I started to believe that surfacing these feelings could be a first step toward dismantling them. At the end of the survey, I asked parents to email me if they'd be willing to be interviewed for my book. Hundreds reached out. For the next three years, I traveled throughout the country, speaking in depth to parents and students in places like Cleveland, Ohio; Yarmouth, Maine; Jackson, Wyoming; Mercer Island, Washington; Los Angeles, California; and Wilton, Connecticut.

Nearly all the parents I interviewed were college-educated professionals; otherwise, the families in this book are diverse: they are of different races and ethnicities; some are in heterosexual relationships, others in same-sex relationships; they are liberal and conservative, single dads and stay-at-home mothers; they hail from cities, suburbs, and rural communities; they are teachers, nurses, lawyers, PTA presidents, bankers, and psychologists. Despite their varied backgrounds, all these families were trying their best to navigate the complex world of achievement.

Eventually, I went in search of kids who were thriving despite the pressures of our modern achievement culture: What buffers do they have in their lives to cope with the stress? What mindsets and behaviors do they exhibit? What do their parents focus on at home? What is their school like for them? What, if anything, do these healthy achievers have in common? I interviewed people in focus groups, after PTA meetings, or over margaritas at Moms' Night Outs, but mostly, I spoke with parents and students one-on-one in coffee shops, at their dining room tables, in their offices, riding in cars between drop-offs, and via Zoom. Once I got back home, I continued the dialogue with these families, often waking up to long, insightful emails from them that began, "I was thinking more about what we talked about . . ." I've stayed in touch with many of these families and followed some students from high school into college while writing this book.

My survey and the resulting connections gave me so much material, both personal stories and patterns that could be traced between them. What emerged from my research hit me like an ice bath: our kids are absorbing the idea that their worth is contingent on their performance—their GPA, the number of social media followers they have, their college brands—not for who they are deep at their core. They feel they only *matter* to the adults in their lives, their peers, the larger community, if they are successful.

I use the word "matter" deliberately here. Since the 1980s, a growing body of research finds that mattering—the feeling that we are valued and add value to others—is key to positive mental health and to thriving in adolescence and beyond. "Mattering" offers a rich, almost intuitive framework for understanding the pressure assailing our kids—and how to protect them from it. It is as profound as it is practical. It doesn't involve spending more money on tutors or coaches or adding another activity to an already overpacked schedule. Instead, it offers a radical new lens for how we as adults—

parents, teachers, coaches, and mentors—see our kids and communicate to them about their worth, potential, and value to society.

Mattering is not mutually exclusive from high performance. When we matter, we are more likely to participate in positive, healthy ways in our families, our schools, and our communities. In my research, I found that it was students who felt a high level of mattering that set the healthy high achievers apart. Mattering informs the language we use, the messages we reinforce, and how we handle failure. It can help any adult sick of the hamster wheel and looking for an alternative—one that doesn't excuse a child from fulfilling their potential but also doesn't destroy them in the process.

When I started my reporting, I worried that parents and students might not want to be open and vulnerable about a topic that sits so close to the heart. I couldn't have been more wrong. Over the past three years, two hundred people have let me into their lives, and I am forever grateful. I've spoken with students who were incredibly candid with me and who trusted me to tell their stories. I've met with families who have lost a loved one to suicide. I've spoken with community groups trying to pave a new path for their youth. I've spent time with parents who have learned from their missteps and are sharing them in the hope that we all can learn from their pain. The pages of this book reflect what I learned. I've written this book for you, but I've also written this book for myself, in my effort to raise healthy and successful kids in a culture that increasingly forces us to choose only one of those outcomes.

I have attempted to take an honest look at my generation's parental anxiety from the perspective of someone right there with them in the trenches. Of course, no one book can describe the experiences of all parents. Achievement pressure will affect individuals differently depending on their backgrounds and lived experiences. And as much as I sought out diverse perspectives, this is not a sociology, history, or public policy book, nor does it dive deeply into topics that deserve more scholarly treatment and books all their own.

This is a book aimed primarily at parents who have the privilege to choose where they live and where their children go to school, and the adults in the community who work with these children daily. Of course, the choices these families make about schooling, activities, and sports affect the opportunities of other families who do not have the means to keep up, further widening the inequity of our society. I've listed resources in the back of the book for readers who want to go deeper on important subjects like systemic racism, marginalization, discrimination, and privilege that relate to achievement culture but are beyond the scope of this book.

To lay all my cards on the table: I am also a product of high-performing schools. I am a white Ivy League graduate raising kids who attend these "high-achieving schools." This book is an attempt to use that privilege to shine a light on a problem hidden in plain sight and to highlight solutions. My hope is to change the conversation we're having about achievement pressure, to move beyond unhelpful finger-pointing toward a better understanding of how the forces making us unhappy are bigger than any one family or school or community.

This book begins by looking at how we got here and what society's increasing achievement pressure is doing to our kids. From there, it discusses practical solutions and outlines an attainable, empathetic path toward raising healthy and, yes, successful children. Finally, I've gathered insights and advice from leading experts about changes we can make beyond the walls of our homes, including what schools and communities can do to help buffer against the toxic pressures of our achievement culture.

What I have found in my reporting is that there are actions we can take now, in our homes, classrooms, and teams, to counter the increasing anxiety, depression, and isolation young people are experiencing. These actions require shifts in thinking, past the harmful messages that society sends day in and day out, messages that often seem inescapable and inevitable. As the adults in our kids' lives, we need to course correct toward behaviors that will protect them and launch them into adulthood better equipped to handle life's ups and downs—and to thrive when we are no longer around to guide them.

1

Why Are Our Kids
"At Risk"?

Life Inside the Pressure Cooker

A
manda should have felt elated: She was a varsity athlete,
the president of the debate club, and about to graduate from
her competitive high school with top grades. She had just
received an early acceptance letter to her college of choice, an elite
university with an admissions rate of a mere 10 percent. It had taken
six full years of sacrifice and singular focus to finally reach this moment. Now she could do anything. She'd made it. But instead of
overwhelming pride, what she remembers is shock and anxiety. The
Saturday after receiving her college acceptance, she brought a bottle of Smirnoff vodka to a friend's house and partied all night—not
to celebrate, but to numb a quiet desperation she couldn't quite name.

Amanda grew up on the West Coast in a small, relatively affluent town reminiscent of so many of the communities around the
country I visited while researching this book: a beautiful downtown
kept up by high taxes, parents who work long hours in white-collar
professions, kids who work just as hard on their homework and
devote their weekends to traveling club sports. As a child, Amanda
loved school. She was "great at being a student," she told me, and she
enjoyed learning—until seventh grade arrived. "Then people started
telling me that I had to do this activity or take that class for my
college application, and life became about setting yourself up early
to get into the best college you could," she said.

For four long years of high school, Amanda maintained an intense schedule filled with year-round sports, after-school clubs that
focused on serving the underprivileged in her community, and a
maxed-out course load of honors and AP classes. Her parents had
instilled a strong work ethic in her and her siblings. Her dad worked
twelve-hour days as a lawyer at a tech company, while her mother
volunteered in various leadership positions for the PTA. Their
house was always impeccably maintained. Amanda remembers the
frenzy that would take place whenever guests were coming over,
even just to drop something off—everything had to be exactly right.
Holidays were particularly serious affairs, prompting her mother
to spend weeks decorating, striving to create storybook memories for her kids. Even family vacations were planned with the
same methodical precision—nothing left to chance. "Achievement in all areas of our lives was what mattered most to my parents," she said.

When it came to Amanda's school performance, her parents
were careful not to make the conversation directly about grades.

Instead, Amanda said, "it was more subtle, under the guise of 'You're not fulfilling your potential.'" Bringing home a C or even a B on an assignment would be met with a quiet, buttoned-up coldness. Their message was clear, she said, even without being explicit: *We know you can do better.*

Many of her friends felt the same way. "We live in a community where your grades, how you look, your weight, where you travel, what your house looks like—everything has to be the best, to be perfect, and to look effortless," said Amanda. Classes at the high school were competitive and demanding, she recalled. Teachers expected a high level of performance from their students, as did coaches during after-school practice.

Most days, it looked like Amanda could juggle it all—until suddenly she couldn't. By the end of junior year of high school, with college applications looming and the pressure mounting, Amanda would stay up late working, then lie awake, gnawed by anxiety. The next day, utterly exhausted, she'd skip classes and head over to the music room to play Bach or Chopin on the piano and temporarily escape.

Amanda was depressed, even if she didn't recognize it at the time. Her life had become rigid, with little time for simple pleasures or even rest. The unrelenting pressure led to the development of an eating disorder that toggled between anorexia and bulimia. Every time she ate a "forbidden" food—secretly bingeing on cookies or ice cream in her room to numb the pain—her lack of self-control only reminded her that, yet again, she'd failed to measure up. Her self-worth would go up or down depending on the number on the scale or the score on a test. "I always felt like I had to maintain this perfect image at home, at school, and online, so I wasn't genuinely connecting with most people, especially my parents," she said. "It was a very lonely time."

Amanda's mental health issues flew under the radar because, despite everything she was going through, she still managed to bring home straight As. Weekends brought fleeting relief. "My friends and I worked so hard all week that we felt like we deserved to let go," she said. They'd binge drink, sometimes to the point of blacking out. Amanda said there was a tacit agreement in town between some parents and their teens that you could do whatever you wanted on the weekends as long as you were performing during the week. Some parents, she told me, would supply the booze and even join them in the drinking. Amanda's parents had a different perspective: "They thought hanging out with my friends was a waste of time, so I'd have to fight with them to be able to go out. Being productive and successful was the number-one priority and anything else, even friendship, was secondary."

By the time Amanda left for college, she'd embraced a "work hard, play hard" mindset. On campus, she found an environment even more competitive than in high school. She struggled to maintain straight As. Her eating disorder worsened, her drinking picked up, and she dabbled with drugs to escape her shame at never quite measuring up. The pressure from her parents migrated from grades to summer internships. After graduation, Amanda landed a dream job in advertising and moved into a beautiful apartment in San Francisco. She was thrilled.

But that familiar drive—to achieve more, to reach higher, to be the best among her peers—followed her. "I was working all the time, getting promoted, but had no sense of balance in my life or healthy ways to cope with all the stress," Amanda said. She turned to old, unhealthy habits instead. One night, after binge drinking and snorting cocaine with friends, she sat on the curb outside her apartment building and considered suicide. "I had this desperate feeling like I just couldn't take it anymore," she recalled. "I was completely exhausted and just wanted to end it."

Amanda's depression deepened, and she soon started drinking during the workday. While driving home one night, she was pulled over by the police and charged with a DUI. After nearly a decade of excessive drinking and drug use, her arrest forced her to deal with her problem, and also forced her parents to accept the reality that their daughter, who seemed to have it all, felt utterly vacant inside.

Amanda went into rehab. Now she's been sober for two years. She's seeing a therapist and slowly unpacking the heavy weight of two decades' worth of expectations. "All of my life, I have felt like I had to be perfect, or people wouldn't love me," Amanda said. It's a mindset that is so ingrained in her that she doubts it will ever entirely leave: "I still want to perform, I still want to achieve, but now I'm trying not to punish myself quite so much when I don't."

An "At-Risk" Group?

When Suniya Luthar first began studying the lives of American teenagers, her work focused on the challenges of living in the inner city. As a researcher at Yale in the 1990s, Luthar put together a study that followed a group of teens whose lives were impacted by poverty, crime, and substance abuse. In need of a control group with whom to compare her findings, she sought out teenage subjects in a nearby affluent community, tracking the same variables: rates of depression, rule-breaking behavior, and the use of drugs and alcohol.

Much to her surprise, she found that the upper-middle-class suburban youth were doing worse on many of the study's measures: they were significantly more likely to use alcohol, marijuana, and hard drugs than the average teen and relative to inner-city kids; suburban girls, in particular, were suffering from much higher levels of clinical depression, and both genders showed slight elevations of clinically significant anxiety relative to norms. To Luthar, the results of the study seemed counterintuitive. To others, they seemed simply wrong. "Initially, there was resistance to the idea that these kids who have it all, who are given every opportunity, could possibly be doing worse than the average American kid, not to mention kids living in poverty," Luthar told me. People couldn't wrap their heads around the study's findings. Americans assume that wealth equals well-being, Luthar said, or at the very least that it protects kids against these kinds of hardships.

In the years since this groundbreaking study, Luthar and other scientists have discovered that what places a child "at risk" for clinically high levels of anxiety, depression, and substance abuse is not growing up in an upper-middle-class family, but rather growing up in an environment of unrelenting pressure. A 2018 report by the influential public health and policy experts at the Robert Wood Johnson Foundation (RWJF) named the top environmental conditions negatively impacting adolescent wellness. Among them were poverty, trauma, discrimination, and "excessive pressure to excel." According to the RWJF report, a "family and/or school environment characterized by extreme pressure to succeed or to outdo everyone else—often, but not exclusively, occurring in especially affluent communities—can affect youth in significantly deleterious ways, including causing high levels of stress and anxiety or alcohol and drug use and dependence." Students who are marginalized—whether due to race, class, ethnicity, or identity—can feel an additional, formidable layer of stress, making it even harder for them to thrive.

These competitive schools, where the average standardized test scores lie in the top quarter of scores nationally, are often located in communities where many family incomes fall within the top 20 or 25 percent nationally—roughly above $130,000 a year, depending on the area of the country. Of course, these schools and communities also include families whose incomes aren't in the top quartile, and students can suffer from constant pressure to achieve just as intensely. In other words, it is not a family's income but rather the environment a child is raised in that can harm development and impact overall health. For all their advantages, many of the high-performing students I met described themselves as anxious, depressed, and lonely. As one student explained, "I was severely depressed in high school and most of the time was barely keeping it together, partly as a result of the toxic culture around grades and achievements in my high school and within my group of friends."

One survey of 43,000 students from across the country by Challenge Success, a research-based organization affiliated with Stanford University, found more than two-thirds of the high schoolers reported being "often or always worried" about college admissions. When you live in a community of high achievers with strict definitions of success, when friends are competing for the same leadership positions, for the same teams, for the same acceptances to increasingly exclusive colleges, you grow up in an environment of outsized expectations.

You might suppose that mental health struggles resolve once these students get into college. But that doesn't appear to be the case. Even before the devastating effects of the COVID-19 pandemic, mental health issues on college and university campuses were a growing concern. Survey data from before the pandemic found that three in five college students reported experiencing overwhelming anxiety, and two in five reported being too depressed to function within the past year. In 2020, a fifteen-month investigation by a Harvard task force found that students there suffered from "high levels of stress, overwork, concern about measuring up to peers, and inability to maintain healthy coping strategies. Extracurricular activities, rather than providing unqualified relief, often represented another source of competition and stress." What starts in high school continues in college.

High levels of stress—whatever the source—also put young people at greater risk for poor long-term physical health. When we perceive danger, our bodies secrete hormones such as adrenaline and cortisol to temporarily sharpen our focus. Once the imminent risk passes, our body is designed to return to its baseline to recover. Our bodies aren't designed to handle chronic psychological stress, the kind that never lets up. Living in a state of constant vigilance, with a steady flow of the associated neurochemicals and hormones, can cause both short-term and long-term damage, including heart disease, cancer, chronic lung and liver diseases, diabetes, and stroke. An increased risk of substance abuse also appears to last well into adulthood. One study found that by age twenty-six, former students of high-achieving schools were two to three times more likely to struggle with addiction than their middle-class peers.

"Critics of this generation say they are being coddled and over-protected, but I actually think it's quite the opposite," Luthar said. "They're being crushed by expectations to accomplish more and more." These students are playing out their young lives in a kind of gilded pressure cooker—shiny on the outside, punishing on the inside. Every win sets even higher expectations: harder classes, tougher tournaments. Even activities that are supposed to be fun and stress reducing, like playing a sport or a musical instrument, become a means to an end: padding for life's résumé. Speaking to young people crystallized for me just how poisonous these pressures are. One New York student recalled bursting into tears in her third-grade classroom because she thought getting a C on a math test had ruined her chances of getting into Harvard and "living a good life."

Despite best intentions, we adults can magnify the pressure. Over the past thirty years, as the world has grown both more competitive and more uncertain, parents have bet big on the belief that childhood success—the grades, the trophies, the résumés—is the surest, safest pathway to a secure, happy adult life. This wager has redefined childhood, family priorities, and the rhythm of daily life. While it's easy to dismiss the parents who spend every waking hour optimizing their children's lives as over-the-top outliers, countless parents in communities around the country find themselves struggling to figure out how far to go to keep up with rising expectations.

Instinct compels us to do right by our kids, but where does "right" turn into something else? Is it spending upward of 10 percent of a family's income on their child's sport? Or hiring a math tutor not because their child is struggling but because they want to give them an edge over their classmates? Or getting an iffy medical diagnosis to score their child extra time on standardized tests?

What is a parent to do in places like Weston, Connecticut, or New-
ton, Massachusetts, where, according to one *Wall Street Journal*
article, 25 to 30 percent of students are diagnosed with a learning
disability that allows them extended test-taking time? (Compare that
to 1.6 percent similarly diagnosed in low-income communities.) Parents who "play the game" are left wondering whether their child is
genuinely happier; parents who don't, or can't afford to, are left wondering how to overcome an unlevel playing field that disadvantages
their child.

As a parent, I've fallen into this achievement trap myself. There
are days when I'm overcome by the pride I feel for my kids. I marvel
at the unique humans that they are and are still becoming, and I'd
give everything to help them find joy, happiness, and purpose. Other
days, I'm overcome by anxiety. Like clockwork, every August, as I
draw up the after-school schedule of sports and extracurriculars,
these fears hit me: Have I signed them up for the right activities and
sports, or is there something better out there? Are my kids too busy?
Are they not busy enough? Am I doing enough? Too much?

When William, my oldest child, started sixth grade, I somehow
became convinced that the clock was running out to find his "passion." It seemed like so many parents I knew had already figured out
what made their kids uniquely tick: there was the violin prodigy,
the soccer star, the budding chess aficionado. I'd heard about third
graders who were participating in School Scrabble Championships.
One boy I knew was so obsessed with ancient artifacts that his
mother signed him up for a summer on an archaeological dig. What
latent interests and talents was I neglecting in my own three kids?

William had always loved architecture and design. When he
was younger, he'd cover the floor of his bedroom with "cities" of

wooden blocks, building structures that resembled Greek temples. As he got older, he'd spend full afternoons imagining new worlds to create with his Legos. When we traveled, he would always be looking up, noticing, and pointing out unusual facades of buildings in the cities we toured. Wasn't it my duty to help foster this passion?

In a parental frenzy, I googled architecture and design classes in New York City and started at the top, both literally and figuratively. I called the Cooper Hewitt, Smithsonian Design Museum, once the home of industrialist Andrew Carnegie, situated on the Upper East Side's Museum Mile. When I earnestly asked whether they offered classes for sixth graders, they said no, they didn't. I detected a light chuckle in their response. I made my way down the list. One school that offered an introduction to architecture class asked if my son had a basic understanding of CAD—computer-aided design software used by architects, inventors, and engineers to design bridges, skyscrapers, rockets, and more. I said no, not yet.

Undeterred, I kept digging. Eventually, one program did bite. The person who answered the phone told me that if my son wanted to sit in on an intro to architecture evening class aimed at older high school and college students, and if I stayed and sat next to him, he could enroll. When I excitedly shared the news with William, he looked me straight in the eyes.

"Mom, I love architecture," he said. "Please don't ruin it for me."

■ ■ ■

In generations past, having two employed parents with college degrees, as my kids do, generally meant that your family was upwardly mobile, if not already financially secure. But my parental anxiety to make sure my kids were not "falling behind" wasn't a personal quirk, as I have come to learn. This anxiety was a symptom of a new, broader cultural trend that has mainly taken root in communities like mine, filled primarily with college-educated professionals. Growing up, our parents might have encouraged us or bought us a pair of running shoes, but they mostly watched our success from the sidelines. Today, many modern parents feel tasked with *making* their kids a success, pushing them, if they must, to the front of the pack. And this trend has not come without a cost, to both parents and kids.

Being pushed like this can feel dehumanizing. A senior at a high-achieving public high school in Brooklyn, New York, sent me an editorial he wrote for his school paper. He wrote, "Many of us have to resort to fake personalities with fake passions in order to not fall behind in 'social status' and the college process." Pressure to stand out, he said, has had a paradoxical effect on his generation, forcing students to be someone they're not and feign passions to appear attractive to top colleges. Students become disaffected learners, consumed by getting good grades and accolades instead of taking a genuine interest in the subject matter. "In the hopes of seeing us for who we are, they've made us become who we aren't," he concluded.

The psychologist Erik Erikson pointed out that an adolescent's most crucial task is attaining a sense of personal identity. But that process is undermined when adolescents feel they must be high performing or perfect to be loved. Adolescents become overly reliant on others for a sense of who they should be and how much they're worth. And when personal worth seems to depend solely on getting ahead of their peers, kids may fail to develop a sense of internal meaning and purpose. This can make achievement unfulfilling and lead to burnout and cynicism.

It's not just the students who feel stuck in this grueling race. Many parents I interviewed said that they, too, felt trapped by hypercompetitive societal norms. An overwhelming 80 percent of the over six thousand parents I surveyed agreed that the children in their community were "under excessive pressure to achieve." When asked about where that pressure came from, more than 80 percent pointed to *other* parents as the primary source. One wrote, "Where we live, it is competitive on all levels. Many have endless resources to 'outdo' your child if they choose or need to. Your kid comes home stating what everyone else is doing, eating, wearing, participating in, going on vacation, etc., and you feel that you must keep up and provide those same opportunities because that is all they know. It's the environment that they are growing up in."

I asked these parents to rank the things they most wanted for their children: happiness, success, having a sense of purpose, and being a compassionate member of society. I also asked them what they thought were the top priorities of *other* parents in their community. Nearly 80 percent of parents believed that "academic and professional success" was one of the top two priorities of other parents. But only 15 percent of parents named it as their own first or second priority—a discrepancy that may reflect just how much parents feel pitted against one another. While many parents may feel stressed and concerned about the pressure that's being put on our kids, no one wants to be the first to drop out of the race—or can even conceive of how they would.

None of the parents I surveyed said that what they ultimately wanted for their kids was to be captain of the football team, a straight-A student, or a Rhodes Scholar. They simply wanted happy, productive, and fulfilling lives for their kids. Even Amy Chua, the author of *Battle Hymn of the Tiger Mother*, has said, "If I could push a magic button and choose either happiness or success for my children, I'd pick happiness in a second."

But there is no magic button, and the path to happiness is increasingly understood as a high-stakes drag race to "success." For parents, the logistics alone can strain even the most solid of marriages. And there are times we simply can't juggle it all, when Saturdays and Sundays are triple booked with soccer games, school projects, and chess tournaments. Standing on the sidelines of a soccer game in the freezing rain, I have looked around and wondered: *How is everyone else pulling this off week after week, year after year, with multiple children? Why are we even doing this?*

The Pressure Is Everywhere

"When parents ask me where all of the pressure on these kids is coming from," Luthar likes to say, "I ask them: Where is it not?" Relationships that once protected students and kept them grounded—with parents, coaches, teachers, peers—can be added sources of pressure nowadays, she said. None of these individual people are at fault. Adults, from teachers to school administrators to coaches, also feel pressure to succeed, to achieve top spots in their field, and to prove their mettle once they're in those prominent jobs, Luthar said.

Coaches, for example, are now part of a nearly twenty-billion-dollar competitive youth sports complex, one that pushes kids to specialize in one sport year-round at a very young age, even at the risk of overuse injuries, in order to sustain enrollment. In an editorial written on behalf of over 200,000 New Jersey youth sports participants, student athletes implored high school coaches in their state to rethink the stressful demands being placed on them. Their requests were heartbreaking in their simplicity: one mandatory day off per week during the sports season to recharge and "sleep," "catch up on homework," and "spend time with our families."

Meanwhile, with housing prices linked to public school performance rankings, school administrators can feel pressured to maintain their school's state ranking, a worry that can trickle down to pressure on students. In a letter to parents, the principal at Harley Avenue Primary School in Elwood, New York, got right to the point: the kindergarten talent show was canceled, and the reason why was "simple." She wrote, "We are responsible for preparing children for college and career readiness with valuable lifelong skills and know that we can best do that by having them become strong readers, writers, coworkers, and problem solvers." Accordingly, the talent show was nixed so that teachers could spend more time on career readiness—for five-year-olds.

Private school administrators, too, can feel pressure from their boards and alumni to protect their school's brand and market share, which increases the pressure on current students to maintain high standards, even as competition for honors and prestigious college seats ratchets up everywhere. In his book *At What Cost? Defending Adolescent Development in Fiercely Competitive Schools*, the psychologist David Gleason recounts what one head of school told him privately: "If we actually gave in, and a developmentally reasonable schedule emerged, we might achieve a healthy balance for our students at the cost of our school's distinctiveness; we might lose our edge of excellence and become a vanilla school, and who would want to come to a vanilla school?"

Our wider consumer culture reinforces the idea that your child is an investment, and that the expected return should be measured early. Colleges have long acknowledged top scholars via diplomas with distinction, dean's lists, and honor societies like Phi Beta Kappa. High schools have the National Honor Society. In 2008, the National Elementary Honor Society made its debut to honor the best and the brightest elementary school scholars. Sports, while always inherently competitive, are not immune to achievement creep. All-star rankings in basketball, for example, now include the top fourth graders in the nation, and semiprofessional, specialized training starts as early as six years old. Music competitions, dance competitions, arts competitions, and even high school bands have become more demanding, if not all-consuming. It's hard to find a hobby— Minecraft, mountain biking, macramé—that can't be turned into an exhausting pursuit of excellence. As a joke, my son and I once googled "Rubik's Cube competitions"—yep, they exist, too.

Busy schedules inhale all downtime, sucking up the idle after-school hours or weekend days once spent with friends and family. Birthday parties are missed for all-day chess tournaments or out-of-state lacrosse games. I remember my son's travel soccer coach sending me a stern warning after my son missed a game to attend his great-grandmother's ninetieth birthday party. Katie, a mother in Alaska, wrote to me that for the past eight years, her kids have missed holiday celebrations with their extended family because of soccer tournaments. "My kids don't know the joy of a traditional Thanksgiving meal with family gathered around a table," she wrote.

Growing up in a culture that teaches our children that certain types of people matter more—those on the varsity team, those with the most As, those with the most likes, or those who fit into the "idealized norm"—can set students up to chronically question their own importance and worth. For Amanda and her parents, the effect of all those years of mounting pressure, of not meeting unrealistic expectations, of never feeling like she was enough, was devastating. Her parents have sought therapy, too, and taken ownership of the pressures they put on Amanda and her siblings. "My parents are working hard on rebuilding our relationships," she said. But it will take time. "They think they have failed me as parents."

Parents Feel It, Too

A mutual friend introduced me to Catherine, a mother of two boys in a suburb of New York City. Catherine had taken my parenting survey and wanted to talk more about the issues it had raised. I drove out of the city to meet her after dropping my kids off at school.

Catherine greeted me at the door and warmly welcomed me into the living room. As I sat on the couch, I saw, on the coffee table, a tray of cookies and tea she'd prepared. She took a seat toward the other arm of the couch and took a deep breath. After a sip of tea, she began to tell me her story.

"My husband and I knew our son was smart," Catherine said, as her brown eyes softened and a faint smile of reminiscence came over her face. "I didn't buy into the pressure in the community to be on my kids at all times, worrying about which activities were the best and making sure I was constantly enriching all of his talents." Instead, their afternoons were spent playing Monopoly or riding bikes around the neighborhood.

Catherine lives in a town full of beautiful old colonial homes set far apart on large, two-acre lots. Well-tended lawns with oversized soccer nets and driveways crowned with basketball hoops are as much a staple here as the SUVs that cruise around town orchestrating pickups and drop-offs. Each hour is marked by the faint rumble of the commuter train rolling through. But most families don't move to this town simply for its quaintness. They're drawn to the community for the schools, which are nearly always ranked among the best public school districts in the state and feed into some of the best colleges in the country.

Catherine, like many of the mothers I subsequently met, put her career on hold to raise her two children. She was active in the community, always the first to volunteer to serve as class mom or field-trip chaperone. In the early years of raising her older son, Catherine told me, she took a hands-off attitude to parenting. It was only as he finished elementary school that she began to feel a duty to make sure he was living up to his potential. Her husband had attended Yale, and with the promise her son showed, Yale felt within reach for him, too. But getting into Yale today—with an acceptance rate of 4 percent—is different than getting into Yale forty years ago, when acceptance rates were around 25 percent. Meeting these increased expectations would require a shift in her parenting.

"My son said it was like a switch went off one day in middle school," she said. "I went from just being his mom to being totally focused on how he was performing—and that was incredibly jarring for him." Catherine's perceived burden of care deepened as her son entered high school. Starting in the ninth grade, she said, mothers of kids in the honors classes became focused on doing more with their boys' talents. They ensured that their kids were enriched outside of the classroom: that weekends were spent learning and that summers were maximized with skill-building camps. "I began to really second-guess what I knew to be true about being a parent," she said. "I thought, well, maybe I'm supposed to be more involved with his schoolwork, maybe I'm supposed to do all of his chores so he can focus all his attention on studying, maybe he's supposed to go to computer camp instead of just chilling out at the pool." Other parents question and judge you, too, Catherine said, if you aren't doing everything you possibly can to help your child succeed.

As I listened to Catherine, I found myself nodding in recognition. "The worry and anxiety I began to feel about my own parenting became my primary focus," she said, "even above paying attention to his own well-being, I'm sad to say." By her son's junior year, Catherine said, most of their interactions and conversations were about his performance and his college admissions. Anxiety constantly nagged her. Instead of just being happy to see him at the end of the day, she said, "I'd pepper him with questions as soon as he walked in the door: *How'd the test go? What homework do you have this weekend? How are you going to budget your time? Did you read that college guide I earmarked for you?*"

Catherine was micromanaging her son to squelch her own anxiety, she said, her voice noticeably quieter, and she wasn't available to him for what he really needed: a relief from all the academic pressures he was feeling at school. It took a complete shutdown for her to see the truth. As the stress of senior year picked up, her son "stopped going to school, stopped getting out of bed, and just completely disengaged," she said. "It got to the point that we didn't know if he would even be able to graduate high school." The close relationship Catherine had cherished with her son was now in shambles.

With the help of medication and intensive therapy, he did graduate on time and was well enough to go to a small liberal arts college two hours away in a neighboring state. But early into his freshman year, the depression and anxiety ratcheted up again. He coped just as he did in his senior year, by staying in his room playing video games all day, skipping class. He flunked out. Everything she had done to help her son succeed had backfired.

The next few years were rocky, Catherine told me. Now in his late twenties, her son is about to graduate from a local college with a degree in economics and already has a job lined up. Looking back, she said, she barely recognizes the person she became, one who got so swept up in her son's performance that she nearly crushed him.

As she spoke, I found myself wanting to lean in to comfort her. All parents want their kids to reach their potential; aren't we tasked with making sure that happens? Sensing my compassion, Catherine moved closer and reached out for my hands. Then, as if issuing a warning from one mother to another, she looked me straight in the eyes. "I thought it was my job as a mom to push my son to be the very best he could be," she said. "I have so many regrets."

I felt a chill go up my spine. I thought about William, who, at the time, was getting ready for high school. I identified so much with what this mother was telling me: the anxiety, the desire to want our kids to have what we had, to guide them to fulfill their potential. It's not just a desire; we feel like it's our duty as parents to set them up as best we can to live a full, successful, meaningful life. As Catherine pointed out, it's not just that we judge ourselves; others judge us if we're not doing all we can to help our kids. But when to push, when to step back—where is that elusive line between healthy high expectations and excessive pressure? There was nothing about Catherine that was remotely unlikable. She was gentle, loving, kind, and thoughtful. This generous woman was sharing her biggest regret and deepest shame, in the hope that she could help my family and others avoid the same fate.

2

Name It to Tame It

Unpacking the Deep Roots
of Parental Anxiety

*Apart from economic payoffs, social status seems to be
the most important incentive and motivating force of social
behavior.* —JOHN HARSANYI, NOBEL PRIZE LAUREATE AND ECONOMIST

The texts from friends started pouring in before I even saw
the headlines:

Just wow, can you believe this?!?!?!?
Really?!? You can buy sports recruiting spots now???
What a horror show.

The breaking news story had all the makings of a Netflix true-
crime documentary—which it eventually inspired. As the high
school class of 2019 anxiously awaited college decisions, the U.S.

Department of Justice announced criminal charges against dozens of people involved in a nationwide conspiracy to influence college admissions. The investigation, code-named Operation Varsity Blues, led to charges against parents on both coasts, among them celebrities and wealthy business executives. Parents and accomplices to the illegal scheme were indicted for racketeering in an all-out effort to secure acceptances to elite universities like Yale, Stanford, and the University of Southern California for their kids. An estimated twenty-five million dollars had changed hands, and some of the criminal charges carried sentences as heavy as twenty years in prison.

The public reaction was united in its contempt for the accused parents. These were famous actors, financiers, and power players with abundant money and clout already. Yet they wanted the credential of a name-brand college for their kids so much that they were willing to break the law. The *Full House* actress Lori Loughlin and her husband paid the college consultant William "Rick" Singer half a million dollars to nab recruiting spots on the USC rowing team for their daughters, even though neither girl rowed. The former *Desperate Housewives* star Felicity Huffman paid to have an SAT proctor fix the answers on her daughter's SAT to gain additional points. According to news reports, Singer played on Huffman's parental anxiety, hinting that her daughter "would face worse admission odds because she wasn't a legacy, an athlete, or the child of a major donor and their efforts would level the playing field." In a statement accompanying her guilty plea, Huffman described how her worries had pushed her over the edge: "In my desperation to be a good mother, I talked myself into believing that all I was doing was giving my daughter a fair shot." Most of the children of these parents had no knowledge of their parents' actions, at least until the story broke. When Huffman's daughter found out, she said to her mother, crushingly, "Why didn't you believe in me?"

It was tempting to dismiss the Varsity Blues cases as extreme outliers, but in truth, the parents' desperation was uncomfortably familiar. Many of the parents I met confided that they were consumed with anxiety over college admissions (albeit anxiety that never turned into illegal payoffs or federal indictments). One Midwestern parent told me about hiring a middle-school math tutor, not because their child was struggling but to make sure they would test into the advanced math track in seventh grade—and eventually place into AP Calculus BC in their senior year, to increase the chances of landing in a good engineering program. Another parent talked about enrolling their child in a summer course on AP Chemistry so their daughter would do well the following year at school. Another couple told me they bribed their son to stick with soccer even though he'd lost interest, because it wouldn't look good on college applications to drop a sport junior year. They were banking on getting him into Amherst, where his mom had gone. Another mother confided that she went on Prozac to manage her anxiety during her daughter's college admissions process.

This angst isn't just a one percenter obsession, nor is it isolated to a few ultra-selective colleges. Some families I met were consumed with their kids' GPAs and extracurriculars not because they were gunning for admission to an elite school but because standing out translates to scholarship dollars. "Most of the stress my kids and my husband and I feel is because college is so expensive," wrote one woman who took my survey. Meanwhile, she explained, as the cost of private schools becomes increasingly outrageous and more families turn to public universities, the competition at affordable state schools has become more cutthroat, too. All of this leads to more academic pressure, sports pressure, and peer pressure for kids, while parents are besieged by costs for activities, tutors, and college visits. "It never ends," she wrote.

College fever has even trickled down to the pre-K set. Some New York families feel compelled to hire consultants to help their child get into a "good" preschool, so the kids are positioned for a "good" grade school that will feed them into a "good" high school . . . and so on. A mother of two in Brooklyn described touring a prospective day care center for her eight-week-old baby and seeing the pennants of elite colleges decorating the wall above the cribs. When she asked the day care director about the pennants, the director responded, "We hold ourselves to a very high standard of care here."

The stress is contagious. At a school fundraiser, I sat across from a woman I'd never met before, who regaled our table about what it had taken to get her son into UPenn. She had hired a college counselor for her son in eighth grade to avoid missteps—"Don't wait until high school," she warned. She stressed the need to find our child's "spike," the thing that would make them stand out from the crowd. Are they a budding naturalist? If so, get them volunteering with conservation groups, writing letters to Congress about water pollution in a local stream, organizing their own marine club at school.

The conversation made me so anxious that I lay awake that night thinking about my kids' spikes, or, rather, their lack thereof. Could my youngest's interest in Greek mythology—James knew all the Olympian gods and their stories by heart—be the start of something pointy? And then my mind went racing: Maybe he's a budding classicist? James is a wonderful storyteller and writer. Maybe he could start by writing and publishing his own modern myths, and then in high school he could head up a classics club and grow his spike by taking Latin and Greek?

Then I came to my senses. James was nine. This was absurd.

Six months after the Varsity Blues headlines, I found myself at a tenth birthday party for a friend's son. The parents had rented out a gymnasium. As we watched the kids play dodgeball, I struck up a conversation with the birthday boy's grandfather, visiting from out of town. When he asked me what I did, I told him I was writing a book on achievement pressure. "Is it a how-to?" he asked. "As in, how do you pressure your kids so they'll get into a good college?"

The grandfather was only half kidding, but he got more serious as he talked about how much more stressful it is to be a parent today than it was when he was raising his kids. The birthday boy's father, who had been standing with us, joined the conversation with a challenge for me: "I hope in this book you're going to go beyond the stereotype of parents living out their unfulfilled dreams through their kids and actually get to the root of why we're all doing this."

The Deep Roots of Status Anxiety

Here is an uncomfortable truth: to our brains, status matters. It's a truth that dates back to our earliest ancestors. The higher an individual's status in their community, the greater their access to important advantages—first choice of food, first choice of shelter, first choice of mate—that ensured their long-term success and that of their children. That deep-rooted drive for accomplishment can still act like a puppeteer pulling our strings, even today.

Modern status seeking plays out when kids jockey for popularity and pick teams at recess. It plays out on the dating scene and at cocktail parties, where adults display status with what they wear, what they do, and who they know. Social media like Instagram exploits this love of status, with some users obsessively curating the perfect image in the hope of securing more likes and more followers. While social status is deeply ingrained in our psychology, not everyone is motivated by the same displays of status. Your neighbor may care about driving a fancy car. Meanwhile, maybe you're fixated on winning the PTA presidency. "You can say that we shouldn't care about status, but if you fill a room with people who say they're 'anti-status,' they would soon create a social hierarchy based on how anti-status they are," wrote Loretta Graziano Breuning in *I, Mammal.*

We live our modern lives with old wiring we can't easily change, Breuning explained to me. Our instincts are a system designed to ensure survival and reproduction. Whether we're aware of it or not, our sensitivity to status shapes how we parent. We pay a lot of attention to even the smallest status markers, anything that serves to rank our kids the littlest bit above or below their peers. Even a slight rise in status—seeing our son score the winning goal or our daughter in the lead role of a school play—rewards us biologically with a pleasant cocktail of dopamine, serotonin, oxytocin, and endorphins. Conversely, when our brain thinks we're doing something that is not to our reproductive advantage—when we're in a state of "status descent"—we experience anxiety and stress, explained Breuning. Our brain punishes us by releasing painful neurochemicals like cortisol. That's why a drop in status hurts—whether it's having an Instagram post go unliked or having your child rejected by the

University of Michigan. Those status pangs can cause us to do or say things that are not in our best long-term interest just to stop the pain, like arguing on the sidelines with a child's coach. "Parents don't think about it explicitly, but raising or maintaining a child's status is a basic form of reproductive success," Breuning said.

At a bustling New York City restaurant, I met psychologist Richard Weissbourd of the Harvard Graduate School of Education, a frequent source for my reporting. When I asked him what pushes parents to extremes in the name of college acceptance, Weissbourd smiled. "Sure, it's easy to point to outlier parents, the ones who are hiring SAT tutors for middle schoolers or starting nonprofits for their kids so it looks good on the college application," he said, "but they are not really the problem." The parents that really concern Weissbourd are the ones who organize their entire relationships with their children around their kid's achievements, a hidden curriculum that becomes the main, if unspoken, focus of their parenting. According to Weissbourd, this might look like telling your child that all you care about is effort, then asking how everyone else scored on the test. Or it could mean saying that going to an elite college doesn't matter, then extolling the virtues of a cousin who got into Brown. What Weissbourd said next prompted a light-bulb moment for me: the real problem, he said, is that high achievement is now seen by many parents as a life raft in an unpredictable future.

In the United States, we are taught that we live in a meritocracy, in which success is supposedly earned through hard work and ability. Add in a little luck, the American myth promises, and anyone can climb the ladder of success. It is an appealing promise—especially for those in white, affluent communities where the climb starts a few rungs up. Of course, as in any hierarchy, there is room for only a few at the top—and that's when a parent's status anxiety can get triggered.

When you think of status, you probably don't picture a mom sacrificing her sleep to help finish a science project on time or scouring the Internet for private classes that might draw out her kid's spike. But such behavior exemplifies what the researchers Melissa Milkie and Catharine Warner call "status safeguarding," a term that describes the decades-long project of ensuring that our offspring don't suffer a generational decline in standing. As Milkie described it to me, safeguarding involves the everyday parenting work of mapping out optimal school activities, hobbies, and social and emotional skills that we hope will improve our children's life chances and eventual happiness.

Safeguarding generally falls to the mother, who is tasked with forging a unique path to success for each individual child. To be sure, many fathers contribute to status safeguarding, but it's mothers, the researchers note, who continue to perform the bulk of the cognitive and emotional labor for children. This invisible labor involves the minutiae of life—making sure the football cleats still fit (and where you last saw them), insisting on piano practice before the next lesson (and keeping an eye on the time)—as well as anticipating potential problems. When a child missteps, "whether not getting above-average grades, not receiving appropriate attention from teachers, or not seeming happy with friends," Milkie writes in her study, a safeguarding mother might intervene by hiring a tutor, requesting a parent-teacher conference, or finding a therapist to help bolster social and emotional skills. Ironically, Milkie points out, all the sacrifices a mother makes to launch a child successfully into the competitive labor market often have a high cost in her own career and compensation—and thus her own status.

In our calmest and most logical moments, we like to think we would resist the worst impulses of status-seeking parenting. Our kids are bright and talented, we tell ourselves. They will be fine, even if they don't make the team or ace the test. But when we feel a threat to our survival—or to the survival of our children—our brains trigger an alarm. This biological tripwire can generate false positives, especially in fast-paced, competitive environments. Randolph Nesse, a professor emeritus of psychology and psychiatry at the University of Michigan, aptly calls this sensitivity "the smoke detector principle." Like a smoke detector that goes off when we burn a bagel, evolution has wired us to feel stressed even when our survival isn't actually in danger, because the potential cost of not responding is too great. Our brains aren't great at distinguishing between a real threat, like someone with a gun, and a perceived threat, like our child getting cut from the A team, denied a scholarship, or rejected from their first-choice college.

This fierce protectiveness does not align with present-day reality. But it's why after a night of hearing about what "we" needed to do to get our kids into an elite college, I tossed and turned. It's why one good friend confessed to getting angry after her daughter didn't make the soccer A team: "I found myself raising my voice at her because she didn't really try," she told me. "And then I spent the rest of the night beating myself up for doing that." It's why we can react so strongly to how much playing time our kid gets on the field or how well they do on one Spanish quiz. And it's why we will sign up a sixth grader for a high school architecture course—and offer to sit next to him to make sure he pays attention.

How Scarcity Affects Us

America's self-understanding as the land of opportunity rests on the premise of an ever-expanding pie, so to speak. Everyone can get a slice, and as long as the pie keeps growing, each successive generation can wind up better off financially than the last. But our collective self-image is due for a revision. Today two-thirds of Americans no longer believe that a steady improvement over generations is a given. American parents worry that resources for their kids are becoming increasingly scarce, and the data supports their belief. White middle-class children who were born in 1940 had a 90 percent chance of outearning their parents. For children born in the 1980s, however, the chances of earning more than their parents fell to 50 percent. In the past several decades, it's only gotten worse. Millennials on average have lower earnings, fewer assets, and less wealth compared to what other generations had at their age.

As with status, scarcity lights up our minds in complicated ways. When we perceive that there are not enough resources to go around, our brains default to a "scarcity mindset"—a one-track fixation on what we lack that can cause us to miss the bigger picture. When essential resources, like food and shelter, were once constrained, the scarcity mindset served as an evolutionary advantage, focusing our attention on what was most important for survival. This same focus gets triggered now when we perceive uncertainty—such as when we think our child might not have a shot at a good college. We become more conservative, more controlling, and more liable to indulge other protective impulses like status safeguarding.

So, as neurotic as contemporary parenting extremes may seem, such behaviors are in fact instinctual responses to insecurity, whether real or perceived. The effects of money on feelings of scarcity are in some ways obvious: money determines where we live, the schools we send our kids to, the enrichment we can provide them. But as researchers have discovered, it isn't just an individual's income that affects their parenting decisions; it's also the macroeconomic climate in which they live, such as the degree of inequality that exists in their country. This is why outwardly comfortable people in the upper middle class can toss and turn all night feeling anything but.

To better understand the weather patterns of money and parenting, I reached out to Matthias Doepke, a professor of economics at Northwestern. Doepke grew up in the 1970s in a middle-class home in a West German village, where his dad was a civil servant, and his mother was a former schoolteacher who stayed home to raise her children and work on the family farm. "My parents, like most other parents at that time, were very hands-off about my schooling," he said. They never asked about his homework or grades or tried to influence his time outside school. After class, the biggest stress he faced was deciding which of his friends' houses to hang out in.

Doepke's relaxed childhood was the norm in most industrialized countries at that time. In West Germany, there was little incentive for kids to spend hours on homework or for parents to invest their own time in building their kids' résumés, because those actions didn't yield much of a return. "If you wanted to go to university, you just went to the one closest to you," he told me. "There was no concept of going to a top college. If you wanted to enroll in a particular program at a university outside your area, you could enroll as long as you passed high school, and I mean minimally passing."

In fact, going to a university didn't even offer a clear edge. There were many other paths a student could pursue, such as apprenticeship programs, that were just as respectable and sometimes led to higher salaries than a college degree. Because the economic returns were comparable, the choice came down to the individual's particular talents and interests.

Doepke is now raising three children of his own in an affluent community in Evanston, Illinois, just outside Chicago, and his family life is starkly different from the one he grew up in. Doepke is more hands-on as a parent than his own parents ever were. Compared to them, he spends much more time managing his kids' day-to-day lives, from planning playdates to signing them up for music classes and sports to gently making sure homework gets done on time. His parents, he told me, had done none of that. It made him wonder: Why had his own parenting style turned out to be so different?

To explore that question, in 2017, Doepke teamed up with Fabrizio Zilibotti, an economics professor at Yale, who also happened to be a father noticing the same generational differences in parenting. The two looked at broad economic and social trends across countries and across decades and sketched out a theory: Do the prevailing economic incentives in any given time and place directly influence parents' behavior, from the number of children they have to the style of their parenting? To begin, Doepke and Zilibotti combed through two large samples of data, the American Time Use Survey and the Multinational Time Use Study, both of which used daily diaries broken down into fifteen-minute intervals to document exactly how adults used their time.

What they found was that since the 1970s, the amount of time average American parents devote to engaging with their children has doubled, with the largest increase among "academic" activities, like reading to children and assisting with homework. Present-day parents are also spending much more money than their predecessors did on resources like extracurricular activities and tutors geared toward college applications. Importantly, these trends have occurred alongside rising economic inequality, in particular a widening gap between college-educated workers and high school graduates. Doepke points to data showing that in the 1970s, college graduates made only about 50 percent more, on average, than Americans lacking a college degree; forty years later, they made about twice as much.

Across national borders and generations, Doepke and Zilibotti found that a country's level of income inequality, social mobility, and return on educational investment informed parents' behavior. To help categorize this behavior, the economists turned to the psychologist Diana Baumrind's groundbreaking framework of parenting styles, which outlines three main approaches: permissive (which allows room for kids' freedom and self-discovery), authoritarian (which restricts kids' autonomy, demanding obedience and a respect for work), and authoritative (which attempts to encourage good behavior through communication and clear limit setting). A country's underlying economic conditions, they found, had a direct correlation with its parenting approaches. In Scandinavia, for example, where there is not a big return on educational investment, the prevalent style today is permissive. In the years after the industrial revolution, when securing a future for your kids meant raising obedient factory workers, the pervasive style in many developed countries was authoritarian. This gave way to an authoritative style in some high-income countries—including the United States, the United Kingdom, and Canada—starting in the 1980s, when parents shifted their focus to raising kids to be desirable white-collar workers: innovative thinkers with college degrees. For parents who feel pressured by increasing economic precarity, a permissive style feels like a risk they can't afford.

What surprised Doepke and Zilibotti was that the rise in authoritative parenting was strongest among more affluent and well-educated parents. Weren't their kids the ones most likely to go to college anyway? Why were these parents so intense? They found two reasons. First, affluent, well-educated parents had the time and means to parent intensively, to hire tutors, and to spend time driving to enrichment classes. But the second and more significant reason was that the "slope of potential social decline is steepest at the top." Doepke explained that well-off parents can feel especially compelled to safeguard against a drop in their child's socioeconomic status.

At home in Evanston, Illinois, Doepke tries to provide his children with some of the freedoms he experienced as a child, like unstructured playtime and more leeway to meet friends without adult supervision. But he remains an involved parent, partly in response to the prevailing economic climate. He and his wife are raising kids who will likely live in an increasingly unequal society—which is one reason as parents they will continue to find themselves cheering on the sidelines of soccer games every weekend.

Weaving Individual Safety Nets

Doepke and Zilibotti's research crystallized how much the world has changed for parents over just a few decades. White middle-class parents in the 1960s and early 1970s could afford to focus more on their children's happiness and less on skills-based achievement because life itself was generally more affordable back then. It was easier to buy a house, afford medical insurance, and get a decent public education. After World War II, many families achieved security through broad economic expansion, government policies such as federally subsidized mortgages and free college tuition for veterans, and strong labor unions that could guarantee benefits such as a comfortable pension. Parents could expect that even if they made some wrong turns, their children would enjoy a safe, middle-class life. There was slack in the system. But starting in the 1980s, the combined influence of technology, globalization, the decline of unions, and government policy—lower taxes, privatization, and deregulation—ushered in a sharp increase in inequality. What's left now, as one woman put it, is the feeling that there's an express elevator headed up—if your kid doesn't get on it early, they'll be left on the ground floor forever.

These intense anxieties likely aren't costing parents sleep in countries with more robust social services and less pronounced income inequality, where the kind of life Doepke enjoyed growing up is still plausible. A friend of mine is raising his daughter in Norway, a country with much less economic inequality than the United States, and her lifestyle is very different from my kids'. There's no pressure to join travel soccer at age seven or to specialize in one sport. Free, unstructured play is seen as a necessity rather than a luxury. Despite Norway's own rising cost of living and increasing competitiveness, the stakes still feel much lower than in the United States, likely because of the country's government-guaranteed safety net.

Here in the United States, without those guaranteed safety nets, parents strive to ensure their children's future social and economic status by "weaving an individualized safety net" for each of them, as the researchers Milkie and Warner have put it. Parents make day-to-day decisions in an attempt to maximize their children's personal achievement and happiness, while constantly anticipating any potential obstacles to success and well-being. One mother, for example, shared with me that she views her kids' education like "concierge medicine"—not one-size-fits-all, but bespoke. Instead of doing the same homework as every other kid in the class, her children, at mom's request, get supplemental homework for the weekends. With the help of additional tutoring, their math skills are years ahead of their classmates'. Of course, this raises the bar in class to such a high level that students who aren't getting extra help are effectively disadvantaged.

Building an individual safety net involves a lot of grunt work, money, and mental labor, whether it's shepherding kids from activity to activity or making constant calculations in our heads about which hobby, class, or sport holds the most promise. And it's exhausting. When my daughter wanted to play the piano, I spent time and energy interviewing several teachers looking for a great fit. I then spent time and energy encouraging her to practice. When she wanted to give up after a few months, I spent more time and energy urging her to stick with it. The words of Amy Chua, author of *Battle Hymn of the Tiger Mother*, kept haunting me: "To get good at anything you have to work, and children on their own never want to work, which is why it is crucial to override their preferences. This often requires fortitude on the part of the parents because the child will resist; things are always hardest at the beginning, which is where Western parents tend to give up." Eventually, after raised voices and cajoling and bribing, I relented. I let Caroline quit, just as my own parents let me quit piano when I was her age.

While parents have always been responsible for launching the next generation, this responsibility has never felt so fraught or so lonely. We sense fewer and fewer guarantees for our children. We have, as the researcher Thomas Curran at the London School of Economics pointed out, absorbed social and macroeconomic conditions into our parenting. Parents engage in anxious, controlling, overly involved parenting—ranking eight-year-olds in soccer, coaching five-year-olds for standardized tests to get into gifted programs—because we have become "social conduits," socializing our kids to prepare them for the economic inequality and cutthroat competition that await.

And we feel trapped. On the one hand, we want to give our children happy childhoods with more freedom to play and quit piano if they want to—childhoods like the one I had, childhoods they can look back on with nostalgia and comfort in the years to come. But we also feel a tremendous burden to prepare them for an increasingly competitive world. As one mother put it, most of her anxiety comes from trying to teach her kids everything they need to know to thrive, when all she really wants to do is enjoy them and enjoy being a parent.

Some minority families report experiencing this pressure even more due to substantial racial wealth disparities in the United States. Wealth can be used both as a cushion in hard times and a safety net that can be passed down from generation to generation. One report found the median Asian American wealth was $91,440 compared to $134,009 for white families, with Asian Americans at the bottom of the income distribution having less wealth and higher rates of poverty than their white counterparts. Researchers at the Federal Reserve Bank of St. Louis found the median white family had $184,000 in wealth, compared to $38,000 for Hispanic families and $23,000 for Black families.

According to one Brookings report, the gaping disparity in net worth between a typical white family and a typical Black family is so large because of "the effects of accumulated inequality and discrimination," such as not being allowed to own property for generations and other differences in opportunity "that can be traced back to this nation's inception." Compared to their white counterparts, Black parents face a starker reality: their kids, even in affluent neighborhoods with similar educations, have a higher risk of falling down the economic ladder than their white peers because of discrimination.

Many Black parents have always felt a sense of scarcity, irrespective of socioeconomic status, explained Chrishana Lloyd, a senior research scientist at the nonprofit Child Trends and the mother of three teenage boys in northern New Jersey. For Lloyd, "intense parenting is about survival. I want my kids to be safe—not the greatest, not sitting on top of the world. Can they be whole? And intact? And be in spaces that are not going to tear them down?"

When Status and Scarcity Collide

There may be no better illustration of status and scarcity than competitive college admissions. In a civics classroom, we might talk about education as a public good, intended to mold informed citizens and strengthen democracy. In reality, higher education has become what economists call a "positional good." This means its value lies less in the actual education provided and more in the fact that not everyone has access to it. An acceptance letter to Amherst or Pomona is a more powerful status symbol than, say, a Gucci handbag.

Access to those status symbols is increasingly narrow. During a presentation I attended for parents in Connecticut called Taming the College Frenzy, Susan Bauerfeld, a mother and psychologist, and Victoria Hirsch, a mother and college counselor, drove this point home mathematically: There are roughly 27,000 high schools in this country. So, alone, the 54,000 valedictorians and salutatorians of those schools could fill the incoming classes of the twenty top-ranked colleges and universities twice over. The sobering math elicited a few gasps from parents who hadn't thought about scarcity in such stark terms.

Colleges know that scarcity serves as a proxy for desirability. Increasing their enrollment capacity to meet rising demand would only harm their status. Instead, some schools go to great lengths and expense to court students whom they know they will ultimately reject, a technique known as "attract to reject." The more applicants a school turns down, the higher it rises in the selectivity rankings. At the fifty most competitive universities in the United States, admissions rates dropped by 45 percent between 2006 and 2018, from admitting more than a third of applicants to less than one in four. Among the top ten universities, admissions have dropped even more dramatically, from roughly 16 percent to as low as 3 percent.

Nowadays, there is a common perception that if a kid waits until high school to start building a college résumé—as was standard a generation ago—they're too late. In her book *Playing to Win*, the sociologist Hilary Levey Friedman points out that today's children face real "credentials bottlenecks" if they wait too long to hone their skills because they're competing against kids who have spent their entire childhoods preparing with tennis lessons, math workbooks, and travel soccer teams. That competition is why a parent might—and I am not naming any names here—conduct a frenzied search for an architecture class that would admit a sixth grader.

Some parents believe that not just any good college will cut it—to maintain our status, our kids must get a particular sweatshirt. Maybe it's an Ivy or an alma mater. Many parents I met had a mental list. In the early stage of researching this book, I called an old source of mine, a sports psychologist and a father of two teenagers living in the Boston area. Many of the patients he sees are children in distress. Parental pressure, he told me, arises from the fact that the long-term goals of raising a child no longer appeal to parents. What is right in front of you—that shiny object, status—is so compelling that even the most well-meaning parents struggle to resist. "The sad truth is," he said, "if some parents were given the choice of pushing their child so hard that they would get them into Harvard but also cause them to develop a depressive or anxiety disorder, some would say 'I'll do it.'"

Part of the reason we get so wrapped up in our kids' achievements is that we're worried that our children won't be able to get into the kind of college we attended, Harvard's Rick Weissbourd told me. In a parent's mind, either consciously or unconsciously, this registers as a drop in status and triggers that smoke-detector alarm. Instead of doing the hard work of self-reflection, many parents accept that eliciting achievement is their sole mandate. Parenting becomes all about shoehorning their children into a small number of elite colleges, Weissbourd said, not prioritizing raising good, ethical future adults.

Status safeguarding can push parents to surprising extremes, even if it's not as extreme as the Varsity Blues scandal. One father I spoke with, who lives in Nashville and has a sophomore in high school, keeps track of every student in his daughter's class: their estimated ranking, each of their parents' colleges, notable extracurricular activities, and how philanthropic the family is. The father told me, "You don't want to waste your energy on a college where you're competing against kids who are in the big donor category."

In 2019, crisis gripped Washington, DC's well-regarded Sidwell Friends School after parents reportedly left anonymous voicemail messages for the school's college counselors, bad-mouthing rival students in the senior class, apparently in the hope of increasing their own child's chances of getting into a specific college. Two of the school's college counselors quit in response, and the head of school, Bryan Garman, issued a stern letter to parents. The college counseling office, he wrote, would no longer "consider anonymous and/or unsubstantiated calls made about a student's behavior; will not respond to calls issued from blocked telephone numbers; does not respond to any inquiry for student records unless that request is made by the student or an approved family member or guardian."

Whether our efforts are motivated by neurochemistry or good intentions, they leave many of our children feeling like commodities. Their lives become high-budget productions meant to attract the attention of admissions officers, scholarship committees, and football recruiters, not unique and imperfect stories just beginning to unfold. At the critical stage of adolescent development, as they are grappling with questions of identity—*who am I?*—they begin to question their place in society. They begin to feel valued not for their intrinsic worth, but for their external appeal, for their résumés. Surrounded by our achievement culture, they begin to wonder: Do only certain people matter in this world?

3

The Power of Mattering

Untangling Self-Worth
from Achievement

Rebecca tightened her grip on the steering wheel and blinked away the tears clouding her vision. She pulled over to the shoulder to compose herself before going home. It wasn't a terrible day at work or a personal loss that had her crying in the car, but a heated meeting at her daughter's school. The gathering had been quickly organized by school administrators to calm an eruption of parent frenzy. But as Rebecca leaned her head against the wheel and sobbed, she felt anything but calm.

At the time, Rebecca and her family were living in Denver. That week, she and the other parents in her daughter's kindergarten class had each received an email from the school announcing their child's scores on an IQ test. The results would be used to determine which kids entered the elementary school's gifted program. But some parents weren't happy. There was confusion about the reliability of the tests and a pervasive sense that the consequences of admission to the gifted track extended far beyond elementary school. The chosen few would be set on the right track for a successful, happy life—while everyone else fell behind. Perhaps none of the parents were thinking in those dire terms. But in Rebecca's highly educated community, as in others I visited around the country, parents can lose their cool over anything that appears to put their child at a disadvantage.

Rebecca's daughter had scored in the average range on the test, Rebecca told me. "Which is fine, of course," she quickly added. But the less-than-perfect score had triggered an unexpected, overwhelming reaction in her. It was the first time she'd encountered such a blunt evaluation of her child's capacities, and it caught her off guard. It felt as if a dam had broken inside her, and all the pressure she experienced growing up—getting straight As, skipping a grade, needing to excel at all times—came flooding back. And then she felt guilty and embarrassed about her reaction. This was when Rebecca realized that if she didn't get a grip on her parenting anxieties, they would get a grip on her children—something she knew firsthand.

Rebecca is a clinical psychologist who has treated adolescents in communities across the country—in the Bay Area, Los Angeles, Denver, and now Chicago. Her patients often arrive suffering from debilitating physical symptoms like migraines and gastrointestinal issues stemming from the extraordinary expectations placed on them. As a psychologist, she knows the limitations of standardized tests and understands why we shouldn't obsess over them. But as a mom of three, her kindergartener's "average" score affected her more viscerally.

Today, an avalanche of metrics, measurements, tracking, and sorting can gradually overtake a young person's existence inside and outside school. For Rebecca's daughter, this avalanche began in kindergarten, but middle school is generally when the rankings pile on for everyone. One mother in Illinois told me her daughter's school sorted the sixth-grade honor roll into three levels—highest honors, high honors, and regular honors—"to ramp up the sorting early." In high school, the sorting isn't just over grades but the difficulty of classes and the number of Advanced Placement classes you take— and how you will maintain a GPA that's *higher* than a 4.0. Outside class, you can't be just a good athlete who enjoys your sport, or a musician who loves your instrument—if you're going to attract acceptance letters or scholarships, you must be the *best* athlete and the *most accomplished* musician.

As if being measured at school and in extracurriculars weren't enough, kids today also clock into a third shift: managing their social media metrics. While teens have always wondered how they measure up against their peers, social media now offers a public and objective tally of popularity: the number of photos you're tagged in, your follow ratio (how many people you follow versus how many follow you), how many likes and comments your posts receive, even how quickly these metrics pour in. One mother I spoke with expressed concern over her daughter, a sophomore in college, who was using so many filters on her Instagram photos that her own mom hardly recognized her. The mother pulled out her phone to show me the difference between her real daughter and her daughter's online self: the Instagram version had longer, skinnier legs, a smaller nose, larger eyes, and an airbrushed face.

Of course, tracking and sorting aren't new. Growing up, I knew who the fastest runner, the strongest arm-wrestler, and the best mathematician and tennis player in my class were. But today, rankings feel more urgent and ever present. There is now a pressing need for children to score in the 99th percentile on a standardized test at age five, to make the A travel team in the fifth grade, and to tend social media profiles like a thirteen-year-old brand manager. Our generation took the SATs and ACTs and watched our GPAs, but our children are living under a tyranny of metrics.

"Average Excellence"

It's not only that there are more areas in which a child needs to be "exceptional"; it's also that the bar for what is "exceptional" keeps rising, offering our kids more and more ways to feel like they are not enough. Children absorb constant messages from our achievement culture that they need to be thin, rich, smart, beautiful, athletic, and talented to be worthy of likes, love, and attention. Like dutiful soldiers, our kids comply with these crazy demands. Over time, they internalize them. One student I interviewed dismissed his nearly straight-A report card at a competitive high school as "just *average* excellence."

For today's kids, it's less about "measuring up" than "measuring over." *Everyone* needs to stand out from the crowd. The pressure to excel is why parents in Denver were so up in arms over kindergarten test scores.

The researchers Thomas Curran, at the London School of Economics, and Andrew Hill, at York St John University in the UK, have spent the past decade trying to better understand factors that make people more or less vulnerable to mental health issues. What they have uncovered is a startling rise in perfectionism in young adults over the past forty years. They report a striking 33 percent increase over time in the level of unrealistic expectations placed on them by society and by well-meaning but pressuring parents.

Both Curran and Hill are quick to clarify that they're not blaming parents, who place excessive expectations on kids because they think that is what society demands. The problem resides in the potential gap between what a child can actually do and what a parent or society expects of them. Parents are reacting anxiously to a hypercompetitive world, with intense academic pressures, extreme inequality, and innovations like social media that feed unrealistic ideals of how we should look and perform, Curran explained.

A parent's pressure might manifest as hypervigilance about a child's grades, intrusive involvement in a child's schedule, or excessive criticism of their failures. The parent-child bond is the most important relationship for a child's mental health. When a child cannot meet a parent's high expectations, that bond becomes jeopardized. Criticism feels like rejection, a loss of love. The relationship transforms from a safe place into a danger zone. The fear of not being lovable as they are can push a child to pursue or present an idealized, perfect version of themselves in order to win the security and affection they crave.

Over time, young people internalize too-high expectations and come to depend on them as indicators of self-value and parental love. In kids' eyes, these metrics are marks they must hit in order to earn their worthiness. Not hitting those marks—whether it's because of inevitable setbacks or an impossibly high bar—can become an indictment of who they are.

When we talk about pressure, perfectionism, anxiety, depression, and loneliness in kids, what we are really talking about is an unmet need to feel valued unconditionally, away from the trophies, the acceptance letters, the likes, and the accolades. When we say that "pressure" is detrimental to children's (and parents') well-being, what we mean by "pressure" is a set of circumstances that cause our children to wrongfully perceive their value as contingent on achievement. When an adolescent believes they must sustain a certain level of success in order to earn their parents' love and affection, they feel inadequate, and this interferes with a healthy, stable identity.

Feeling Valued

It was the legendary social psychologist Morris Rosenberg who first conceptualized the idea of mattering, in the 1980s, while studying self-esteem among adolescents. Critical to the well-being of these high school students, Rosenberg found, was feeling valued: those who felt they mattered to their parents enjoyed higher self-esteem and lower rates of depression than peers who felt they mattered less.

When you feel like you matter, you are secure in the knowledge that you have strong, meaningful connections and that you are not going through this life alone, explained Gordon Flett, a professor at York University in Toronto and a leading researcher on perfectionism and mattering. Mattering expresses the deep need we all have to feel seen, cared for, and understood by those around us, notes social psychologist Gregory Elliott of Brown University. Elliott describes the feeling of mattering this way: Do people take an interest in you and what you have to say? Do you have people who can share your triumphs and support you after setbacks? Do people depend on you and rely on you for guidance and help? As long as we live, this instinctual need to matter never changes.

You've likely never heard about the specific framework of mattering, but you've surely felt it. Mattering occurs in life's big moments, like being celebrated with heartfelt toasts by friends. It's found in everyday moments, too, like when you're sick and a friend brings over a pot of homemade soup. The feeling that hits you when you open the door is *mattering*, that you are deeply valued by your friend and worthy of love and support. When a teacher assigns a child a classroom chore like watering plants, that child feels like they *matter*, that they are counted on and capable of adding important value to their little world.

Mattering has many layers. It begins with mattering to our parents and then extends outward to our community and the wider world. The more we feel valued, the more likely we are to add value, and the other way around—a virtuous cycle of interdependence that can continuously feed our sense of mattering, notes the community psychologist Isaac Prilleltensky. Mattering is what he describes as a "meta need," or an umbrella term that captures feelings of "being valued," such as belonging, community, and attachment, as well as feelings around "adding value," such as self-determination, mastery, and competence. Put them all together, he says, and you experience mattering.

No one is born knowing their inherent value. We form this perception over time, based on how we are seen and treated by the people in our lives, most critically by our primary caregivers. In other words, self-worth isn't developed in a vacuum. It functions as a social barometer, a way of tracking how we're doing in the eyes of others and becomes the story we tell ourselves about how much we are valued by those around us. When we are made to feel that we matter for who we are at our core, we build a sturdy sense of self-worth. We learn that we matter simply because we are. Mattering is a pathway back to our inherent worth. It tells us we are enough. Mattering won't solve everything, but it goes a long way toward addressing many of the emotional and behavioral problems facing our youth today, says Flett. High levels of mattering act as a protective shield buffering against stress, anxiety, depression, and loneliness. What is so appealing about mattering is how actionable it is. As parents, teachers, coaches, and trusted adults, we can dial up and nurture a child's sense of mattering so they can meet the challenges they have ahead.

On the other hand, when we are chronically made to feel like we don't matter, when we are abused, ignored, or made to feel marginalized, we can behave in ways that force others to take notice of us—whether that's obsessing over a perfect image, overworking, developing an eating disorder, or acting out in extreme ways (a school shooter being among the most visible and tragic examples). A lack of mattering is a strong predictor of depression, anxiety, substance abuse, and suicide. When we don't feel like we matter, we can turn inward: we give up, drink to escape, and even self-harm. People low on mattering tend to overgeneralize and catastrophize their thoughts, said Flett, convincing themselves that they don't matter now and will never matter in the future. Flett's research suggests that as many as one-third of adolescents in the United States and Canada do not believe they matter to others in their communities.

Our world of metrics and impossibly high standards directly undermines our children's sense of mattering. To be clear, every single parent I spoke with for this book loved and valued their kids deeply. The problem, I found, was that too many kids perceived their value and worth to be contingent on their achievements—their GPA, their number of social media likes, or their college's brand—not for who they are deep at their core. If children "matter" only to the extent that they follow their parents' directives or live up to their parents' standards, they will not experience true mattering, writes Gregory Elliott in his book *Family Matters*.

We are in a crisis of the self. The formative years are when a child builds a stable foundation for a secure, sustainable adult identity. What we are doing instead is inadvertently sending a devastating message: In order to be valued, you must audition for it, work for it, and keep earning it. Only then will you matter in this house, at this school, in this world.

In his book *The Psychology of Mattering*, Flett notes seven critical ingredients to feeling like you matter:

1. **Attention:** Feeling that you are noticed by others

2. **Importance:** Feeling like you're significant

3. **Dependence:** Feeling like you're important because others rely on you

4. **Ego extension:** Recognizing that someone is emotionally invested in you and cares what happens to you

5. **Noted absence:** Feeling like you're missed

6. **Appreciation:** Feeling like you and your actions are valued

7. **Individuation:** Being made to feel unique, special, and known for your true self

Not What You Say, but What They Hear

Despite our loving efforts, we are unintentionally denying our kids a key release valve to their gilded pressure cooker: close, nurturing, caring relationships that deliver mattering. In my research, I have found that it's not enough to love our kids unconditionally, as we do. To matter, our kids must also *feel* that the love is unconditional. That feeling is formed not by what we say but by what our kids hear—and they are natural prodigies at translating our doublespeak, like when we say that grades aren't everything but then ask how the test went the minute they walk in the door.

"Many parents perceive their children feel that they matter when in fact their children don't feel that way or they are not sure whether they matter," Flett told me. He spoke of one school board survey showing that only 8 percent of parents believed their children felt that they didn't matter, when, in fact, 30 percent of the students reported feeling that way. You may think your own children know just how much they matter to you, but my student survey tells another story:

- Astoundingly, more than 70 percent of the young adults I surveyed reported that they thought their parents "valued and appreciated" them more when they were successful in work and school.

- More than 50 percent went so far as to say they thought their parents loved them more when they were more successful, with 25 percent of students saying they believed this "a lot," the highest degree the survey allowed.

- When I asked respondents to agree or disagree with the statement "I feel like I matter for who I am at my core, not by what I achieve," a surprising 25 percent of students agreed either "a little" or "not at all."

In other words, one in four of the students in my survey believed that achievement, not who they are as people, is what is most important to their parents. When a friend of mine asked her son if he ever thought he was more loved or liked when he did well academically, he told her, "Well, everyone's mood does seem better when I bring home an A."

My survey also asked students, "What is one thing that you wish adults in your life knew about the pressure you feel/felt in high school?" As a parent, the responses were hard to read:

- I wish they would have understood that grades are not everything. Their pressure to be an overachiever was the catalyst for my depression and anxiety issues.

- It felt like my worth was tied to my grades.

- I wish my parents knew that it's okay for me to get less than perfect grades sometimes. It's okay not to be exceptional in everything.

One student wrote that they wished their parents understood how the pressure they exerted was "more mentally abusive" than "helpful." Others described more subtle forms of criticism: "My mom would compare me to my friends—and my friend's parents would compare them to me—and that kind of comparison was really damaging to my mental health and the way I viewed myself." When you criticize a child, they don't necessarily stop loving you, psychologists say; they stop loving themselves.

We all know the stereotypes: the critical or withholding mom, the overinvolved sports dad. Most of us know that such behavior is destructive, and we consciously try to avoid it. Still, it's natural to get swept up in feelings of pride when our kids shine and to button our lips when bad news hits to avoid piling on. But these reactions can send subtle messages, and they can make a big impression. One New York City student poignantly decoded them for me. "I know that when my report card comes and my parents take a few days to talk to me about it that they're not pleased," he said. "They think they're being helpful by not being critical, but their silence hurts just as much." As he spoke, I felt my cheeks blush, knowing that I'd probably done similar things to my own kids without realizing it. I had celebrated their wins but kept quiet when they bombed a test. I was disappointed *for* them, not *in* them—but how could they know that? Nothing could make me love my children more or less. But did my kids understand it that way? Seeing it from this student's perspective made me want to run home and set the record straight.

When I mentioned this story to the psychoanalyst Robin Stern, associate director of the Yale Center for Emotional Intelligence, she told me about a similar experience with her own kids. Stern would include handwritten notes in their lunch boxes—"Thinking of you" or "Hope you're having a great day"—signed with her signature two-word pep talk: "Personal excellence." Recently, she and her children, who are now young adults, were talking about those lunchtime messages. Her daughter said to her, "Yeah, no pressure with those notes, Mom."

Robin was mortified. "That was not at all how I meant them," she told me. "I wanted them to stay on their own path and not worry about how the kids around them were doing. But my kids interpreted my pep talk as pressure."

The difference between what we say and what our children hear is magnified in the teen years. Like all of us, teens come wired with a negativity bias. Simply put, adverse events elicit a stronger neurological response than positive ones. Criticism, research suggests, has a much greater impact on us than positive feedback does. Moreover, psychologists have shown that teenage negativity overperforms that of other age groups, making teens hypersensitive to threats in their environment, even imagined ones. This bias also means that the subtle messages our kids receive regarding achievement—a raised eyebrow, a question about how a test went—can come across as excessive pressure. *Perceived* parental criticism, which a parent may subtly wield in an effort to mold and control a child's behavior, is linked to poor mental health outcomes.

Feeling controlled and routinely criticized can make an adolescent feel less accepted by a parent, which weakens their relationship. When that relationship feels weak, a child can in turn feel like they matter less. The consequences of associating love with achievement can last far beyond childhood. It can set our children up for a lifelong pattern of accepting themselves only with strings attached: *I'll be worthy when I get straight As, lose ten pounds, get 100K followers.* In a world that already values achievement, our kids don't need the adults in their lives to push for their excellence. What they need to hear is the opposite: that their worth is absolute and their value to us never fluctuates.

The False Self

As Gregory Elliott says to his students: "What gets in early gets in deep." When a parent is critical (*Why can't you be more like your brother?*) or when love feels conditional (*I expect all As this semester*), a child begins to feel defective. To cope with those painful feelings, they learn to hide who they really are, their true self, in order to become the person they believe their parents want or need them to be. In other words, the child makes a subconscious trade: they abandon their real self to stay connected to their parent through the long, vulnerable years of adolescence. It can lead kids to develop what psychologists call a false self—an artificial persona that serves as a coping strategy to get the love and support the vulnerable child needs to survive.

While a pressured child may put on a good show, inside they harbor shame over not feeling lovable as they really are. Over time, a false self can lead to choosing the wrong friends, partners, or careers—essentially, to living someone else's life. At their cores, people in such situations feel unlovable and unknown. In the most extreme cases, the heavy burden of a false self can cause a young person to feel suicidal. As one student who had been hospitalized for an attempted suicide told me, "It wasn't even like I was killing myself. I was killing this fake person I'd created, someone I didn't even know."

Beth, a single mother of two adolescents in Los Angeles, was raised by parents who provided her all the material things she wanted, even if it meant sometimes emptying their bank accounts to do so. She was a nationally ranked athlete, top ten in her age bracket, for much of her high school career, and she attended a highly competitive all-girls school. Despite all the trappings of a wonderful life, home never felt safe for Beth. Early on, she had intuited that to get her parents' love, she would have to live the life *they* wanted, even if it meant betraying herself. Beth understood, albeit subconsciously, that her job was "to be the trophy child," to win, look perfect, and "be someone my parents could brag about to their friends."

When Beth did pursue interests her parents didn't value, or when she stumbled in reaching a goal, she felt rejected by them, even scorned. "I was the kid who wanted to talk about my feelings, who was sensitive, and my parents would shut me down," she said. On the other hand, when Beth followed her parents' directions and performed at the top of her game, she was met with love and approval. To cope, she did her best to appear perfect, but this was isolating and lonely. Presenting a flawless image forestalled healthy vulnerability. "It prevents you from reaching out," she told me.

Beth had always wanted to be a child psychologist, but her parents pushed her to go to law school, offering to pay for her schooling as an incentive. "Being a lawyer was not who I was nor who I wanted to be," she told me. She suffered from panic attacks all through law school and took medication to cope. After graduation, she got a job at a top Los Angeles firm with A-list celebrity clients, which thrilled her parents. But walking into the lobby every day, she felt like she was carrying a "big, bulky gorilla costume around my body," she said.

"Conditional regard" is the psychological term for parental affection that depends on a child meeting certain expectations, whether academic, athletic, or behavioral. Researchers distinguish between two types of conditional regard: positive, like when children feel their parents provide more warmth and affection than usual when expectations are met, and negative, when affection is withheld after expectations aren't met. Psychologists have shown that conditional regard undermines a child's self-esteem. Instead of figuring out who they really are, adolescents fixate on pleasing others.

To be clear, conditional regard and unconditional love aren't mutually exclusive. Conditional regard is determined by a parent's behavior and a child's interpretation of it. For example, you will still love your child unconditionally if they bomb a test or flop on the field in front of college scouts. But you may pull back a bit all the same. Your expression of disappointment can signal conditional regard. To our kids, that coldness feels like being loved less.

This kind of parenting can be passed down from generation to generation. In one study that tracked parenting styles and well-being over three generations, researchers recruited 124 mothers with college-aged daughters to complete questionnaires about their parents' use of conditional regard around academic achievement. The mothers answered questions about their own self-esteem, how they coped with stress, and their attitudes toward parenting. Meanwhile, their daughters were surveyed about their mother's use of conditional regard, evaluating statements like "As a child or adolescent, I often felt that my mother's affection for me depended on my academic success."

The researchers found that if grandparents used conditional affection to encourage academic achievement, the mothers went on to use the same conditional affection with their own daughters, even though this strategy had had negative effects on the mothers, eliciting anxiety, shame, low self-esteem, poor coping skills, and resentment toward their parents. The daughters likewise reported experiencing conditional regard—a kind of emotional family heirloom.

Of course, having unconditional positive regard doesn't mean that parents can't have expectations about a child's behavior. Psychologists say we must be mindful about how we express those expectations. When a child acts in ways that are inconsistent with our values or hopes, we need to signal warmth even while expressing disappointment. In other words, we need to separate the deed from the doer. You still love the person, but you don't love the action. When we're able to clearly separate the two, a child doesn't link their worth to their behavior, whether "good" or "bad." This creates room to make mistakes and grow up without fear of failure.

In reflecting on her childhood, Beth realized that both of her parents tied their own self-esteem to her successes. Researchers call this phenomenon "child-contingent self-esteem." The connection between parent and child is complex enough to permit two-way traffic—parents sway their kids' self-worth and adjust their own self-worth depending on their offspring's accomplishments. Psychologists have developed an assessment to measure child-contingent self-esteem that involves asking participants to rate how much they agree with statements like "My child's failures can make me feel ashamed."

A parent's tendency to invest their self-worth in a child's performance is influenced by both their personality and perception of the social environment. In my survey, I asked parents what it means in their community to "succeed" in raising kids. Their answers reflected some commonalities, succinctly stated by one parent: "You are judged by the success of your child's academics and athletics." Another wrote that success in their social setting meant that "their child is the best at everything."

Even young parents had a sense of what "success" was supposed to look like. One parent of an eleven-month-old wrote about how her peers were very focused on milestone achievements as a yardstick for parent success—and how parents feel responsible when their kids don't hit the developmental mark.

For Bill, a father of two boys in Mid-Coast Maine, recognizing how stress from day-to-day parenting affected his own self-esteem proved illuminating. "For a few years, it felt like every Sunday there was an article in *The New York Times* about how parents are doing it wrong," said Bill. "Every time I read those articles, I felt bad, and when I felt bad, I was actually a worse parent." He lost his patience with his kids, became overly critical of their behaviors. The expectations conveyed by media triggered deep feelings of inadequacy, vestiges of his own childhood.

Bill recalled reading a piece of advice that helped turn his behavior around: parenting is about the child, not the parent. For example, Bill explained, he might have the thought *If I were a better parent, they would get better scores on their SATs*—without even realizing that he was thinking it. That subliminal thought would sometimes lead him to overreact or to say things he didn't mean. "What [kids] will hear in the frustration or anger in my voice is not that *I'm* a terrible parent, it's that *you* are a terrible person, even if I don't say it," Bill said. In the everyday grind of parenting, when so much seems to be riding on our shoulders, it can be hard to be so reflective. Bill came to realize that recognizing the self-critical voice in his own head allowed him to challenge and control it, rather than having the emotion control him. "I consciously made the decision to do my own psychological and emotional work so that my kids don't have to do it for me."

For Beth, it was only by grappling with her upbringing through therapy that she slowly shed her bulky gorilla costume. As an adult, she went back to school to become a therapist, the job she had truly wanted all along. "In order to be the kind of parent I wanted to be for my own daughters, I realized that I had to look back at my past and reparent myself," she said.

In her own home, Beth has purposefully created an environment where the public masks we all wear are left at the front door and where her girls can be themselves, however messy or imperfect that looks or feels. Her daughters know they belong unconditionally at home, she told me. And they know that who they are—their emotions, their hopes and dreams—matter to their mother. At dinner, family conversations are often about the highlights *and* lowlights of their days. Beth opens up about her own struggles to model vulnerability. She told me, for instance, that she had talked to her girls about how nervous she was to be interviewed by me, but that she was going to fight through the feeling. As our chat ended, Beth said she couldn't wait to share it at the dinner table that night.

Beth has learned firsthand that coming to terms with our past and repairing our own self-worth can bolster the self-esteem of the entire family. Beth told me, "I knew that if I wanted my girls to grow up with self-worth, with a true sense of who they are, I'd have to model it myself."

Good Warmth, Bad Warmth

Children thrive in warm, loving environments. Decades of research show this. But there is a difference between what the psychologist Madeline Levine calls "good warmth" and a more controlling "bad warmth." Good warmth is the love, understanding, and acceptance a parent communicates to a child as they change and grow, writes Levine in *The Price of Privilege*, and good warmth is cultivated by taking time to get to know our kids in intimate and specific ways. Bad warmth, on the other hand, can look like overinvolvement in a child's life, like doing for your child what they can do for themselves. To a child, bad warmth feels conditional. For instance, it might involve showering a child with effusive praise about a grade or performance as a way to keep kids invested in what the parent deems important. Bad warmth can be tempting in its convenience and quickness, a short-term strategy that a tired parent might use to get a child to conform to expectations.

Okay, you may be thinking, *but what if my child does need a bit of a push when they aren't living up to their potential?* Most kids want to do well in school, Levine says, so get curious, not furious, about what's going on under the surface. Rather than getting upset, spend your energy getting to the root of the problem. Listen to them, ask probing, open-ended questions, and take time to figure out *why* they're underperforming. How we manage our emotions when our kids inevitably disappoint us is one of the greatest challenges parents face, writes Levine: "While it is tempting to deal with our disappointment and anger by being critical, research is very clear that just as warmth and connection are the silver bullets of parenting, criticism and rejection are the deadly ones."

In other words, the way we express our concerns and expectations makes a difference in our relationship with our kids. Leigh, a New York mom, told me the story of how she developed good warmth with her fifteen-year-old son, Jake. For months, Leigh and her husband constantly battled with Jake over inconsistent grades. Sometimes he'd buckle down, study, and ace his tests; other times he'd goof off, play too many video games, and bring home Cs. His first report card freshman year was straight Bs. "I know that Bs are fine," she told me, "but my son has big dreams, and he's actually capable of reaching those dreams, but those grades are not going to get him into the kind of college he wants." This tension turned into a nightly battle.

The friction caused Jake to become even less motivated to do his work. He became sullen and withdrawn, so much so that Leigh reached out to a therapist for advice. The therapist asked her to track her interactions with her son. "The majority of our conversations were around convincing him to do something that he didn't want to do, like pushing a boulder up a mountain," she said. Too many of their interactions had an agenda, the therapist told her. For kids in high-achieving communities who absorb pressure all day, the therapist warned her, home needs to be a warm place to recover.

Still, it's a parent's job to set some standards. Mattering doesn't mean letting our kids off the hook. Realistic and attainable standards communicate to our children that we are invested in their development, *that they matter to us*. Leigh's therapist suggested that she avoid fixating on a particular grade and instead focus on her son's work habits, how and when the work got done. Leigh and Jake made an agreement. If he sat down at a desk and tackled his homework following a short after-school break, without distractions on his desk like his phone, she would stop nagging. They would try this for a few weeks and see how it went. Meanwhile, Leigh actively worked on reversing the negative-to-positive ratio in their daily interactions. She focused on having several encounters each day that carried no agenda, like going for a walk, cooking together, or affectionately rubbing his head when they passed in the hallway. By being deliberate about her interactions, Leigh was able to move their emotional ledger well into the positive. "It's not perfect, and sometimes I still find days when things feel more negative than positive, but I really try to keep that ratio in my head," she told me. On days when she hits the right ratio, when they do something fun together that has no end game, she said, "The whole climate in the house changes for the better for both of us."

Leigh was also learning how to use good warmth in their relationship even in the midst of a conflict. If a school night had some tension, no matter what, she made a point to pop into his room at bedtime to hug him and remind him: *I love you the same no matter what.* When a parent has this kind of positive relationship, they become the go-to person for their child, a safety net for their child's mental health. When the vital parent-child relationship thrives, the child senses their intrinsic value and feels reassured psychologically and biologically that they are safe and not alone. Close, supportive relationships aren't just a lifeboat in rough seas; they are also the most effective source of strength and resilience for reaching higher. Something else happened when Leigh loosened the reins and focused on maintaining warmth: Jake took more ownership over his schoolwork, and his grades went up. Leigh, who had been raised with parents who criticized her as a way of showing love, had learned a different way to parent. When I asked her what Jake thought of the change, she told me, "He said that he was happy to get his mom back."

Our children feel freer to express their true selves when we focus less on molding them into what our communities regard as "exceptional" people and more on seeing and loving them for who they are right now, their wonderful, "ordinary," authentic selves. Our job as parents isn't to push or drag our kids to excellence. It's to correct the lies that our society tells them: that they matter only if they're performing, if they're achieving. Our job is to let them know they are enough, right now, in this moment.

Get a PhD in Them

While the problems with being critical and withholding are obvious, researchers have also found that praise can function as bad warmth. Like criticism, praise is a form of judgment and can make a child vulnerable to shame when they don't measure up. As one student in my survey explained, "Being told that I was especially good at something felt like I had to then work really hard to maintain if not exceed the levels at which I was already doing it . . . [or] I would be worth somewhat less."

Parents might feel like they can't win: we want to set high standards for our kids, but both criticism and praise have the potential to cause harm. Thankfully, the sweet spot for showing unconditional love and positive regard is a lot bigger than you might think. As Harvard's Richard Weissbourd notes, "The self becomes stronger and more mature less by being praised and more by being known." Our children feel they matter to us when we know them deeply and uniquely.

That advice has stuck with me. Yet sometimes parents—well-intentioned, loving parents—struggle with knowing their kids for who they are. Some of us may want our kids to carry on our legacy. Fathers who loved sports, for example, might be crushed to learn their sons don't. Mothers who performed on the stage might be disappointed to find their daughter is too shy to ever stand up in a crowd. This disappointment clouds our vision of our child, causing us to see who they aren't instead of who they uniquely are.

So much parenting energy is often spent on identifying and fixing our kids' weaknesses: who needs help with social skills, or with math or writing. But a mother I met in Maine used a different strategy. She told me about how she really got to see her kids for who they were by becoming a "strengths spotter," by noticing when her kids were at their best. Instead of looking at her kids' deficiencies, she told me, she shined a light on their best aspects and found ways to use those strengths to drive their growth.

Interestingly, researchers estimate that two-thirds of us don't know what our own strengths are. We tend to lack awareness of the gifts we have to offer the world. This mother in Maine told me about an online survey she had taken with her kids that helped to map their top "character strengths," their most prominent positive personality traits. The VIA survey, standing for "Values in Action," was created by the renowned psychologists Martin Seligman and Christopher Peterson, along with a team of fifty-five scientists over the course of three years. The survey, available on VIA's website, https:// viacharacter.org, takes about ten minutes to complete. It can be eye-opening for any parent who has wondered about their kid's natural strengths, or their own.

As much as we love our children, we are sometimes blind to their strengths, partly because of negativity bias and partly because those strengths are so central to their personalities that they become invisible. That's why it's helpful to take note of what other people point out about your children. For example, I've taken to literally annotating teacher comments on our kids' report cards, underscoring what others see about them. I highlight their strengths—"supportive to classmates" and "diligent"—and then comment in the margins, "I see this too!" or "Totally agree!" I keep these annotated report cards in each of my kids' baby boxes—huge containers full of important keepsakes. We revisit these boxes every couple of years, and it's fun to see how their strengths have been evident to their teachers all the way back to kindergarten.

Amy, a junior at Yale, said her parents helped her become aware of her best traits by writing her "strength letters" annually, beginning on her tenth birthday. More recently, they've begun sending the letters before milestones: college drop-off, her first summer away from home, the beginning of her gap year. Now the stack of letters is so fat, she told me, that the drawer gets stuck when she tries to open it. Over the years, she has gone back to reread the notes "as a reminder of who I was at that stage of my life, what my passions, habits, and personality quirks were then." Notably, the letters rarely focus on individual achievements but on ways in which she has demonstrated curiosity, grit, or compassion. She added, "They took note of who I was, even when there wasn't an accompanying medal to bring home or an A to show for my hard work, and those letters proved to me that my parents saw me, the full me. That level of attention was proof of their love."

The Puppy Dog Principle

To show our kids how much we value them, we must attune ourselves to the emotional and physical nuances of our communication. Mattering can be communicated through what Gordon Flett calls "micro-practices": Do you light up when your children walk in the room or do you pepper them with questions ("How'd you do on that test?") to relieve your own anxiety? For the mother and psychologist Susan Bauerfeld, mattering means greeting your children at least once a day like the family puppy: with total, unabashed joy. This includes being physically affectionate with them and playing with them.

Gordon Flett offers tips to convey mattering to kids in his book *The Psychology of Mattering*:

- Respond in a warm and sensitive way

- Explicitly tell kids how much they matter to us

- Express unconditional acceptance, particularly after a failure

- Show warmth through affection

- Engage in mutual activities

Flett warns of ways parents can unintentionally convey a sense of their kids not mattering:

- Being overly focused on themselves

- Treating some kids in the family as more or less important

- Rewarding kids with praise and expression of warmth when certain expectations are met

- Engaging in harsh criticism

- Comparing kids negatively to others

- Invalidating emotions

Physical touch and affection emphasize how much our children matter to us. Or, as NYU professor Scott Galloway poignantly writes about his own loving mother, "For me, affection was the difference between *hoping* someone thought I was wonderful and worthy—and knowing someone did." In fact, studies have shown a link between warm parental affection in childhood and future mental and physical health. One study out of Notre Dame found that children who were raised in a physically affectionate household reported less depression and anxiety and higher levels of compassion as adults.

So much of our lives as parents consist of getting our kids to do things they don't want to do, teaching them lessons, setting them up for future success. But something gets lost when our relationships don't include enough time just enjoying each other, delighting in what is inherently lovable about our kids. That's why playtime as a family is so critical. When we don't carve out time for play, we lose out on some of the highest-quality interactions we can have with our kids—getting immersed in something together, as equals. Play has no agenda and offers a judgment-free place for our kids to be, to learn, and to become their ordinary selves. It can be hard to protect that time, of course. My husband, Peter, instituted a family rule: at least once a week, all of us must participate in something he branded NOFAs, or "nonoptional family activities." It's a signal to the kids that play and family time is a priority in our house: yes, we value hard work, but we also value having fun together. Our kids need to learn and cultivate the skill of using downtime as a way of replenishing themselves and their relationships. Past NOFAs have included game nights, picnics at the beach, bike rides, and working through one-thousand-piece puzzles.

Peter is a strategic thinker, so he paired NOFAs with OFAs (optional family activities) to offer the kids some agency. The branding helped to get buy-in, as did allowing the kids to participate in choosing activities. Sometimes we even play video games as a family, if that's what one of the kids chooses. Before you balk at the idea of having to learn about Fortnite: one recent study found that the more frequently family members play video games together, the more family satisfaction and family closeness they report. It's less about what the activity is and more about the closeness you feel as a family doing it.

Maintaining this closeness, especially with older kids, requires parents to push back against the negative, unfair stereotypes that surround teens: that they are prickly, sullen, and moody and don't want us around. Yes, developmentally our kids are pulling away and forming their own identities, but that doesn't mean parents should be pulling away, too. Parents, research finds, remain the most important source of support for our teens in these critical years. And this sometimes requires us to knock on closed bedroom doors to issue an NOFA. Keeping this relationship strong offers our kids not only support now, it also serves as a model for the kind of warm relationships they can replicate in the future.

Make the Implicit Explicit

Of course we want our kids to strive to be the best they can be. But we need to be mindful about how we communicate that desire so that their inherent value—their mattering—is never in question. Parents cannot assume their kids know that they matter, Flett told me; we must engage in what he calls "proactive mattering promotion"— explicitly telling our kids how much they matter to us.

Here's a "mattering lesson" I learned from a mother I interviewed. One night, when her hard-working teen was excessively worrying about an upcoming test, this mother pulled out a twenty-dollar bill from her wallet. She crumpled it up, put it on the floor, theatrically squashed it, then dunked it in a glass of water. Picking up the soiled, soggy money, she said to her son, "Remember, like this twenty-dollar bill, our value doesn't change, even when we're dirty and bruised and soaking wet, like when we get a bad grade or get cut from the team or mess up in a million ways."

Knowing this has shifted the way I talk about achievement in our house. What I have discovered is that parents must keep up a steady beat of unconditional mattering to drown out the harmful messages of our culture. One night before bed, for example, Caroline talked about how she and her friends were worried about their upcoming report cards. After listening to her concerns, I took a minute to point out her strengths. I told her that I saw how much time and care she put into her schoolwork every day, how organized she was, and how engaged she was in her education. I knew she was doing her best, so I wasn't particularly worried about what was on the report card. If the upcoming grades didn't reflect the time and effort she put into her work, then we would figure it out together, I said. She seemed to lower her shoulders a bit in relief.

Then I grabbed a Post-it note from her desk drawer and scribbled on it:

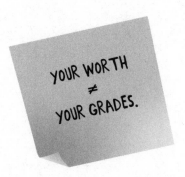

YOUR WORTH ≠ YOUR GRADES.

I handed it to her along with an explicit statement of what too often remains implicit: "My love for you never changes. It doesn't depend on how you behave, what you look like, or any grade you get."

Fighting the messages sent by our "never enough" culture takes constant and consistent reminders. It is not solved over one bedtime conversation, with one Post-it, or even with a hundred. But I am hoping that over time the message will sink in. And I think it's starting to. That sticky note I gave Caroline so many months ago is now taped to the keyboard on her laptop, serving as her own constant, gentle reminder.

4

You First

Your Child's Mattering
Rests on Your Own

The morning unfolded like a TV sitcom. For two weeks in a row, I'd been waking up at an ungodly hour—before 4:00 a.m.—to meet looming deadlines. I remember stumbling into the kitchen to make breakfast for the kids, gently placing the eggs in the pot, putting the pot on the stove . . . and then forgetting all about it. Almost an hour later, everyone awoke to the screech of fire alarms and the smell of smoke.

By 7:15 a.m., I'd lived a full day. So when my eight-year-old asked me to come watch him practice basketball after school, I didn't immediately jump at the opportunity. Sensing my "no," James issued a full-court press. "It's what *aaaaalllll* the other moms do," he pleaded, scooping soggy Cheerios into his mouth. *All the other moms sit and watch the practice? For real?* Maybe it was the sleep deprivation, or the mom guilt he'd triggered, but I heard these words coming out before I could stop them: "Yes, of course, I'll be there. Wouldn't miss it!"

So I stopped work early that day, threw on enough concealer to cover my dark circles, and devotedly, if begrudgingly, made my way to the gym—to watch him *practice*. The gym was swarming with so many kids that the coaches cut the gym in half to accommodate everyone. I got myself as comfortable as I could on the steel bleachers. And then, for the next two hours, a dozen other mothers and I proceeded to stare at the partition screen that cut through the middle of the gym. Of course, James was on the other side of the screen, practicing on the far court. But I saw nothing, and I got zero credit for making it there to cheer him on at a *practice*. And now I'd have to make up for those wasted hours.

Indulge me, if you will, in a little thought experiment: Imagine your child was moving through life as I was that day. They were waking up before 4:00 a.m. to do work, desperately filing assignments, killing themselves to please their teachers, their friends, you. What might you say to them? Remind them that what they do or don't do doesn't affect their worth? That they are worthy of care and compassion? Yes, these are the wise words of a parent who knows how to make their child feel like they matter. But there's also what *they see you do*.

Kids learn and internalize mattering not just by absorbing our words, but by absorbing our actions, how we *model* mattering. A "take my advice, I'm not using it" approach backfires. Our kids see the dissonance between our words and our actions when we exhaust ourselves, trying to secure the best for them. Think about it: We want our kids to know that they are more than just their grades, but we ourselves prioritize good outcomes, in their lives and our own. We want our kids to lean on us for support when they are feeling overwhelmed, but we shoulder everything alone. When we put every family member's needs above ours because that's what "good" parents, particularly mothers, do, we are showing that we don't think *we* matter—even if we think we're showing our love.

To raise our kids well, I have learned from talking to experts, we have to examine what we're doing, not just what we're saying. Do I behave as if my worth is unconditional, do I practice being kind to myself, do I act like my interests are just as important as theirs?

Your kids need this from you, but you also need this for yourself. Because you matter, too.

The Tipping Point

Wearing no hat, no gloves, and no scarf, I stepped off the train wildly underdressed for the chilly New England fall day. Earlier that morning, I had rushed out of my apartment to drop off my bundled-up kids, a huge cello, and an oversized science project at school— and I myself had forgotten to bundle up for the gusty weather.

For the third time in as many months, I had come to Wilton, Connecticut, a suburban town in the southwestern part of the state, with beautiful homes, winding streets, and stone walls that stretch for miles. I'd come to meet with a mother of three named Genevieve Eason. She had moved to the town in 1999 for the same reasons that have attracted many families: the community's storybook charm, its commuter-friendly proximity to New York City, and its schools, which rank among the best in Connecticut. Genevieve sat across the table from me at a lively Italian restaurant, recalling just how thrilled she and her husband, Rob, had been to find a place like Wilton.

Every day at 6:00 a.m., Rob left to catch the train to his finance job in New York, while Genevieve stayed home and kept the household running. A graduate of UCLA, she set aside her ambition of working in wildlife conservation to take on the stay-at-home role, very much a privilege, she pointed out. "I imagined a career sitting in tall grasses or hidden in the bushes observing wild animals and taking notes on their behavior," she said. But now, she poured herself into giving her children what she hoped would be "the perfect childhood," as free as possible from life's many road bumps. The stay-at-home life suited her: she soon found herself channeling, as she put it, "a lot of Martha Stewart," taking pride in her cooking and keeping a well-decorated, well-organized house.

The demands of raising three children filled her days and then some: her time and energy went to chauffeuring them to various activities, supervising their homework, offering them emotional support through friendship woes, and making sure their needs at home were met. "I was in touch enough to not want to live through my kids," she recalled. "But I also wanted them to be healthy and happy, to find their unique talents." As she saw it, her role was to support her children so that they could live up to their potential. "If they wanted to quit an activity, my job was to make sure they didn't," she explained. She made sure that they practiced their musical instruments, that the math enrichment worksheets came home, and that the kids exercised and ate well. Even her adult friendships orbited the kids and their lives; it was easier to maintain a social life that way.

But when the kids' friendships shifted in middle school, much of her own social group fell by the wayside. There simply weren't enough hours for her or Rob to nurture many relationships of their own. Yet she didn't dwell on all she'd given up—a career, her time with friends. Everybody had a job to do, and hers simply required these sacrifices. Besides, she reminded herself, these responsibilities wouldn't last forever. Mothering was her profession now, one she should enjoy while it lasted, and some days—when her children beamed with pride performing in a dance recital or triumphantly waved a straight-A report card—she felt as though she, too, was hitting her stride.

As the kids grew older, their schedules grew as well. Genevieve did what she could to maintain a sense of balance for everyone, but the reality of what it takes to be a high-achieving student in Wilton hit her the summer before her oldest, Savannah, began her sophomore year. Except for PE and choir, every class her daughter planned to take was either honors or AP. Fearing Savannah might be biting off too much, Genevieve suggested she meet with the school's guidance counselor for advice. But her daughter prided herself on being strong academically; in sixth grade, she had been invited to take an accelerated math class two years ahead of grade level. She did not want to pass up opportunities in high school. So Genevieve let it drop. "I didn't want her to think I didn't support her or believe in her," she explained.

Even though life continued to be hectic and sometimes stressful, things seemed to be going well at home—until, almost overnight, they weren't. Ten days into Savannah's sophomore year, she tiptoed into her parents' room in the middle of the night, gently woke up her mother, and whispered, "Mom, I need your help." Tears dripping down her cheeks, Savannah told her mom she was so stressed about schoolwork that she was contemplating suicide. Genevieve spent the rest of the night with her. Early the next morning, she called the pediatrician, who dispatched a crisis social worker to their house.

The social worker gave Genevieve and her husband a directive: they were to remove academic responsibilities from their daughter's plate. Genevieve had wanted Savannah to have the autonomy to make her own choices, but the social worker was clear. Savannah felt pressured to take on the challenges, and she could not step back herself. So, the following day, Genevieve went to school and helped Savannah withdraw from the advanced classes that were causing her the most stress. "It sounds ridiculous to say now," she told me, "but at the time, it felt risky, like we were giving up something very important to her future."

Genevieve was now shouldering a new, formidable layer of parental responsibility, both all-consuming and emotionally draining. On top of looking out for Savannah, she was still running the house and trying to meet the needs of her other two kids—her middle child, too, was now showing early signs of excessive school pressure. Looking for insight, she went into therapy. "I was always asking my therapist what the 'right' way was to handle this problem or that problem," she told me. She was often short-tempered, particularly with Rob, "who really had to walk on eggshells around me." The stress—the stress of making sure her daughter was relieved of stress, the stress of making sure her other two children felt seen, too—started to take a physical toll. Her body began to hurt, with an intense pain running from her jaw down through her back. Her dentist informed her that she was suffering from TMJ, or pain and stiffness around the jaw joint, often a product of tension, and suggested she take up yoga or Pilates. She found this laughable. When was there time? "It was like, 'Great, now I have to add 'self-care' to my to-do list,'" she told me.

Aside from the teachers and administrators at school, she told almost no one about what her family was going through. Savannah didn't want anyone to know just how much she was struggling—she worried about her reputation among her friends and their parents—and to respect her privacy, Genevieve kept these struggles to herself. Instead, she'd wake up alone in the middle of the night worrying. "I knew there was something wrong, and that meant that I was doing something wrong," she said, "which meant that I was somehow a bad mother."

Intensive Parenting

It is easy to believe that sacrifice is the only way we can secure a decent life for our kids. To be a "good" parent today is to be an all-consumed parent, norms primarily defined by white, affluent parents who have the time, money, and privilege to engage in "full-contact parenting." Some parents move houses, neighborhoods, towns for their kids, even change careers or give them up entirely, if they can afford to. Like Genevieve, when I had my children, I temporarily sidelined my career to raise them, a choice many mothers never get. For our family, it made economic sense. If I stayed working, my modest salary would cover childcare but little else. My husband's higher salary could support us in a way that mine never could.

When I left my job, it was not only to raise our kids, but also to support Peter: he had received a work opportunity in London. As he went about networking in a new country, I went about running our lives. If I wasn't working a full-time job, I decided, I would instead devote myself, as Genevieve had done, to making our family life perfect. Instead of researching stories, I researched ideal sleep routines, the best ways to introduce new foods, the healthiest sunscreens, and the philosophical differences among parenting styles and preschools. I devoted my education and talents to my kids and their successful future. Parent-teacher conferences felt like my year-end reviews.

As parents, we listen and chauffeur and chaperone and coach and cheer and help with homework and attend games and even practices. Each effort, each sacrifice might seem worthwhile on its own, but when we take them together, we can see an exhausting pattern: what sociologists call "intensive parenting." Intensive parenting is a parenting style that puts children's needs at the front and center of family life. Being a parent, of course, has always meant putting your needs second. But this kind of parenting demands an excessive level of sacrifice, which more often than not leaves our own basic needs unmet. It also sets the bar so high that it's virtually unreachable for all but the most privileged parents who have the time and resources to parent this way.

Despite advances in gender equality, the responsibility of launching a "successful" child still weighs more heavily on mothers, research suggests, no matter their employment status. Since the mid-1970s, the time mothers spend on childcare has gone up 57 percent, despite the fact that 71 percent of mothers now work outside the home. That can mean that working mothers are spending more time taking care of kids than stay-at-home mothers did in the 1970s. Additionally, panel studies—long-term studies that follow the same people over time—find that the number of hours spent on children's activities has gone up the most for college-educated mothers, more than it has for college-educated dads or non-college-educated mothers. The sociologist Sharon Hays has argued that our society has developed unrealistic expectations for women's home lives as a way of compensating for our uneasiness with the self-interest required of a woman developing her career. These expectations developed as more white women entered the workplace and Americans struggled to define what it should look like for a mother to care about her work inside and outside the home.

While mothers in particular have been found to fall into this style of intensive parenting, fathers are increasingly adopting it as well. According to Pew Research, since the mid-1970s, the time fathers spend on childcare has almost tripled. Modern fathers know they matter to their child's well-being. The "good father effect," as sociologists call it, finds that more involved dads make a positive impact on their children that can last through the years. The expectations we have for ourselves, that our partners have for us, that society has, are changing and expanding, and that's exciting, said Matt Schneider, a stay-at-home father of two boys in New York City and the cofounder of City Dads Group, a support network of fathers. As a society, we are starting to reconsider the lines between the traditional roles of father and mother. "But dads are thirty years behind women in trying to figure this all out," said Schneider.

Same-sex couples can struggle, too, with dividing labor once children come on the scene. When Lynn, a mother of two from Portland, Oregon, was first married, she and her wife were "pretty equal" in the division of labor. But once they had their first child, very quickly Lynn assumed the role of the lead parent, bearing

80 percent of the household and childcare, while her wife focused more time and energy at work earning money to support them. "The truth is, same-sex couples wrestle with the same dynamics as heterosexuals," Abbie Goldberg, a psychology professor at Clark University, told a reporter for *The New York Times*. She added, "Things are humming along and then you have a baby or adopt a child, and all of a sudden there's an uncountable amount of work."

At the same time, the networks that parents have historically relied on for help—extended family, committed neighbors—have eroded. People move away from their families and neighborhoods for jobs, leaving behind critical sources of support. One woman I interviewed had relocated with her family to a new city and told me that when she first moved in, she had to put her real estate agent down as an emergency contact on her child's school form because she knew no one else in the area.

These one-person villages have increased the burden on individual parents to do everything, and be everything, for their families. And we are feeling the pressure. Time and time again, the mothers I spoke with shared the lengths to which they go for their kids. For some, this looks like sleepless nights and concealer-caked days. Others bear a more existential toll. Victoria, a mother of five in New York, was so devoted to managing her children's busy schedules that she trained herself, inadvertently, to hold in her urine all day. It's not that she fought the urge, she explained; it's that she didn't feel the urge in the first place. Victoria had trained herself not to have needs at all because "not having needs meant that I couldn't be disappointed if they weren't met," she said.

Another mother with three kids under ten shared a similar sentiment. "After fighting so hard every day to keep some sense of my old self alive," she told me, "I've decided to just give up and surrender to motherhood for now." When I asked if she was happier as a result, she replied, "No, but I think I'm less stressed, because I no longer think about how I'm going to carve time out of the day for me." As she spoke, an image flashed before my eyes of her old self lying, lifeless, under a pile of laundry, just waiting to be found.

The researcher Suniya Luthar calls parents "first responders" to our kids' daily struggles, and paying constant attention to their roller-coaster feelings and social and academic pressures can take a toll, particularly when we don't have time to recover before another problem hits. There are plenty of weeks like this: your daughter doesn't make the cut on the soccer team, your son bombs his math test, and one of them gets left out of *another* Friday-night party. We want to be, and should be, a constant source of empathy for our kids, but the nonstop snags of everyday parenting do add up, even on a biological level: one study found that the more empathetic a mother is, the more likely she is to experience chronic, low-grade inflammation, a physiological process which is believed to raise the risk of serious health issues like cancer and heart disease.

Intensive parenting is also associated with heightened feelings of isolation and a greater sense of burden. More recently, Luthar has found that college-educated, overextended mothers can be particularly susceptible to chronic stress and burnout. In fact, the parents most at risk for anxiety and depression in these competitive communities are mothers with children in middle school, when the children start to pull away from parents and there is less emotional return on our sacrifices. In *All Joy and No Fun*, the journalist Jennifer Senior details how mothers who chose to stay at home, along with parents who didn't engage in meaningful hobbies or have fulfilling jobs, were particularly vulnerable to a decline in mental health during these years. She writes, "It was as if the child, by leaving center stage, redirected the spotlight onto the parent's own life, exposing what was fulfilling about it and what was not."

Adolescence is also, incidentally, when the pressures of high achievement start to really kick in. One study, conducted by Luthar and her colleagues, analyzed surveys from over 2,200 college-educated moms across the country. Luthar found mothers with middle-school-age children reported "the highest levels of stress, loneliness, and emptiness, as well as the lowest levels of life satisfaction and fulfillment."

"Good mothers put their needs last, right?" Genevieve asked me with a smile the day of my visit. And I thought back to how I'd left the house that morning without a scarf while my kids were probably sweating under the layers I'd protectively draped over them. We've come to accept that how we parent, what we do and what we don't do on any given day, will directly impact our child's well-being and success—and that the sacrifices we make are an implicit measure of our love for our kids. But where does that leave us?

Bowling Alone

After Savannah's crisis, Genevieve's focus shifted, as she and Rob put their energy toward creating a home environment where their kids could escape the pressure of not feeling "good enough." Genevieve found her daughter a therapist, and took a more active role in helping her daughter manage outside pressures. Genevieve was there to tell her that she had spent enough time studying for a test, that taking on another extracurricular activity might encroach on what little free time she had, that a good night's sleep would help her finish the paper more than an all-nighter would.

Genevieve felt lucky, even grateful, to be able to support her daughter in what seemed like such a healthy way, but secretly she wondered if other families were also struggling. She had no one to ask. At that time, mental health wasn't something you talked about in Wilton, she told me. "It was important to maintain a facade."

Despite the increased support, in the winter of Savannah's senior year, on New Year's Eve, Rob found Savannah in her room, holding scissors to her wrist. She had kept her struggles with the college admissions process and the stress of senior year to herself. Savannah was so depressed that her parents had her admitted to a hospital. "I was worried that I wouldn't be able to keep her safe at home," Genevieve said.

To protect her daughter's privacy, Genevieve told almost no one about what had happened. She felt all the lonelier, holding it inside, until one unremarkable afternoon in the middle of the school's parking lot. She and a mother she barely knew were walking to their cars when the other woman suddenly disclosed that she was worried about her own child, who was struggling with academics and social comparison. Then, blushing, the mother caught herself. "Well, your daughter is so beautiful, smart, and popular," she told Genevieve. "You wouldn't understand."

All at once, Genevieve realized she was not alone. Here they were, giving their kids their very best—and somehow it wasn't enough. Neither of them knew how best to help their children. But standing there in the parking lot, all Genevieve could think to say was "Oh, things aren't always as perfect as they seem."

Soon after, she spoke with a mental health counselor in Wilton, who confirmed that Savannah's struggles were becoming increasingly common in the community. Instead of feeling comforted, Genevieve was furious. *If we know this is happening, why aren't we doing something about it?* she wondered. As medication helped Savannah improve, Genevieve and her daughter decided to forgo the secrecy. If other people weren't talking about mental health struggles, then Genevieve would be the one to start. Through their church, she organized a Mental Health First Aid course, which offered training on how adults could respond to mental health crises.

In attendance one evening was Vanessa Elias, a mother of three adolescent girls, whose oldest had also threatened to harm herself over academic pressure. Vanessa, too, had been keeping her family struggles a secret, and she, too, was exhausted: one week, she'd counted thirty-seven drop-offs and pickups from activities, sports, and school. "I felt like a failure as a mom," she told me. But that day at the church, as she listened to Savannah open up about her experience, she felt hope. Someone was finally—*finally*—speaking to her struggles. Afterward, Vanessa approached Genevieve: "I think we should get to know each other," she said.

I met Vanessa during one of my visits to Wilton, when she picked me up in her minivan to take me around town. She is self-deprecating and sarcastic, with a warmth that puts you immediately at ease. As we drove, she told me a story from when she had first moved to town, about five years ago. A neighbor had called asking for a cup of flour. "It made me feel warm and fuzzy inside that I could help," she said. "It made me feel connected." The next day, Vanessa pulled up to her house and saw a bag of flour leaning against her front door. The neighbor thought she was being helpful by repaying the favor so quickly. But Vanessa read it differently. "It felt like a slap in the face," she told me. "It felt like you can't owe anyone anything, have any kind of dependency on someone else—it was as if she couldn't deal with having a cup of flour hanging over her head."

It's a small moment, perhaps a funny thing for Vanessa to remember, but it represents a bigger idea, one that I heard over and over again in my interviews all over the country: the expectation that today's parents must be independent and self-reliant. This mindset seeps into even the tiniest crevices of our lives, into places you may not consciously realize but innately feel, as with Vanessa and the flour. People pride themselves on being capable, and no one wants to appear dependent on anyone else, Vanessa said. As she rounded a wide corner, gripping the steering wheel, she added, "I call it living in our own little silos of hell."

This lack of intimacy in affluent communities can feel all the more alienating for parents of color. Some of the Asian mothers I interviewed talked about enduring the harmful stereotype that they were all "Tiger Moms," accused of harming the mental health of their kids and ratcheting up the competition for everyone at school. Several Black mothers I spoke with said they have felt isolated in majority-white communities, where, for example, addressing race at school has created tension among some parents.

Working mothers talked about how it stung to appear as if they couldn't give their kids as much time as stay-at-home mothers. One stay-at-home mother, meanwhile, told me she felt less valued because she wasn't bringing in a salary; in her community, staying home was seen as a "lifestyle" choice, frowned upon as displaying a lack of ambition. Many moms talked about the burden of abundant opportunities. "We are supposed to be working full-time, being a fully present mother, staying in shape, living in trophy houses, and raising trophy kids," one woman told me.

And yet what all these relatively affluent mothers had in common was this: there was an unspoken assumption that being materially successful should somehow protect against distress, that high levels of education should provide the skills to eliminate worry and loneliness. Given the many resources at our disposal, we wrongly believe we *shouldn't* need help. "As a management consultant, I help solve problems for a living," one mother in Washington, DC, told me. "And then I feel totally incompetent when I can't figure out how to manage my own family's problems."

Our viciously meritocratic mentality—that old pull-yourself-up-by-your-bootstraps thinking—has pushed us toward an overworking, overproductive lifestyle that dominates the energy and attention we used to give to other things, like our friendships. For decades now, sociologists have charted the decline of social structures, from churches and civic groups to bowling leagues. They have documented how we are "bowling alone," disengaging from the larger community. Instead of spending time together building trust and cooperation in leagues, at religious institutions, in local clubs, we are bowling alone in our own siloed lanes.

Just Perfect

When I became pregnant shortly after moving to London, I spent months planning the perfect arrival for our son. At my doctor's suggestion, I wrote a birthing plan, a document that laid out exactly how I wished the delivery to go. I wanted to hold off on the epidural until the last minute, so that I could have the freedom to move around as I labored. But labor didn't go as planned: William came like an earthquake. My water broke, and after a desperate taxi ride through Hyde Park, I barely made it to St Mary's Hospital in time. In my sweatpants, I dragged myself up the hospital steps, the same spot where a perfectly put-together Princess Diana had been photographed holding *her* William decades before. Within two hours of my water breaking, I arrived in the delivery room fully dilated. There was no time to read the birthing plan, let alone get an epidural.

It was not quite the introduction to motherhood I'd envisioned. I was determined to make up for the rocky start. We held tiny, beautiful William as if he were made of glass, beset with love and wonder, and I resolved to become my very best self for this child. I read every parenting book I could get my hands on and considered going back to school to become a child therapist—not to practice, just to feel "certified" that I could mother right, relying on the latest research and theories. As William grew, I offered him endless energy, eye contact, playground visits, and reliable routines. I bought him gender-neutral toys. Knowing that his vocabulary was directly affected by how much I spoke to him, I talked all day long, narrating our lives: "Now Mom is cooking William hamburgers."

Other mothers I'd gotten to know in London and New York acted out their perfectionistic tendencies in their own idiosyncratic ways. In London, as a new mom, I was amazed at how many prams (flat strollers) were assembled with freshly ironed baby linens—and at how there was never a single sign of spit-up in sight. In affluent communities in New York, the more "perfect" mothers were the ones who fit back into their skinny jeans just days after giving birth.

Performing the "perfect mother" act can be exhausting. A "good" mother, we've come to believe, isn't just committed to being the best she can be. She must hide any cracks in her mask. Showing need, we fear, will reveal weakness—and weakness makes us vulnerable. It puts our status—our family's status—on the line. A "good" and status-safeguarding mother, then, must maintain an I've-got-it-together veneer for the sake of her family. "You can't just have friends over on a random Thursday to have a glass of wine and catch up, because your house is a mess and you'd have to serve some beautiful hors d'oeuvres, get flowers, and put on a nice outfit," said Genevieve. "You don't just invite people over in your sweatpants."

And so, instead, we exhaust ourselves. We go to basketball practice with enough makeup to hide just how much we're wearing ourselves down. Because at the end of the day, it all has to be worth it, right? We make these choices, and willingly pay the costs, because our kids matter to us—deeply. Surely they pay off?

I posed this question to Melissa Milkie, a sociologist at the University of Toronto and a mother herself, who has been studying the rise in intensive parenting over the past three decades. "It's complicated," she replied. There is little strong evidence to show that the sheer amount of time mothers spend with children is linked to better outcomes. Rather, research finds that the quality of time and type of activity matters more. And mothers do not have to be the only ones who provide quality activities for their children. I, like many moms who could afford to, had put my career, my social life, and my own wants and needs on hold for the betterment of my kids—yet here was Milkie telling me that my sacrifices *may have a negligible effect*. I nearly dropped the phone.

It gets worse, Milkie explained: some research suggests that intensive parenting may actually have a *negative* impact on our kids.

"Having mothers who are exhausted and burned out is not likely to benefit their kids," she said. I thought of Wilton, a town filled with loving, child-focused parents just like Genevieve. When the community's parents invited the researcher Suniya Luthar to survey Wilton's students, she found that 30 percent of them were experiencing "internalizing symptoms," including clinically significant levels of depression and anxiety—compared to a national norm of 7 percent. Moreover, 20 percent of Wilton students had "much above average" levels of these symptoms, compared to the national norm of 2 percent. The data from Wilton wasn't unique, Luthar stressed. It was consistent with other high-achieving schools across the country. And we're not talking about the occasional blues here. We're talking about eating disorders, habits of self-harm, anxiety, depression, and thoughts of suicide.

It's not that we parents aren't doing our best, Luthar said empathically; we are not being neglectful or unloving. But all the ways that we are overstretched—work deadlines, financial anxieties, emotional turmoil, satisfying our child's every need—can deaden our ability to be sensitive, responsive parents, she explained. We are more likely to be moody and critical and controlling, and less attuned to our children's emotional cues. Anxiety, depression, and exhaustion impair our perspective and patience, as well as our ability to be consistent; to set healthy boundaries, limits, and schedules; and to find the energy to start fresh the next day when we fall short.

Most alarmingly, our kids can misinterpret our stress and impatience: they may internalize the belief that something must be wrong with *them*. "A feeling of not mattering is often rooted in the smaller actions or lack of responses that accumulate on a daily basis," notes researcher Gordon Flett. Feeling like you don't matter or that you matter less than, say, a parent's career or social life can contribute to a child's negative view of themselves as not worthy enough to be valued. Kids can feel the difference between a parent who works two jobs because they need to financially and a parent who chooses to work rather than spending time with them. Feelings of low mattering can make a child feel isolated in their own home, even among close families. Psychologists refer to this phenomenon as "proximal separation"—when "a parent is physically there but emotionally unavailable because they are too stressed and distracted" by work or other concerns.

A feeling that you matter to your parents is an adolescent's first and often greatest source of well-being, Flett told me. Among boys, it has been found to have an even stronger impact than mattering to one's friends. One of the most influential factors of parental mattering "is the extent to which the parent is psychologically present," Flett writes in his book *The Psychology of Mattering*. When we run ourselves ragged to secure every benefit for our children, we deny them that crucial presence.

Kids do not need parents who take self-sacrifice to the extreme. They need parents who have some perspective on the fraught high-achievement culture they find themselves in. Our kids need parents who have the wisdom and energy to call out the unhealthy values of achievement culture for the threats they are. And kids need to hear consistent countercultural messaging: about their inherent worth, about the delight they give their parents, about their meaning and purpose as a part of a larger world.

In the past, psychologists interested in helping at-risk kids focused on specific interventions. They told parents what they should and shouldn't do: set limits that are firm but reasonable; convey affection, but in the way your child needs it; know your child's friends and their parents, but don't be intrusive; push your child to do their best at school, but don't be too demanding; give honest feedback, but without being critical. Being a parent is like walking a tightrope, said Luthar. But as it turns out, there isn't a magical list of dos and don'ts that can teach a kid to weather life's storms. What makes the biggest difference is simply having psychologically healthy adults in a child's life—parents, teachers, coaches, mentors who are not struggling with untreated depression, anxiety, or high levels of stress. Decades of resilience research makes this clear: a child's resilience depends on their primary caregiver's resilience. At home, the primary caregiver is usually the mother. This directive, Luthar said, has turned child development upside down. To help the child, first help the caregiver.

Being a mom is a tough job, made even harder when we must swim against the powerful tide of community norms. To love a child well—to walk the fine line between supporting a child and respecting their autonomy—a parent must, of course, have the emotional and physical resources to do so. You need a mental calmness, a composure, which is impossible to maintain unless you yourself feel supported. To be good parents, we need to take care of ourselves. But to take care of ourselves *first and foremost*? The idea can be hard to wrap our heads around. After all, it directly contradicts how society tells us—especially women—to parent.

I discussed this contradiction with Luthar when we met for fish tacos in Phoenix, Arizona. Luthar is a petite woman with expressive brown eyes and the authoritative demeanor of someone at the top of their field. Across from me, she elaborated on the preeminent importance of a mother's own mental health. As she spoke, I scribbled on my yellow notepad, nodding along. But soon I felt her staring at me, anticipating my skepticism. When I looked up, her eyes narrowed.

"Why are mothers so resistant to this message?" she asked. "Why don't they understand the importance of taking care of themselves first?"

"Are you talking about a 'put on our own oxygen mask first' kind of thing?" I asked, thinking I finally understood her point.

"*No*," she said emphatically. She leaned over the table. "I'm *not* asking women to add yet another thing to their long to-do lists. What I'm talking about is finding people who will put that oxygen mask on *for you*."

I leaned back, took a sip from my margarita, and tried to process her words. Luthar stared at me. Then, utterly exasperated, she added: "If you won't do it for yourself, *do it for your kids!*"

The Friendship Solution

What we need, Luthar explained, is not the kind of "me time" marketed to tired women by the multi-billion-dollar self-care industry. The trick is not running a bubble bath twice a week, or getting your nails done, or taking up yoga, or finally trying out that meditation app that's been sitting on your phone, unused, for a year. Instead, the trick is prioritizing the rich relationships that allow us to feel deeply loved and cared for, just as we strive to make our children feel with our own caregiving.

Friendship buffers against the wear and tear of daily stress, lowering anxiety and regulating emotions. Social support, research finds, short-circuits our body's natural threat response; experiments have shown that when a companion is in the room, our stress is reduced. It sounds hokey, but our relationships act like a shock absorber, reducing the brain's response to pain. One study found that if two people are standing together, looking up at a hill, the incline doesn't look as steep as it would if they were each alone.

Do our friendships on the PTA count as authentic and supportive? Do our marriages? What exactly are the ingredients for this kind of bond? Luthar, as a scientist and a mother, was interested in this question, too. In an effort to help women get the most out of their relationships, she has studied the effects of research-based support groups for mothers facing high levels of stress in their daily lives. Based on an earlier successful program for mothers in poverty, Luthar developed a twelve-week program for college-educated, professional mothers called Authentic Connections Groups. Luthar tested the program with medical practitioners—physicians, nurses, and physician assistants—at the Mayo Clinic in Arizona. During weekly one-hour meetings, Luthar pursued two goals: to establish close bonds—among the women within the group and with chosen "go-to people" outside—and to introduce new skills for effective parenting. After twelve weeks, participants reported significant improvements in mental health and well-being, and even showed decreased levels of the stress hormone cortisol. These gains were not just sustained but improved over the three months after the Authentic Connections Groups program concluded. Remarkably, not one woman dropped out, despite their busy schedules. Many kept meeting long after the study was over. Subsequent studies by Luthar and her collaborators have shown the same patterns in both in-person and virtual Authentic Connections Groups across the country.

What Luthar discovered is that mothers don't need hours of time together to form the kind of authentic friendships that bolster our mattering and resilience—we just need deliberate time. The women in Luthar's studies benefited from just one hour a week of intentional connection. One participant described how eye-opening it was to find that "you can create real connections in such a short time."

One parent in Maryland, a mother of two named Margo, explained that building these close connections early in her time as a parent saved her. Twelve years ago, when her daughters were toddlers, she connected with three other mothers whose kids were the same age. Ever since, the group has remained close, comparing notes as their kids have entered adolescence. "Whenever I share something hard that I am going through with one of my children," she said, "they always meet me with understanding and validation that they are dealing with similar issues, too." Just knowing that she isn't alone helps her relax and avoid excessive self-criticism. "It allows me to get past the worry and be more present with my children," she told me.

This talk of authentic relationships is all well and good. But in practice it may feel impractical. There are only so many hours in the day, and parents have only so much energy to give. It can feel impossible to meet a friend for coffee or to intentionally share your worries when you have to drive your kids to and from gymnastics four days a week and act as a homework helper, screen-time monitor, and short-order cook.

It's not that the parents I met in these affluent communities didn't have friends. It's that they didn't have the bandwidth to deepen the intimacy of their friendships enough to become a source of relief for one another. When life gets hectic, it's easy to move friendships to the back burner. In my own survey, 60 percent of parents agreed with the statement "Because of parenting demands, I don't see my friends as often as I'd like." Or, as one mom put it, "Everyone is so busy, no one has time to hear my sob story."

There are different ways to go about this, but I'd like to recommend two key practices that have helped parents I interviewed keep friendships strong and healthy. They may strike you as simplistic, but in our overextended lives, you'll be surprised by their power. Here's the first: put your friends on the calendar.

Friendship is a gift we give ourselves. Friendship has a deep, healing power that I didn't fully appreciate in my twenties, when my friends and I were more focused on just having fun together. Research has found that time with our friends may make us the happiest, happier than time with anyone else, including our children, relatives, parents, and even spouses. And yet friends are the first ones to take a back seat when life gets hectic. We take them for granted, thinking they'll always be there, until one day, maybe they're not. Without intentional focus and attention, even close friendships can fade away over the years.

Consider how deliberate you are with your family's schedule and needs—how you write down when that specific karate instructor is teaching or pull up your calendar to put in a playdate. What would it look like for you to be just as deliberate with the friendships that sustain *you*? We're willing to carve out the time we need to work on our marriage, our relationship with our kids—why not our friendships, too? Can you apply the same intention that you give to all the permission slips, reading assignments, and after-school sign-ups to the cultivation of friendships? There's an assumption that real friendships just happen—that they don't require work and attention.

But this assumption is a false one, and it holds parents (especially women) back from taking a more active and thoughtful role in pursuing and building deep, sustaining relationships. We don't need a lot of time, remember, just commitment.

Vanessa has come to realize this. "Unless we put ourselves on the calendar first, it's like trying to save money at the end of the month: there will be nothing left over," she said. She herself has developed a go-to committee: a friend in Pennsylvania named Jen, with whom she has a Zoom call every Wednesday (Jensday, Vanessa calls it), and an old friend from high school, whom she meets every Friday for lunch. "Before, we would go four months without seeing each other," she explained, but their newly consistent commitment has brought them deeper connection—and helpful insight into their daily lives. "I feel more joy. I feel heard, seen, and understood," Vanessa told me.

It can feel counterintuitive, focusing on your relationships outside of the home for the sake of the people within it. But many of the mothers I spoke with testified that their lives are kept afloat by this intentionality. "My friends and I live really busy lives; most of us commute into work and have a house full of children and responsibilities that eat away our time and energy," a mother of two adolescents in a New Jersey suburb told me. Life can make it hard to find time together, she continued, but she and her friends commit to having dinner at least once a month, and that dinner is written in pen. "I've also come to realize that *which* friends I spend my time with really impacts my parenting," she continued. "I make a conscious effort to invest in friendships that make me feel good when I'm with them and who bring out the best parts of me, so that I can bring those best parts of myself to my parenting," she said.

"After these dinners, my kids see me coming home happy, relaxed, and rejuvenated, and I can more easily share myself. I have something to give them."

Vanessa asked me, "You know that phrase 'You're only as happy as your least happy child'?" She said that was once her parenting style: She would ride shotgun next to her girls on their emotional roller coasters, feeling first-hand the ups and downs of their adolescence. When a daughter opened up about social drama or pressure at school, she'd internalize her pain—and then spend the next day emotionally spent. "My kids don't need me climbing on their roller coaster," said Vanessa. "They need me to be their rock when they're whipping around." Her regular check-ins with friends have helped her become that rock; they make her feel grounded. Now, when her kids are struggling, she is a more mindful listener and a better resource to them.

Don't Worry Alone

To build these kinds of life-sustaining relationships, a second critical practice is the willingness to be vulnerable—*and* the willingness to accept support. We're comfortable telling people we're looking for a new job or trying to lose a few pounds, but in our hyperindividualistic society, we're often reluctant to admit we need support. Psychiatrist Edward Hallowell, a father of three, writes in his book *The Childhood Roots of Adult Happiness* that there is one rule he puts above all others when it comes to worrying about a child, or about anything else: never worry alone. It's simple yet profound advice that I have implemented as my own family mantra.

If there's a silver lining of the pandemic, it's that it has made us realize how much we need relationships in our lives, how much we need to lean on each other for solidarity. Suniya Luthar's Authentic Connections Groups work so well in part because they normalize asking for help. They are built on the principle of giving and receiving support. According to Luthar, we can take this idea beyond the support-group setting; the key is to be explicit with your needs. "You must literally ask someone to be your go-to person, the person you call when you're upset and need support," she said. If this feels cringey, think of it this way: vocalizing your need shows that you trust the other person, and it also holds you accountable to lean on them when you need it. Luthar points out that your go-to cannot be your spouse or partner—our relationships with them are often already overtaxed, due to the disbandment of our traditional villages.

Instead, we can create a go-to committee. Luthar suggests the following roadmap: Decide on a couple of friends who make you feel safe and who you think might be comfortable being open. Suggest meeting once a week on a designated day and time and protect that time. Then set expectations: the goal is to be heard, understood, and comforted in a caring context (not so much to offer advice). Take turns running the group each week, starting with a simple prompt, such as "How is your week?" or "What's on your mind?" The space should be a place to share things you're struggling with, but also a space to celebrate joys. End on a positive note, with each person offering up something they're grateful for or a mantra they plan to keep in mind over the week.

Margaret, from an affluent community in Oregon, told me that it was her friends who got her through a difficult time in her marriage. When she and her partner of twenty-three years were unexpectedly separating, Margaret said, "I very intentionally reached out to my friends because I knew that they would be the best resource to get me through that difficult time. And once I was able to get through that time, I was obviously able to be a much more focused and present parent." Margaret's friends would show up every day to take her for walks or to have a cup of coffee. There was also a steady stream of texts, calls, and Zooms throughout the day for the first four months or so after she and her partner separated. Inspired and buoyed by her friends' support, Margaret started a file on her phone called "Friends' Wisdom," where she collected the best, most supportive texts. She'd read them over and over again whenever a wave of grief would hit her, until they became almost a mantra: "I can do this. I am resilient." The quicker she was able to get through the anger and grief, she thought, the better chance she would have of building a solid coparenting relationship. "Ninety percent of my recovery from the separation was because of my friends," Margaret told me. They were a net of social support that carried her through.

Asking for help is powerful precisely because high-achievement culture discourages it—reaching out can disarm those around us, causing them to drop their defenses, too. It's also critical to our mattering: when you ask for help, you recognize that you are important enough to have your needs met. At the same time, you communicate to your friends that *they* matter to you, which bolsters their own mattering. "We have a culture that sees asking for help as a weakness," noted Vanessa. "But anyone who has ever asked for help knows how much humility and strength it takes." Because she and her friends talk openly about what they are wrestling with—time crunches, guilt, communication with their kids—they can remind each other of their worth as individuals, not just as supermoms.

Fewer than two weeks after meeting each other, Genevieve and Vanessa read an ad calling for volunteers for the Wilton Youth Council, a nonprofit that offers programs on parent education and student well-being. Looking for insight into their own families, both mothers started showing up to the monthly meetings, which tackled big topics such as substance use and anxiety. At last, they had found a community of like-minded parents and professionals that felt honest—and safe. "I finally found a place where people could talk about things without judgment," Genevieve said. "It put Savannah's story into a broader societal context and validated my sense that cultural forces beyond my control were at play."

Vanessa and Genevieve were so clearly invested in the mission of the WYC that they were asked to run the program the following year. The two jumped at the chance, organizing talks and book clubs so that other parents could learn to be open about Juuling, drug use, suicide. "Parents will say, 'Oh, not my kid.' So we hosted events called 'Not My Kid,'" Vanessa told me, laughing. "There's a lot of denial out there. We wanted to show you're not alone."

Savannah finished high school and left for college on the West Coast. But after a few months, she dropped out and enrolled in culinary school, where she was able to combine her long-standing interests in chemistry and creative arts into a career. Genevieve was able to swallow her anxieties and fully support her daughter. She had the clarity to see what her child really needed, even if it didn't fit the achievement list she'd once held in her head. Savannah is now working as a pastry chef on the West Coast, and while she still has her difficult moments (as most twentysomethings do), she is thriving.

When Genevieve looks back, she sees that she and her daughter were experiencing the same thing. "Savannah didn't want people to see her as 'less than' or unable to measure up," she said. "And I worried that if my kid was really struggling—and she truly was—people would blame me." A successful child meant you were a good mother; an anxious or depressed child, on the other hand, meant you didn't have enough family dinners, or weren't strict enough, or were too strict, or were a helicopter mom who had pushed your child beyond their limits, she said.

By joining the Wilton Youth Council and opening up to others, Genevieve found that her family's struggles were not unique. The WYC gave her hope, she told me, that so many dedicated, compassionate, and knowledgeable people were working to combat the negative effects of achievement pressure. "We've become good at catching kids as they fall off the cliff. We know the warning signs and how to get them help," Genevieve told me. "Now we have to do something to stop herding them to the cliff in the first place."

5

Taking the Kettle
off the Heat

Confronting Grind Culture

A ndrew was planning his schedule for the fall of his junior
year in high school, one that he knew would be critically
important for his college applications. As a sixteen-year-
old growing up in an affluent community outside Seattle, Andrew
played travel soccer, mentored kids in his community, and thought
he might want to be an engineer one day. Looking through the course
listing, he scanned for the math and science classes. If he could add
another class to his schedule, doubling up on AP science classes,
he believed it would improve his odds of getting admitted into a
top engineering program.

Which classes you were taking, and the rigor of your schedule, was a big topic of conversation at school. "You ask your friends how many APs they're taking, and some people are taking a full load, and then you feel compelled to not slack off, so you add even more to your plate," Andrew said. In his high school, he explained, the expectation among the students was to take advantage of every opportunity available to you.

Andrew was raised on Mercer Island, a small, thirteen-square-mile island about a ten-minute drive over a floating bridge to Seattle. Ranked by *Money* magazine as the best place to live in Washington State, its picturesque parks and miles of hiking trails attract residents who work as executives for some of the country's most profitable companies—Microsoft, Starbucks, Amazon, and Boeing. The community is upscale and many of the residents I met worked long hours to afford to live on Mercer Island so their kids could attend the excellent public schools.

Like his ambitious peers, Andrew knew exactly how he wanted next year's course schedule to look. Now he just needed his parents to sign off on it. His parents, Jane and Mike, said they'd consider it. But Andrew's schedule for next year was already "ridiculous," Jane said, with more than a full plate of honors and AP classes on top of travel soccer and volunteer commitments. By adding even more to his busy day, he would have absolutely no downtime—or even time for a full night of sleep.

After thinking about it for a few days, Jane broke the news to Andrew that they wouldn't be letting him double up on AP sciences. "Andrew was furious," she said. He argued that if he wanted to be a competitive candidate for top colleges, he would need all of these sciences courses on his transcript. Also, Andrew believed he could manage the work, and his best friend was doubling up too. "This was an area where I had a good track record," Andrew told me as he recalled the incident years later. "I felt that this was best for me. I felt like my parents were limiting me."

Despite Andrew's protests, Jane and her husband held their ground. "We always thought that our job as parents was to take the kettle off the heat," Jane said. "Our kids get enough pressure at school, with their peers, and from themselves." Still, in communities where ambition can come to define you, it was easy to second-guess her instincts. When the then high school principal sought to limit freshmen and sophomores from doubling up on science classes—an effort to curb unhealthy achievement pressure—some parents argued it would be harmful for their children's applications to top colleges. The cap was never implemented.

It can be challenging to go against the tide. But Jane knew she was the last line of defense in protecting her children's mental health. She felt it was her responsibility to help her kids set healthy boundaries around school, sports, and extracurriculars. If at any point they looked like they might be at risk of drowning, Jane gave them explicit permission to get out of the water—or pulled them out herself if she had to.

Surrounded by the Grind

For decades now, sociologists have been documenting how our country is splitting along lines of social class, with those at the top end of the socioeconomic spectrum creating communities of "SuperZips"—towns like Mercer Island, where there is a heavy concentration of high-income and highly educated families. When the term was first introduced in 2013, *The Washington Post* located

650 SuperZip communities in the United States, where two-thirds of adults had college degrees and the average household income was $120,000.

Growing up in a community packed with materially successful people who have similar expectations around achievement can turn up the pressure on children. Kids sense a duty to produce a kind of "encore effect"—to uphold their family's status and one day replicate their expensive upbringing. They internalize these expectations. When I asked students in my survey to define what it means to be successful in their community, their responses were incredibly consistent: "nice homes" and "high-paying careers." Or as one mother in Palo Alto put it, "Parents say that they just want their kids to be happy, but what they really mean, and their kids know this, is that they want them to be happy like they are, with the prestigious job and the big house."

You don't have to be a forensic accountant to figure out how much a parent's lifestyle costs. A simple Internet search reveals a house's estimated worth and tax history, the price of a fancy hotel stay in London, the sticker price of a new car, the salary ranges for any number of careers—it's all a few clicks away. "No one wants to live at a lower standard of living than the one they grew up in," said Lisa Damour, a child psychologist who lives in Shaker Heights, Ohio. She sees this pressure heightened in her clients from more affluent families because of the narrowing of the kind of lifestyle they feel they must maintain, the jobs they feel they must do (mostly in finance or tech), and the neighborhoods they feel they can live in.

At a small dinner party, I was seated next to a father with two daughters, and we were bonding over our mutual love of old TV classics like *The Brady Bunch* and *Little House on the Prairie*. It turns out we were both watching these old episodes with our kids to expose them to a simpler life. Over dessert, he asked me: Do you think we've ruined our kids by raising them in a place like New York, surrounding them with *so much* at such a young age? With so much focus on money and personal success, were our kids being saturated with the wrong values?

It's not just New York, I said. Wealth is concentrated now in pockets all over the country: Atherton, California, and Weston, Connecticut; Waban, Massachusetts, and Crystal Bay, Nevada; Kenilworth, Illinois, and Rye Beach, New Hampshire, among the other hundreds of SuperZip communities. Even when we consider ourselves generally even-keeled, the communities we've opted into can make it easy to lose sight of what we think we value. I told the father about one public school I visited in California that had recently hosted a student career fair. The panel was extraordinary: Academy Award–winning directors, C-suite executives, tech moguls, and some of the state's top surgeons and lawyers all gathered in one room to talk to the students about their professions. All I kept thinking when I heard about career night was that *this* was now the bar for success. A senior at the school commented to me, "It's ironic that adults wonder why there's so much anxiety and depression in my generation when they're the ones who have created this crazy environment for us."

When I asked psychologists and researchers what was making young people today more vulnerable than past generations, they all pointed to one thing: the increasingly narrow definition of "success." The problem isn't wanting to be successful, but how we have come to define success as a society and the strict path we've laid out to achieve it. "In affluent communities, you can literally go through a checklist of what's 'the best,' and it creates an intense pressure and competition among peers and families to keep up," said Rachel Henes, a consultant and parenting coach who specializes in working with high-achieving schools and families in the New York City area. "I work with parents of kids as young as preschool who are already worried about getting their kids on this path."

On a surface level, this means kids can come to believe their value rests on achieving the external markers set by their community: where they go to college, what job they land, where they live, what they buy. At a deeper level, they can come to believe something even more damaging: that they are expendable. Their health, their interests, their needs—these are not marked as important. Instead, a "work hard, play hard" lifestyle is the ideal, the expected cost for getting ahead.

And no cost is too much. "If you had asked me at age fourteen if I'd chop my leg off to attend Stanford, I'd have said yes in a millisecond," said a recent graduate of another Seattle-area high school on a local radio show. It was at age twelve that she "became a slave to the goal of being the best" and earning a place at an elite school like Stanford University. The pressure accumulated from her parents, her school, her peers, from messages in movies and books and magazines, until in her sophomore year, when her mental health caved. When she started losing weight and throwing up blood, her parents stepped in and hospitalized her for most of that year. "I would cry in the hospital bed, not thinking, 'am I going to die?' I was crying because my grades were slipping; I was losing that Stanford dream."

Worthy of Protection

As parents, we sometimes think our role is to help fuel and support our kids' ambition. But in a hypercompetitive culture, kids sometimes need the opposite. They need the adults in their lives to occasionally hold them back—to prevent them from sacrificing their minds and bodies on the altar of achievement and to teach them how to build the kind of life they won't need substances to escape.

Mattering, from a child's perspective, means your physical and psychological limits are worth honoring. What the experts in this field have told me, time and again, is that our kids need wise balance-keepers, parents who actively help protect their time, their energy, their health, and their integrity. It is not our role to support every endeavor, in other words, but to wisely challenge, to create guard-rails that tell our kids they are not cogs in a machine but people worthy of rest and preservation, to help them reimagine their ambition in an environment that tells them constantly to secure and acquire more. We demonstrate to children that they matter when we send a distinctively countercultural message: that they are worthy of protecting.

Children need to be taught, explicitly, that true success comes from finding healthy ways—both physically and psychologically—to excel. "As a conscientious student growing up, it took me a while to get to this place where I was essentially asking my children to do less and teaching them to be strategic," said Damour. It was counseling high school juniors in her practice and seeing them get crushed by their inefficient style that convinced her there had to be a better way. As the workload rises through the academic years, if the only strategy they have is to give 100 percent in everything, students become overwhelmed. Our kids need permission to rethink what a good student is and let go of an unhealthy work ethic, she told me: "We have to help kids walk it back a little."

When her older daughter, Ellen, was averaging a solid A in a class, Damour would suggest that maybe she should take her foot off the pedal a bit and apply that gas to other areas of her life, like downtime with friends or investing more in another subject. "You know how to do a really good job when it needs to be done," Damour told her. Now she wanted Ellen to learn how to be energy efficient with her work. For any week of school, she explained, think of yourself as having one tank of gas. If you're flooring it on everything, you'll be running on fumes by Thursday.

The job of a "good student," she explained to her daughter, is to figure out when to give a subject your full capacity and when to pull back—and even coast. Parents can give kids the confidence not to have to overwork. "I told Ellen, you have the skills, you have the grasp of the material, and you have other things to do with your time," she said. "You don't need a 100 to prove anything to anyone." This strategic approach, Lisa told me, makes a huge difference for students' stress and anxiety. As one of Damour's colleagues succinctly put it: the difference between getting a 91 and a 99 is a life.

That balance is what Jane and Mike wanted for Andrew. After weeks of going back and forth with him, the couple arrived at a compromise: instead of doubling up during the school year on AP science classes, Andrew could spend one summer taking a science course on his own, fitting it in between his volunteer work. Jane's priority was for Andrew to acquire the skills he would need to get through college and life in a healthy way: how to balance work with fun, ambition with commitments to friends and family. Summer offered lots of free time, so Jane felt that taking a self-paced class was a solution that would allow his schedule to stay flexible. "Our kids are only under our roof for a short amount of time," she said, "and we wanted to relish our family time together."

■ ■ ■

Driving through Mercer Island, you'll find charming local restaurants and small shops, including the Mercer Island Thrift Shop. Opened in 1975, the store sells gently used high-end furnishings and clothes with the proceeds going to support programs and services for all Mercer Islanders. One parent explained the irony of the store to me like this: we donate our expensive vintage Tiffany candlesticks to fund programs to help support the mental health of our kids who feel pressured growing up in a place like this.

The Mercer Island parents I met were compassionate, thoughtful, and not afraid to mine the data to find solutions for what ails their kids. Each year, students take a health survey to assess their mental health. The community has brought Suniya Luthar into town twice, first in 2009 and again ten years later, to conduct an even deeper survey of their kids. When Luthar surveyed the students just before the pandemic in 2019, she found that the number-one worry among middle school students in Mercer Island was around "achieving in school." Like other high-performing schools across the country, their student data put them in the "at-risk" range for anxiety and depression, as well as for substance abuse. Luthar describes

Mercer Island, and other affluent communities she has visited, as an "I can, therefore I must" culture, which her research identifies as a significant risk factor for young people.

When kids are encouraged to "do it all," they come to believe that their fates rest entirely in their own hands. Having the privilege of choices, as many students in affluent communities do, can give them a false sense of control over their lives. Access to private tutoring and coaching, for example, makes students feel as though they have the power to design their own fate. This belief—that their fate is in their hands—leads to a particular mental burden. Emma, a senior at Mercer Island High School, told me she suffers from severe anxiety, which began around middle school, where she maintained a perfect 4.0 average. "I just felt so much pressure to be the best," she said. Emma credited her anxiety for helping her academically, but she told me that there was only one moment she could think of in the past ten years when she wasn't consumed by it. "I was driving through town with my mom and for a split second, I wasn't anxious. I forgot about everything." She remembers turning to her mom and asking, "'Is this what people feel like on a normal basis?' It was amazing."

What Emma described was something I'd heard from many students: a compulsion to always be improving, doing more, reaching higher. One Texas mother I spoke with talked about a teacher who, with the best of intentions, would hand back her daughter's papers in seventh grade with the feedback "Close, but *not yet*." The teacher's presumed intent aligns with the idea of the growth mindset—a groundbreaking concept pioneered by Carol Dweck that holds that a person's talent and ability can grow with effort. The growth-mindset ideology has become popular in our self-improvement culture. Encouraging such an outlook, this well-intentioned teacher would ask for multiple drafts of the same paper before deeming it worthy. This pattern set the daughter, who was already displaying perfectionistic tendencies, on a path where nothing was acceptable unless it was absolutely perfect, the mother told me. In communities where the norm is to push and push and push, experts say a growth mindset, if not employed correctly, can backfire.

Some teachers, coaches, and parents have oversimplified Dweck's insights, the UK researcher Andrew Hill explained to me. Kids can wrongly assume that if they aren't being successful, it's because they aren't trying hard enough. "These students have a high ability to try really, really hard," he explained. "What they lack are the self-regulatory skills that signal *when to give up*, when to disengage." In a 2018 paper, Suniya Luthar and Nina Kumar expressed a similar contention: "It is not a lack of motivation and perseverance that is the big problem," they wrote, but the "difficulty with backing off when they should." A growth mindset can certainly help students who are underperforming in competitive settings, noted Luthar and Kumar. But the risk for overachieving, perfectionistic students is that the effort to stand out can turn pathological: they come to believe that pushing and sacrificing for that A or squeaking out time for one more activity can be *the thing* within their power that gets them into the college of their dreams.

In some students, this drive can turn into a compulsive and excessive need to overprepare and overfunction. Scholars find that "study addiction" during the school years can be a precursor to workaholism in later life. When a student puts an excessive amount of time and effort into studying, it can impair their relationships and health and can lead to other addictions, like drinking and drug use, in an effort to calm the compulsion. It can also harm performance. One study of college students in Poland found that study addiction was related to higher perceived stress and a trend toward worse academic performance—results that parallel findings among adults who have a compulsion to overwork. These students don't have internal breaks to help them regulate their time and energy. They don't know when it's time to say to themselves, *Well, that's enough for the day.* And it's crushing them.

An Emergency Exit

It was the end of summer vacation for Maggie, a sophomore at a boarding school on the East Coast. She had spent eight weeks in what her mother, Anne, called Maggie's "happy place," volunteering as a counselor at a wilderness camp. Anne, a mother of two in Brunswick, Maine, was putting the duffel bags into the trunk to take her daughter back to school when she caught a glimpse of her noticeably shaking on the gravel, "looking like a frightened deer in the headlights." The demanding academics and social pressure she felt at school—who is wearing thousand-dollar Canada Goose coats and who is having their birthday party in New York City with a chauffeur taking them there and back—was overwhelming Maggie. "I can't go back," she whispered.

Anne knew right there and then that she needed to find Maggie what she called "an emergency exit" from an environment that had become toxic. Within a few days, Anne had found Maggie a spot in a semester-long wilderness school in Maine—that quick pivot was a privilege she recognized. Maggie slept in a cabin heated with a woodstove; the girls needed to keep the fire going at night. Each evening, the six other girls in Maggie's cabin would choose one tiny bunk bed to pile on with a bag of popcorn and tell stories in their pj's. Their boots would be lined up by the door, covered in mud from the day's farm chores.

In the unrelenting chase of what is "best," many of us can unknowingly allow our lives to become defined by materialism. Materialism isn't simply about loving certain logos or buying nice stuff; rather, it's a value system that defines our goals and attention and how we spend our days. And it can leave us not just exhausted but unmoored. Pursuing materialistic goals, like high-status careers and money, causes us to invest our time and energy into things that take time away from investing in our social connections, a habit that can make us feel isolated over time. Ironically, the more isolated we feel, the more likely we are to pursue materialistic goals that we hope, even subconsciously, will draw people to us. Acquiring status markers, we believe, will make us worthy of the human connection we crave. It's a vicious cycle: some people may become materialistic not because they love money more but because they have underdeveloped connections. Instead of attaching to people, they attach to material goods and status markers to fill the void and to try to get the emotional security they're lacking. But this approach can backfire and undermine the very relationships we're trying to foster. In fact, people who prioritize materialistic goals tend to have weaker, more transactional relationships: you do for me, I do for you.

For the past thirty years, the psychologist Tim Kasser, an emeritus professor at Knox College in Illinois and the author of *The High Price of Materialism*, has focused his career on studying how the pursuit of goals like career success, money, and image relate to our well-being. In one study, Kasser and his colleagues surveyed a group of eighteen-year-olds, asking them to rank various goals in terms of their importance: job, money and status, self-acceptance, community goals, and belonging. They also surveyed them for any mental health issues. Twelve years later, when these teenagers turned thirty, researchers revisited the group. At both points in time, Kasser found that participants who were more materialistic were also more likely to be suffering from a mental health disorder. Moreover, he found that those people who became less materialistic over time—whose values had shifted between the ages of eighteen and thirty—went on to experience an increase in well-being.

Kasser explained to me that the connection between materialism and our well-being boils down to this: When we chase materialistic goals, we typically do so at the expense of our basic needs to feel autonomous, competent, and connected to other people. This makes us more stressed and less happy. Regardless of age and socioeconomic status, those who favor status-driven goals, on average, tend to be more depressed and anxious, have lower self-esteem, and drink and smoke more.

While some of us may care more about certain goals than others, we all basically share core values that can be divided into extrinsic and intrinsic goals. Extrinsic values center around personal achievement and enhancing our self-esteem: financial success, image, popularity, conformity. They are focused on other people's opinions, outside attention, and approval and rewards. Intrinsic values, meanwhile, center around personal growth and improving the community and our relationships. The difference lies in the motivation of our behavior. If you're, say, pursuing a career in medicine mostly for status and the high salary, you're pursing it for extrinsic reasons. But if you're pursuing it because you want to help others, that's an intrinsic pursuit. Interestingly, Kasser told me, these values operate like a seesaw: the more we value extrinsic goals, like wealth and status, the less room we have in our lives to pay attention to intrinsic ones, like community goals that focus on improving the lives of others.

Kasser also offered an analogy of a pie, where your values are different slices: one might be material goods, one might be family, another might be career goals, another might be community. If the materialistic slice gets too big, the others get short shrift. Values operate like a zero-sum game: as one set increases in importance, the others must decrease. A great desire for personal success and achievement, then, can crowd out the desire to help others without expecting anything in return. Logistically, a person has only so much time, energy, and attention to spend.

Choosing intrinsic values—like investing in friendships, neighbors, or volunteer groups—has been found to sustain our happiness and well-being in a way that pursuing extrinsic goals, like higher income or higher status in a career, doesn't. Intrinsic values offer nourishing payoffs, like more social support and a sense of belonging, while extrinsic goals can be a little like junk food: they feel good in the moment, but that feeling doesn't last long and too much of it can make you sick. It's not that we don't know and appreciate good values, of course. The problem is that we are bombarded with messages that activate those extrinsic values that are inside all of us, pulling us away constantly from intrinsic ones. Material goods also feed our status-safeguarding instinct, giving us a feel-good neurological release that's hard to override. Our focus on extrinsic values can be activated in a particular moment, like when we log in to Instagram and see friends enjoying a fabulous vacation, or they can be triggered by ongoing feelings of scarcity, like those caused by constant conversations about dropping college admissions rates. One mother described how every time she'd go to a friend's house and admire something they had—a new kitchen, some new landscaping, table settings—she'd leave feeling envious and wanting to make some changes in her own house, even though her house didn't really need updating.

The more parents model that having material possessions, making lots of money, and going to a name-brand school are important, Kasser said, the more children tend to follow along in adopting those same values. If we want our children to shore up on intrinsic values—relational, community-minded ones—the first thing we must point them toward is regular ways of experiencing their value outside their zip codes. We must offer them regular reprieves from a world that cares about advancement and stuff—whether it's offering connection through family dinners or friends' birthday parties, a mental reset through unplugging from devices, or a reminder of our smallness and humanity through excursions into nature.

This is exactly what Anne discovered with Maggie. Over that one semester, Maggie recovered from two years of her boarding school grind. She went from being saturated with displays of status to being surrounded by nature and people who shared her values: a love of the outdoors, an interest in helping the environment. Feeling stronger, she convinced her mother that she was ready to go back to boarding school. This time, though, she was deliberate about the friends she surrounded herself with, making sure their values were aligned. She thrived.

"What was it exactly about this time away that reset Maggie?" I asked Anne, as she and I walked along a hiking trail in the woods of Maine. "There is no judgment when you go into the forest," Anne replied. "The trees are not saying your hair is the wrong color, you're too fat, you're too slow. The trees are just saying 'welcome.'" Paraphrasing a favorite quote by Robin Wall Kimmerer, Anne said, "We talk about tree huggers, but what we don't think about is how the trees love you back." She added, "It's not an exaggeration to say that nature saved my daughter."

Reject the Premise

At the root of grind culture is a foundational belief: a good life is secured by admission to a "good" college. Many of the students I interviewed believed that *High school is a means to an end.* They have been inculcated with the idea that attending a prestigious college is the key to financial success, social status, and happiness. Of course, most adults have the perspective to know this isn't true; plenty of people who go to top colleges have lives that don't turn out as they hoped, and plenty of people who go to less selective colleges have lives that turn out even better than they'd imagined.

This belief also presupposes that a select few colleges are "good"—and the rest are not. Since 1983, *U.S. News & World Report* has sought to sort colleges along these lines in their annual rankings of the 1,500 best colleges and universities in the nation. Their rankings—alongside *Barron's*, the Princeton Review, and others—attempt to flatten each unique college, from tiny liberal arts colleges to massive research institutions, into a single numerical score. In the 2022 *U.S. News* rankings, for example, Stanford earns a score of 96 out of 100, the University of Michigan an 80, and Penn State a 64. It couldn't be clearer, according to these numbers, that Stanford is much "better" than Penn State. Such rankings have developed a remarkable currency with students at high-achieving schools. Paul Tough, in his book *The Inequality Machine: How College Divides Us*, tells the story of a father who printed out the *U.S. News* list, drew a line under the top thirty schools, and told his daughter to apply only to colleges above that line.

But experts who have analyzed the rankings will be quick to tell you that college rankings are, at best, misleading. "Rankings may seem like they are objective measures of quality because they use complex formulae and present their findings definitively," wrote Denise Pope, a cofounder of Challenge Success and senior lecturer at Stanford University Graduate School of Education, in a compelling 2018 white paper. But, she continues, many metrics are "weighted arbitrarily and are not accurate indicators of a college's quality or positive outcomes for students."

Parents and students might be surprised to learn—as I was—what criteria *U.S. News* uses to produce their rankings. In 2022, for example, 20 percent of a school's ranking was based on its reputation among peer institutions. Think about it: How many college administrators have a firm grasp of the inner workings of hundreds of peer colleges? Moreover, how could they possibly keep up with how all these institutions change from year to year? The answer is they can't. What they *can* keep track of is a college's prestige, making these lists a kind of self-fulfilling prophecy.

Graduation and retention rates make up another 22 percent of the ranking criteria. Pope notes that a highly ranked private university typically has a 95 percent graduation rate, while flagship public universities have rates between 65 percent and 85 percent, depending on the school. But the main factors that drive a school's graduation rate involve its students' backgrounds (such as how many come from wealthy families), not the quality of the education itself. As Malcolm Gladwell explained in a *New Yorker* article, the kind of class a school assembles determines its graduation rate. If you admit only the students with the most polished résumés in the country (Yale), then you'll have a very high graduation rate. If your mission is to graduate as many people as you can (Penn State), then you'll inevitably have a lower graduation rate.

Some colleges even manipulate the data to improve their standing, throwing more uncertainty into the rankings. Columbia University made headlines for submitting statistics to *U.S. News* that were deemed "inaccurate, dubious or highly misleading" by one of its own math professors. In retaliation, *U.S. News* dropped Columbia's ranking from number two to number eighteen. "The broader lesson everyone should keep in mind is that *U.S. News* has shown its operations are so shoddy that both of [Columbia's rankings] are meaningless," the whistleblowing math professor was quoted as saying. "If any institution can decline from No. 2 to No. 18 in a single year, it just discredits the whole ranking operation." It's not the first time an institution has been caught up in a scandal over its ranking; Columbia is hardly alone in sending false or misleading information.

Rankings are compelling because, in an uncertain world, we would like to believe that getting a degree from a higher-ranked college, even if it costs more, will lead directly into a high-paying career and greater life satisfaction. But does a more expensive college lead to better career outcomes? Pew Research conducted a study to explore this very issue. Researchers compared life outcomes between graduates who had attended large public universities and those who had attended more expensive private schools. Surprisingly, they found "no statistical difference" in the outcomes. The majority of each group reported about the same levels of personal satisfaction with their family life, their economic well-being, and their job.

In her white paper, Pope also synthesized key research about the life outcomes of those who attended highly selective colleges and those who didn't. She, too, found little evidence that attending a highly selective college translated into greater success. Pope noted one important exception: first-generation and marginalized students who attended a top-tier school were more likely to have higher incomes than peers who attended less selective colleges. Researchers do not agree on the exact reasons for these differences. Some believe it is likely due to the networking opportunities these schools offer students who arrive at school with few connections; others credit it to the fact that low-income students at many of these schools are given scholarships that allow them to graduate with less debt.

If the rankings are shaky, and there's little to no financial advantage, some parents and students might still cling to the belief that attending a top college leads to greater well-being and happiness. In 2014, Gallup and Purdue University teamed up to conduct the largest study of college graduates in US history, surveying more than thirty thousand graduates to measure five key dimensions of their well-being: purpose (how motivated were they to achieve goals?), social (did they have strong, supportive relationships?), physical (were they in good health?), financial (were they effectively managing their finances?), and community (did they have a sense of belonging?). The researchers also measured how engaged they were at work, including whether they enjoyed their jobs and whether anyone at work cared about their development. The researchers found that the prestige of the college they had attended—whether it was highly selective or not selective, public or private, small or large—"hardly mattered at all to their current well-being and their work lives."

However, what did impact later-life success was a student's experience while they were at that school, particularly the quality of their relationships and their level of engagement on campus. Graduates who reported higher well-being and job satisfaction tended to have had highly engaging experiences at college. The study singled out six key types of college experiences that had an outsized positive influence on future success.

1. Taking a course with a professor who made learning exciting;

2. Having a professor who cared about the student personally;

3. Having a mentor who encouraged the student to pursue personal goals;

4. Working on a meaningful project across semesters;

5. Participating in an internship;

6. Being active in extracurricular activities.

If a student had had a strong relationship with a professor who cared about them as a person and encouraged them, the odds that they were engaged with their job more than doubled, as did the odds that they were thriving more generally. Likewise, if graduates had

had an internship or a job that matched their academic interests, if they were working on meaningful multi-semester projects, and if they were actively involved in extracurricular activities, their odds of being engaged at work also doubled. Students at any college—not just the "good" ones—have the opportunity to fulfill all six criteria. The results of this study suggest that the prestige of the college you attend is much less important than how you "fit" into its culture.

A good "fit" means that a student feels significant and important within a campus community, that they feel others are interested and concerned with their well-being and come to depend on them. Put another way: future success and well-being are correlated with how much a student *feels like they matter on campus*. Did they have a professor who made them feel valued? Did they have a semester-long project or an internship where they were able to use what they were learning to add value?

Of course, there is no one formula that guarantees our children fulfilling adult lives, but when parents define success in terms of mattering and well-being—and not simply in terms of achievements—we can better guide them forward, Lisa Damour explained. Knowing that well-being is affected above all else by cultural fit, adults can make a conscious effort to keep their discussions with kids about college less focused on extrinsic goals like prestige and more focused on intrinsic ones, like personal growth. In other words, college conversations should center around a student's values—not around college rankings.

"Parents can start these conversations by rejecting the premise that the path to happiness must be through a top-tier school because it's just not true," said Damour. Instead, adults can offer perspectives on the stressful process of college admissions by deflating the myth that a prestigious college is the key to success. Adults can speak deliberately about what leads to a "good life" based on decades of science. "Whether your kid goes to Brown or a school that ranks lower on the list does not decide midlife happiness. What does? Having good relationships, purposeful work, and feeling competent in one's chosen pursuits," said Damour. "We need to know this, and our kids need to know this, too." Instead of worrying about a wobbly ranking, research points us toward a better use of parental energy: emphasizing not *where* you go to college but *what* you do when you get there.

Materialism and Mental Health

When Tim Kasser and I spoke, I asked him about how affluence and achievement shape our children and their mental health. Short of moving out of these SuperZip communities, I wondered, what can parents do to make sure we're focusing on values that won't harm our kids?

Kasser threw my question back at me. "Well, I don't buy the premise of your question," he replied. "Why not move?"

I paused.

"If you were sending your child to a school where there was lead in the pipes, you would recognize that the child's health was at risk," Kasser continued. "So, if you could, you would probably leave and put your kid in a different school, right?" If you believe, and the research shows, he continued, that sending your child to a very achievement-focused school is bad for their values, bad for their well-being, bad for their ultimate behavior, and you have the opportunity to leave, why *not* leave?

I felt my neck growing tense. As I searched for a response, a fear came over me: How could I raise my kids in an environment I now understood could be toxic? What would it mean to leave? Where would we even go?

Kasser mercifully interrupted my spiral: "But if you decide not to leave, then it should be a thoughtful, deliberate decision." The point, he said, is to give every priority to intrinsic values at home. The more we build and support these at home, the more suppressed our materialistic values will be. It's not enough, Kasser told me, to *believe* in the importance of family and friendships over material comfort. Your actions have to enact this belief—and this requires honest self-reflection. What does your family's life—your schedule, your vacations, your activities, your *stuff*—tell your kids about what you think is important? Do you say you value family but then miss holiday gatherings for out-of-state travel games? Do you talk about the need to volunteer and help others, but leave no time in their schedules to do it?

It's only when we get clear on our intrinsic values that we can develop the wisdom to be effective balance-keepers for our kids. Kasser suggests asking yourself: Have I set up my life in a way that reflects what I think is most important? For example, if my family is most important to me, does my day-to-day schedule reflect that belief? Am I encouraging my children to live the kind of lifestyle I think is important? Are my kids so involved in so many different activities that they never have any free time to sit and relax? If I really want my child to be a kind person who cares about others, what opportunities do I give my child to practice this?

Kasser says that parents should talk about values openly, just as you would about substance use or sex. Instead of one hundred-minute conversation, aim for one hundred one-minute conversations peppered into daily interactions. When you're at the mall and your son is begging for the latest sneakers, Kasser suggests asking: *Do you really need another pair? Will it actually get you what you want?* Similarly, I have found, you can have these same conversations around achievement. *What would getting a higher score on your SATs really mean? Will going to a name-brand college lead you to a fulfilling life?*

Direct conversations about values have been some of the most important talks I've had with my kids. These conversations have pushed me to define what success means to me. When my older son, William, hit middle school, his workload and expectations increased, and he would spend hours trying to write a two-page paper. A lot of time was spent staring at the screen, typing and deleting words. I'd try to encourage him by telling him, *Just try your best.* One day, in frustration, he responded, "Mom, I'm eleven. I don't *know* what my best is."

I thought back to my own adolescence and trying to figure out what it meant to do my *best*—and what a loaded word it is. How *do* we help our kids figure out when enough is enough?

A few years ago, as I was researching an article for *The Washington Post*, I stumbled upon one way to answer this question, using the concept of taking pride in what you do. Pride can be felt two ways: intrinsically, when you're authentically proud of yourself; and extrinsically, when another's opinions tell you how you should feel, what psychologists call hubristic pride. An authentic, healthy sense of pride is linked to genuine feelings of self-worth and accomplishment, like being a good parent or partner or being helpful to your community. Authentic pride makes us feel good about ourselves, writes the researcher Jessica Tracy in her book *Take Pride*, prodding us to figure out who we want to be and what we need to do to become that person. On the other hand, hubristic pride, which occurs when we allow others' judgments to determine how we feel, can motivate us to pursue more hollow goals like money and fame to win the admiration of those around us.

I wanted my kids to focus on feeling intrinsic, authentic pride—and not to be overly distracted by extrinsic, shiny outcomes. And this changed the way I talked to them about measuring their success when I saw they were already working overtime. It isn't about doing your best, I told them. It was a different metric, a different question we needed to ask: Are you *proud* of your work?

This shift in thinking gave me the tools to define what "doing our best" really means for our family—reaching for that proud feeling, rather than just reaching for the A. It helped focus William. He wasn't just working for a good grade; he was working for the anticipation of how proud he would feel for producing good work. Even if he didn't earn the highest grade on a paper, he could still feel proud. The shift changed me, too. I remember one moment in particular. I'd just written an article for *The Wall Street Journal* on the psychological power of nostalgia, of its use as a helpful coping strategy in times of transition. I thought it was one of the best articles I'd ever written, and I couldn't wait to see the reaction from readers. But when I logged in to the online version of my article the next day, instead of seeing activity—comments, shares—there was nothing. Crickets. Only one reader commented, and funnily enough, he too had noticed the lackluster response: "I'm surprised at the lack of comments to this powerful piece."

At dinner that night, I told my family about my confusion and disappointment. Writing the article, I said, had totally changed my perspective, but it didn't seem to have made much of an impression on readers. I was discouraged.

Then William, who had been listening, spoke up. "But do you feel *proud* of it?" he wanted to know.

Deliberate Rest

Time is precious to the relentless overachiever. "My friends are all so productive that I feel bad about myself if I'm not living up to that," said Rachel, one senior at Mercer Island High School. "Being productive is my way of coping with the pressures in my life. I don't know any other way to be." Rachel told me about a boy she recently met who showed her how he carves out time to relax. He put a two-hour block in his schedule and marked it: *Take time for yourself.* "It blew my mind," she told me. "Slowing down feels like such a luxury."

To matter is to realize that we are not machines; we are humans with limits. Monitoring those limits sends a strong signal to our kids: they are worthy of rest and nurturing. Our role as balance-keepers is to insist on this. In conversations, several parents brought up Malcolm Gladwell and the 10,000-hour rule, a study he details of elite musicians in his book *Outliers.* The takeaway for parents was that kids needed intense, deliberate practice—ten thousand hours of it—if they were going to be standouts in a field. What didn't get as much popular press was the *other* finding in that study: that musicians who were at the top of their field also *rested* more than their peers. They practiced for eighty minutes at a time and then took a thirty-minute break. They slept a full eight and a half hours, took naps, and prioritized leisure time—three-and-a-half hours of it a day. "Deliberate practice," the researchers noted, "is an effortful activity that can be sustained only for a limited time each day." To be top musicians, the students should "limit practice to an amount from which they can completely recover on a daily or weekly basis." In other words, just like deliberate practice, they must engage in deliberate rest.

Like these world-class musicians, teens should be getting eight to ten hours of sleep a night, but fewer than 25 percent of teens today are getting the minimum. In one study of teens, those who got more than eight hours of sleep a night were found to be the most mentally healthy, reporting the lowest levels of moodiness, feelings of worthlessness, anxiety, and depression. In a community that emphasizes hustle culture, insisting that your child rest—whether it's closing the books at night so they get a full night's sleep or encouraging them to nap—can feel risky. But when adolescents don't have the skills to decompress, they are more likely to turn to unhealthy coping strategies to manage the stress and anxiety they feel, such as drugs or alcohol. Giving permission to rest communicates to our children that they are worthy of protection, that their being, their physical and mental health, matter. As Lisa Damour told me, "Sleep is the glue that holds human beings together, and it is the hill I will die on as a parent." Rest isn't only about achieving peak performance. Our kids need to learn they are worthy of rest because they are cherished humans, not machines.

To be clear, home conversations about what we value, like taking care of our health, aren't about abandoning achievement or hard work. Rather, they're about offering a whole-person framework: saying in our words and modeling in our actions that achievement is just one part of what it means to live a "successful" life. About ten years ago, my friend Elizabeth and her husband, Scott, who live in New Jersey, were forced to examine their values when, within a few months of each other, they were both offered big promotions at their respective jobs. She works in advertising. He works in finance. The promotions would have meant more prestige and much higher salaries, as well as longer hours at the office and more day-to-day stress.

That week, a small group of us took Elizabeth out to dinner to celebrate. But sitting at the table, we could all see she was conflicted. Elizabeth opened up about it. She wanted a strong family life for her kids, then ages six and four, but she also wanted the job opportunities she'd worked so hard for over the past twenty years. "I am so anxious and sleepless about making the decision," she told us.

To get clarity, Elizabeth went into therapy for the first time. She wanted to figure out what her own personal definition of success was—not her parents', not her colleagues', not her neighbors'. Her therapist had her think about which five areas of her life were the most important to her. Elizabeth listed them: family, friendships, volunteer work, exercise, and work. The way she and her therapist saw it, Elizabeth could excel in a couple of these domains, but not all of them, with young children at home. She realized that for her, success meant living a balanced life—and this meant not *excelling* in one or two domains but being *good enough* in every domain. After weeks of soul searching, she turned down the job. A few weeks later, Scott came to a similar conclusion and turned down the promotion at his company, too.

Was this hard? I asked her. Of course, Elizabeth said. But the exercise was helpful because it forced her and Scott to clarify their family goals: What values did they want to encourage in their boys? And did their day-to-day lives reflect those values? When Elizabeth and Scott thought about what they wanted for their sons, top on the list was that they would be kind, caring members of the community.

In the years since, as their kids have grown, this clarity has helped Elizabeth and Scott make big and small decisions in their family's life: how many hours to devote to SAT prep, how many Advanced Placement courses to take, how the family spends the weekend. When Elizabeth hears the frenetic conversations about achievement by other parents in her community and starts to feel pulled off course, she reminds herself that she wants her kids to do well but in a way that matters to their family. She'll call a friend with similar values and say, "Remind me why we're not doing a travel team this year?"

When it recently came time to talk about summer plans, instead of enrolling her now high schooler in an academic program to enhance his résumé, Elizabeth encouraged him to get a job at the local deli and volunteer at the local animal shelter. "He's so focused on himself all year long—his grades, his performance—that I wanted him to focus more on other people, including those who needed his help," she told me.

"It doesn't mean we're not ambitious—we are," said Elizabeth. "But there are limits to how much we're willing to sacrifice for that ambition." They explain to their sons that ambition can't come at a cost to important relationships and it can't come at a cost to mental health. "I want my boys to know when enough is enough," she said.

Everything in Moderation

I was lucky to spend nearly a week in Mercer Island, meeting families, visiting the high school, enjoying walks in the parks overlooking the water. On my last day, Andrew's mother, Jane, and I met up outside at a café in town. Jane, who owns an online stationery company, and her husband, a tech entrepreneur, moved to Mercer Island to raise a family because they were drawn in by the community feel. She found a close-knit group of like-minded friends through her kids' nursery school, and these friends helped her stay true to her values. "While we do like nice things," she said, "we did not focus on keeping up with the Joneses. We drove our minivan into the ground after thirteen years of owning it." When it came to activities, Jane and her husband allowed their kids to do about half of what their friends did. "My husband's philosophy has always been: everything in moderation," she told me, and this became their family motto in how they wanted to live their lives.

Jane believes her kids, all of whom did well in high school, didn't excel *despite* the balance and boundaries she enforced in the house but *because of* them. Despite not doubling up on AP science, Andrew was now attending his first-choice college on the East Coast and studying engineering. As counterintuitive as it may seem, what Jane saw, and what research finds, is that a balanced approach actually *improves* achievement. In one study, researchers asked hundreds of middle school students to rank the values their parents prioritized. Half of the values centered on achievement, such as attending a good college, excelling academically, and having a successful career.

The other half focused on character traits, such as being respectful, helpful, and kind. Adolescents who reported that their parents valued character traits as much as or more than their performance exhibited greater mental health, enjoyed higher levels of achievement, and engaged in less rule-breaking behavior than peers who believed their parents were primarily focused on how they were performing. Jane's children benefited from having parents who prioritized caring for themselves and others as much as they did their academics.

As our conversation wrapped up and we walked to our cars, I shared my concerns about raising my own teenagers in a similar high-pressure community. Jane smiled and said, "I promise you that we weren't perfect parents." They made their mistakes, but kids are resilient even to our missteps. All of her kids are now in their twenties, she continued, "and I can honestly say that they are living healthy lives."

So, what do you credit it to? I pressed. "Well," she said, "we were clear at home about what we valued as a family and held on to it, even when it was hard, even when other people warned us that we were wrong. Look, we're at the end of it now and it all worked out," Jane said as she pressed her car key to unlock her doors. "We got to enjoy our time together as a family and Andrew actually got to enjoy his high school years."

6

Envy

Coping with Hyper-Competition

erched behind a gated entrance in the Brentwood area of Los Angeles sits the Archer School for Girls, an independent middle and high school. With a kind of cinematic appeal, the iron gates open up to reveal a U-shaped driveway, a sweeping front lawn, and the school's historic 1931 main building designed in the Spanish Colonial Revival style. Originally built as a women's retirement home, the school fits right in with the surrounding architecture of the neighborhood.

Vaughan Anoa'i, one of the students I met during my visit, transferred to Archer in sixth grade and was immediately struck by the sophistication of her classmates. Each response to a teacher's question was so well reasoned and insightful, she said. She began to feel a creeping sense that she was competing against her new classmates. Whenever she took time to slow down, Vaughan said, she'd feel guilty and restless, like she was falling behind. This unspoken competition inevitably got in the way of close friendships, a reality that sometimes left her feeling like she was "stranded on an island."

The competition Vaughan described was a common refrain among the students I interviewed all around the country. It's one of the unique challenges our children face in high-performing schools. Parents move to towns with excellent schools or pay high tuitions because they want to give their kids the best education, the best opportunities, and the best shot at a successful future, but these competitive environments can have unintended side effects.

As if to get it off his chest, Nate, a senior at a competitive public high school on the West Coast, told me early in our interview that he's "haunted" by three grades he's gotten over his high school career that were less than As. When I asked him why three grades across four years upset him so much, he said, "I'm such a generic person, just totally vanilla. There are twenty-five other kids just like me in my class—who play sports, who get good grades—and that's why I need to be perfect, to somehow distinguish myself." Then he added, almost as an aside to himself, "I've often wondered if I would feel and think differently about myself if I'd gone to another school that wasn't so competitive."

Social comparison—sizing up the competition—is an inescapable part of human nature. And local context matters. A sixty-degree day in New York in March is warm; in Florida it's considered cool. Nate was doing the same mental math in his honors classes:

getting a B+ when everyone around you is getting As can make even strong students feel "less than."

In education, psychologists call this kind of social comparison the "big-fish-little-pond effect." When you are a "big fish" (competitive student) in a "little pond" (less competitive school), you have more confidence in your abilities. You feel smarter because you're smarter than the average student. On the other hand, when too many talented students (little fish) are in high-achieving environments (big pond), they can suffer psychological fallout from feeling like they do not measure up. This is the case even among the top 1 to 5 percent of students, like Nate—someone has to be in the bottom half of the AP Calculus BC course. At such high levels of achievement, competition and social comparisons become even more unhealthy. One mother, in hindsight, described the intense competition at her children's private school in DC: "It's a school that makes smart people feel dumb."

So when we talk about the waters of achievement our kids swim in every day—the waters that erode their mattering—these skewed metrics of performance are perhaps the most difficult for our kids to see and name. It's the water they swim in, invisible because it's all they know. These undercurrents make their way into every area of their young lives: school, sports, music, theater, dance, art—causing kids to have to break their necks to distinguish themselves within a very narrow band of excellence. Treading these competitive waters, it's almost impossible for kids to keep any perspective on their worth outside their performance. Or any perspective on how, just by being in these well-resourced schools, "they're already winning a medal, just maybe not the gold," the sociologist Natasha Warikoo, author of *Race at the Top*, told me. The children who are at a real disadvantage, she pointed out, are those who are living outside of these elite communities.

Social comparison within such a narrow range pits classmates in an understood but unspoken competition against one another, where *your* success harms *my* chances, as one student said. "When Harvard's rate is 3 percent, then you have to do the calculation," said one father in a *Town and Country* article titled "This Year's College Admissions Horror Show." "What if you take away all the slots for first-gen students, all the athletes, and the legacies? Then how many are left in that 3 percent? The feeling is: What can kids possibly do? How do they distinguish themselves?"

Competition isn't new. But at elite schools, psychologists are noticing a trend of heightened competition coupled with greater weight placed on early childhood success. When I was in high school in the early nineties, yes, college was on my mind, and I certainly reached for high grades and leadership positions, but these achievements didn't define my childhood, as many of the students I met felt they did. When I asked Nate why he was so concerned with those few Bs on his transcript, he said, "It scares me to think that I may have already screwed myself over for the future."

Like Vaughan, Nate described feeling a constant drive to put in his absolute best effort, whether studying or practicing soccer, which he said dampened any fun or downtime he might have. "The scariest part is that after giving myself some downtime," he said, "if I do something that I'm not proud of, if I don't ace a test or play well in the game, then I will look back at that downtime and berate myself for not working harder, which will then make me less inclined to give myself downtime in the future."

Nate described his high school as "toxically competitive," to the point that it inhibited his friendships. "When another student gets an award, I don't think, *Great for him*; instead, I think that I should have worked harder, that that should be me up on the stage." Another student I met from a West Coast school pointed out that hyper-competition can hinder trust in a community: "When college is such an end goal, you can start to believe that everybody around you is out to get you."

Other students I met admitted to not sharing their class notes even with close friends or improving their own sports stats at the expense of their team's success. John, a student at a competitive New Jersey public high school, told me about a few students in his AP math class who had deliberately sabotaged the class's two top-ranked students. Concerned about rumors of rampant cheating, administrators handed out anonymous surveys asking students to report how often they saw cheating, but not to name names. After class, a few students admitted that they had written down the names of their math "rivals" to put them under a cloud of suspicion and ruin their ability to get a teacher recommendation for college, even though there was no evidence that they had cheated.

Over the years, Vaughan has witnessed adults bring out some of the worst instincts in kids. She talked about her experiences in competitive travel volleyball, where she would sometimes see parents pit kids who played the same position against each other. In some families, there was an unspoken rule: don't make friends with people who play the same position because it can get touchy when it comes to playing time.

The first day that Vaughan walked into journalism class to write for *The Oracle*, Archer's national-award-winning online newspaper, she brought the competitive mindset she learned on the court with her, expecting to have to prove herself worthy of being there. What Vaughan didn't know was that another student in the class, Chloe Fidler, was feeling the same way. Going to school against the backdrop of a place like Los Angeles, Chloe told me, "amplifies the competition." In LA, she explained, there's such an emphasis on material worth that "it's easy to grow up thinking you're not enough because you're not rich enough, pretty enough, or smart enough." This inadequacy only feeds the feeling that you have to outcompete people in order to prove your own worth.

A knives-out reality is contributing to a relationship and mental health crisis. Well before the isolating effects of the pandemic, the number of teens who reported feelings of loneliness had more than doubled, jumping from 18 percent in 2012 to 37 percent in 2018. Even if our kids are well supported at home, they can lose proof of their worth and their sense of belonging when their friendships are hypercompetitive. In a highly competitive context, friendships can become transactional—a pattern that can persist into college and the workplace. "The culture here is very much based on getting to where you want to be as fast as you can," one Stanford student was quoted as saying in the *Stanford Daily*. "It's cool if you can make friends on the way, but you can dispose of them whenever."

Mattering to Friends

Mattering starts at home when we feel valued by parents and family. But when it comes to feeling significant in the eyes of other people, our role in a larger community is also critical. For our kids, this larger community is primarily found at school, where they spend the majority of their waking hours and where their identities are being formed. The National Longitudinal Study of Adolescent Health, which examined the reasons for well-being among more than 36,000 seventh- to twelfth-grade students, found that family connectedness was the strongest protective factor against distress, eating disorders, and suicidal thoughts. But it also found that feeling connected at school—a child's next most important community—was strongly protective against substance use, early sexual initiation, and risk of unintentional injury, such as drinking and driving.

Like parents, peers can be a uniquely protective factor in an adolescent's mental health and well-being. As our kids grow into teenagers, notes Gordon Flett, it's their peers who "are increasingly able to satisfy the need to matter." By feeding each other's sense of mattering, friends grow closer. Knowing that we matter to people who matter to us can protect an adolescent's well-being, while loneliness increases the risk of a host of serious problems, such as depression, anxiety, and substance abuse.

Even just one quality friendship can shield against the harmful effects of loneliness and bolster self-esteem and academic engagement. One study followed 365 students as they transitioned from elementary to middle school and found two key predictors of well-being and performance: first, feeling accepted by peers, and second, having at least one good friend. The researchers theorized that students who feel a sense of belonging don't have to worry about scanning for threats in the classroom and can instead devote those important cognitive resources to their schoolwork, resulting in an academic boost.

The *quality* of friendships during adolescence can also have a long-term effect. Researchers have found that students' perception of mattering to their friends is directly associated with their happiness; friendships with those who know us well and enjoy our company, quirks and all, feed our hunger to feel unconditionally valued. In one longitudinal study, researchers at the University of Virginia found that students who had a close best friend at age fifteen reported less social anxiety, greater self-worth, and fewer depressive symptoms at age twenty-five than peers who didn't have a best friend during their adolescence. These students, the researchers contended, were better equipped to build and maintain supportive relationships throughout their lives. By contrast, adolescents who had experienced a large social network but lower-quality friendships reported higher levels of anxiety by the time they were in their mid-twenties.

As parents, we can't control whether our kids form safe relationships that will bolster their mattering in a deeply alienating environment. We don't always know when our kids are getting pitted against each other or when (perhaps) they're the ones doing the pitting. And there's nothing we can do, or should do, about the class our kid doesn't get into, the play they don't make the cut for, the sleepover they don't nab an invite to. But at home we can emphasize that their friendships are critically important and worth prioritizing. In an environment that promotes competition and disconnection, we need to teach our kids that they are *worthy* of connection, that they can rely on others and enjoy being a source of support for friends.

Vaughan described her mindset when she first transferred to Archer: "I'd rather drown than ask for help." Just like parents in these communities, kids can come to believe that to protect their status, they can't show weakness, rely on others, or even celebrate others' successes. Instead of imparting the value of social connection, parents may tend to focus on what we've been told is the ultimate goal of parenting: to raise independent, self-reliant adults.

While speaking with Kenneth R. Ginsburg, a professor of pediatrics at the Children's Hospital of Philadelphia, I experienced a light-bulb moment that illuminated a path away from this zero-sum thinking that someone else's gain is your loss. Yes, it's important to foster a child's independence, but there was an even bigger lesson to teach my children if I wanted to protect their mattering: how to be *interdependent*, how to rely on others and allow others to rely on them in healthy ways. In my travels, I have found that the kids who thrive in competitive waters have adults in their lives who actively push back against a zero-sum mindset. These adults—be they parents, coaches, or teachers—encourage kids to root for their classmates, to sacrifice for the greater good of the team, to help their friends and learn to ask for help in return, and to confront and manage the uncomfortable feelings that arise from competing with peers. These adults focus on fostering an interdependent mindset, rather than preparing them for some sort of *Hunger Games* situation that will never come to pass.

Make the Thinking Visible

When I met Vaughan and Chloe in person in the spring of 2021, I was struck by how they spoke about their friendship. The insecurity and loneliness they had described feeling was noticeably absent:

they laughed, finished each other's sentences, and knew each other's quirks and mannerisms. Another friend, Thea Leimone, a serious swimmer and member of the newspaper, joined our conversation. As they spoke with me, all three were quick to point out one another's strengths, often expressing their appreciation for one another: "Thea is super motivating," "Chloe gives the best advice," "Vaughan is fiercely loyal." They had an easy, supportive rapport. Each one was mindful if they seemed to be talking more than the others and would quickly pass the baton: "Oh, Chloe, you should answer this one; you always have something really interesting to say about social comparisons."

So, what happened? I wanted to know. If they entered the journalism classroom with a competitive mindset, feeling like they had to prove themselves worthy of being there, how had they moved past that? It was clear to me that the girls were well supported at home; all three spoke of parents who loved them unconditionally, who drove them to sports practices, and who took time to listen to their worries and concerns. It was also clear that they had friendly personalities; they laughed easily and were introspective about who they were. And all three had spent years at Archer, soaking in the collaborative culture of the school. But all three credited their changed philosophy to their journalism class. What was it about this class that had shaped their relationship? I asked.

Vaughan spoke first. As she saw it, their friendship was made possible by the class culture that their journalism teacher, Ms. Taylor, had fostered. Kristin Taylor, who serves as the Archer newspaper advisor and has been teaching for twenty-five years, conveys an effective blend of high expectations and support for her students. When she inherited the newspaper a decade ago, it was a club that met only once a week, and it published only one or two print papers a year. But even then, Ms. Taylor could see that *The Oracle* could serve a bigger purpose—that it could teach her students about teamwork, cooperation, community, and civic engagement. Under Ms. Taylor's supervision, Archer's online newspaper has gone on to win several prestigious national awards.

Ms. Taylor has witnessed how today's competitive pressures can fracture friendships, so she takes a deliberate approach to managing competition in her classroom. Being a part of a close-knit but competitive community can be incredibly stressful, particularly when the elephant in the room—that you're all competing against one another for the same things—isn't openly addressed. Ms. Taylor's job is not only to be honest about someone's writing needing improvement. It is also to be honest about the unspoken dynamics in the classroom. She often addresses things the students feel but can't name: the shame a girl might feel about her first draft not being perfect, say, or the tension over vying for the position of editor in chief. She's aware that underneath all the hustle to outdo one another can be a deeper feeling: envy.

Social comparison is a natural part of being human, but left unchecked, it can make us deeply lonely. Envy diminishes one's sense of mattering. The pernicious thing about envy is that you don't want to show that you're feeling it, because doing so exposes your own deficiencies. Experiments have found that people are less willing to own up to feelings of envy than they are any other emotion. This shame also makes us less likely to open up and receive help from others—undermining the very relationships that would allay our painful feelings. This is partly why, right from the beginning of the school year, Ms. Taylor makes a point of articulating *why* her students are in her class: they have a collective purpose, to learn and practice *together* the role of journalism in a democracy, and in the microcosm of Archer. The girls, she insists, aren't there to win writing awards. They are there to support one another and to make it the best publication they can. If it is going to be great, she tells them, then they have to learn that they need one another—whether for writing, editing, selecting photos, or proofreading.

It's clear to any casual observer that Archer's school leadership has created a strong, supportive culture. The competition inherent in a high-performing school is met here head-on by the faculty, who explicitly encourage the girls to be ambitious, joyful learners. It may seem paradoxical: ambition is inherently stressful and can come at the expense of joy. What Archer is trying to help their girls see is that ambition is a good thing when it's purposeful and balanced. The head of school, Elizabeth English, and the associate head, Karen Pavliscak, bring their dogs to work, as do other adults at the school, fostering a climate of palpable joy. Teachers greet everyone warmly and often by name. There is laughter in the hallways and deep intentionality in the classrooms.

To start, the teachers themselves model collaborative learning, often sitting in on one another's classrooms for ideas and inspiration, what English called "instructional rounds," similar to what you'd see between younger doctors and more experienced doctors at a hospital. Another tenet of Archer's philosophy is to "make the thinking visible," just as Ms. Taylor does when she describes the hidden dynamics of her classroom. Teachers and coaches are another critical source of mattering for our children, especially when they go above the call of duty to help students.

Ms. Taylor's classroom generally exemplifies the best of Archer's school-wide culture. Her insistence on creating connections among her students, on dispelling each girl's illusion that she is a one-person army, caught Vaughan by surprise. Once each week, at the start of class, Ms. Taylor asked each girl to verbally celebrate another girl's positive influence, an exercise they call "share the love." A writer might call out her editor for spending time on her story; an editor might commend the news team for their reporting that week. "It's an instant mood booster," Vaughan told me. "It really lightens the mood and makes everyone happier." In other words, mattering— specifically hearing why you're valued—offers a more proactive, helpful way to instill a sense of belonging for a student.

From time to time, Ms. Taylor also has her students tape pieces of paper to one another's backs and write words of appreciation on them, without signing their names. "I tell the girls to just sit back and bask in that feeling of being appreciated," Ms. Taylor told me. "I tell them to put that sheet of paper in their notebooks, and when they're having a bad day, look at this list of all the things people said about them."

The intentional positivity of the class, the idea that everyone mattered in their own unique way, started changing Vaughan. Working at *The Oracle* became a safe spot, a "utopia," as she called it. She felt her perfectionist tendencies start to soften. "I had this idea that I had to be perfect and do important things in order to be worthy of praise, but what I learned in this class is that I can be appreciated for small things, too, like helping someone with edits for her article or being a supportive friend," she said. The intensity of true collaboration also taught Vaughan the benefits of being vulnerable in her relationships. "I used to feel like I couldn't show emotion, that I had to have this perfect appearance," she said, "but here I learned how to reach out for help and support." Unlike on her travel volleyball team, at *The Oracle* Vaughan didn't feel like she was "trying to run a race against everyone else." Instead, Ms. Taylor pushed every student to become a better version of themselves, said Vaughan.

Chloe, Vaughan, and Thea discovered how teamwork could motivate them, and how envy could be turned into a force for good. "If we had a long-standing project or essay to do, Thea would say, 'Well, I finished the intro, then the first paragraph,' and that pushed me forward to do mine," said Vaughan. "We motivate each other." When inevitable bumps hit the newspaper—a tricky article or a breaking news moment—Thea and Chloe could anticipate Vaughan's anxious response. "They knew me so well that without me even saying anything, they'd know when I was starting to struggle, and they'd step in to help." Soon their friendship had transcended the classroom: the three texted or called one another multiple times every night.

But in the spring of junior year, the girls found themselves in a tricky situation. Applications for next year's leadership positions were due—and the newspaper needed a new editor in chief. Applying for the job is an arduous, multistep process that asks students to explain the decisions they would make in various ethical dilemmas and tests grammar and editing skills. In other words, you had to really want the position to spend hours on the application during the hectic days of junior year. All three girls wanted the top position. "At the end of the day," Vaughan recalled, "we knew only one of us would get it."

Normalize Healthy Reliance

Early in the school year, Ms. Taylor likes to open class with a group discussion about how vulnerable it can make someone feel to receive feedback. She calls on more advanced students to share their experience: What was it like for them when they received comments on a story the first time? How did they learn how to report and write for the paper, and why is feedback so useful? "Oh, my God," an older student told Thea. "The first time I got feedback, I felt so awful and stupid. Then I realized that the editor was trying to help me." Ms. Taylor told me that the discussion seemed to bring visible relief. "We talk about how it takes courage to both ask for input and receive it," she said. "And then there's all this mini modeling going on between the older classmates and the younger ones."

One of the most practical ways to cement our value and that of others is by asking for help, relying on someone's support, and feeling that we are worthy of that support. But in competitive environments, some students can come to believe that admitting that they need support means they are inadequate. It's why so many adolescents suffer in silence, unbeknownst to us, until they implode.

Asking for help can feel especially difficult for our kids because they are so competent in the first place. "My family's very supportive, and they've always made it clear that I can ask for help," Thea told me. "But I am innately very independent, and I've always wanted to prove to myself and to the people around me that I'm smart and capable." Being surrounded by so many other talented kids made expressing any kind of vulnerability feel not just hard but practically impossible—how could she, when no one else was? "I had built this shame around asking for help," she told me.

Chloe felt the same way. New to Ms. Taylor's class, when she received an edit on her first piece of writing, she was mortified. "I considered myself a writer—I enjoyed writing, it was my thing. And at a school like Archer, it felt especially important to me, like I needed to have this natural talent." But, when she got back that first assignment, it was filled with comments from the editorial staff. "I hated it," she said. With Ms. Taylor's coaching, however, she found the practice of inviting input transformative. "To put yourself out there and discover that this can actually make you better—it changed how I felt in class," she told me.

Opening herself up to feedback improved her relationships, too. "It bleeds over, because it teaches you how to bring your newspaper friends into other areas of your life: 'I trust you to give me good advice,' 'I trust you to learn about this situation I'm not comfortable with myself yet,'" she said. Interestingly, she continued, the weekly experience of asking for and offering input made her feel *less* vulnerable. "Because I've gotten so much input from people within this close group, I'm more confident," she told me. "I kind of feel like I can now ask for, and accept, input from anybody."

Vaughan has a passion for journalism, but what motivated her to keep taking the class wasn't necessarily writing stories—it was the people. She came to admire and care for the other girls, and loved being around them. In other words, continuing to work at the paper wasn't simply a strategic move for college applications. These girls wanted to work together because it was fun, and because they had built a friendship that transcended the newsroom. As a self-described perfectionist, Vaughan told me, "I'm extremely hard on myself, but having friends who help me has alleviated a lot of the anxiety I used to feel on a day-to-day basis."

Our kids benefit when we teach them the power of inviting people in. A competitive culture forces our kids to exude self-reliance, to pretend that they can handle everything on their own. But if parents talk about vulnerability and model it at home, if we make home a place where feelings and fears are nothing to be ashamed of, we can bring our kids relief. Like Ms. Taylor, we can convey that it takes courage to invite help, and we can make sure that we'll be our kids' safe base if being courageous doesn't work out as planned. We can coach our kids on the cycle of generosity: Just as it's our responsibility to offer help to friends when they need it, it is our responsibility to ask for help when we need it. When you interrupt this cycle, not only do you deny yourself the benefit of help, but you also deny the other person the benefit of being a helper.

It is on the grown-ups in the room to beat this drum—early and often. With my own kids, I've started emphasizing the help I've needed in my own work and career, and how others have contributed in a real way to any success I've had. Once, when Caroline was struggling with a paper, I told her I knew just how she felt. She dismissed me with, "Oh, but you're a professional writer." I walked her to my desk and, on my computer, pulled up the first edit on an early article I'd written for the science section of *The Washington Post*. It was a bloodbath—red marks everywhere. "Oh, my God," said Caroline, staring wide-eyed at the page. "I can't believe they let you write for them."

"I took it the opposite way, as a sign that this seasoned editor wanted to invest in me," I replied. "They saw my potential, and so that's why they made the effort with the red marks." Do your kids see the nitty-gritty of your vulnerabilities? Do they see your set-backs? Do they see you accepting help?

Surface Deep Emotions

Kids are not always lucky enough to be in a school as intentional as Archer or surrounded by peers like Vaughan, Thea, and Chloe, who are willing to be so introspective. But at home, parents can help their kids surface the uncomfortable feelings produced by competition so they can make healthy choices in their relationships. I'm reminded of a conversation I had with a mother in New York named Allyson, who shared a story about her daughter, Kate. All through elementary school, she told me, Kate was the best of friends with a girl named Melissa. They signed up for the same after-school activities, spent their evenings doing homework together on FaceTime, and had standing plans every Friday and Saturday night. They confided in each other about everything—family troubles, school failures, classmate dramas—and turned to each other in times of stress.

When Kate and Melissa entered eighth grade, suddenly the time the girls had once spent just hanging out turned into an endless competition: they auditioned for the same starring role in the school play, tried out for the same soccer team, tested into the same advanced math class. Melissa's parents said she needed to buckle down if she wanted to attend the same Ivy they had. She needed to focus on the "right" after-school activities, like club lacrosse, rather than the ones her friends did. It was no longer enough to be a high achiever at school—Melissa needed to be *the highest* achiever. When teachers handed back papers, Melissa would immediately turn to ask Kate her score. When one did better than the other, it soured their interactions for the rest of the day. Kate struggled to reconcile wanting to be a friend to Melissa and suddenly wanting to outperform her. Their rivalry bled into other relationships, as the girls started gossiping about each other to friends, trying to secure their reputations and status.

At home, said Allyson, Kate became noticeably more anxious—and so did Allyson. The jockeying by Melissa's parents was stirring up her own competitive juices, and she found herself looking for ways to give Kate an edge. She hired a voice coach for a couple of sessions to prepare Kate for the eighth-grade musical auditions and secured a math tutor, despite it being a subject in which Kate was a solid B+ student.

Everything came to a head one night when Kate was scrolling through her Instagram feed and saw that Melissa had invited a group of girls to celebrate her birthday—and had left her out. Kate was crushed. Before social media, we might learn afterward that we weren't invited to a party. But now Kate had to witness in real time—and in vivid detail—the fun she was missing out on. It was painful enough to be excluded, but now their friendship breakup was officially public. Kate couldn't focus on schoolwork. She didn't want to join family meals. Allyson realized then that to help her daughter, she needed to treat Kate's "online world" seriously.

Finding Kate in her room, Allyson told her daughter about how when she herself logged in to Instagram, she sometimes felt left out or envious. Was this what Kate was maybe feeling? Kate said yes, but she was also feeling embarrassed and betrayed. They kept talking, and as they sorted through Kate's emotions, Allyson made a suggestion. She had recently learned a loving-kindness meditation in her yoga class in which you take a small time-out to send positive thoughts both to yourself and to the difficult people in your life. Would Kate like to try? Allyson asked. Together, they sat on the floor with their backs against the wall and said the meditative phrases out loud, wishing these things both for themselves and for Melissa: *May you be safe. May you be healthy and strong. May you be happy. May you be peaceful and at ease.*

It wasn't a magic spell that fixed everything, Allyson told me, but sitting together in their feelings did seem to soften the pain. The two also talked about how to remove yourself from the situations that trigger painful feelings. So when Kate saw her friends celebrating at the party on Instagram, she removed the app from her phone. Figuring out how to normalize sharing difficult emotions has helped Kate better manage her competitiveness. A year later, her friendship with Melissa has begun to return to its former closeness.

Kate's experience also forced Allyson to investigate her own uncomfortable feelings about Melissa's mother: Why did Allyson feel so competitive? And what did she really want for Kate? Yes, she wanted Kate to do well, but she certainly didn't want to model Melissa's pushy mother, who seemed to condone climbing to the top even if it meant destroying relationships to get there. Allyson saw a more important role: teaching her daughter broader life lessons, like how to manage uncomfortable feelings in a way that doesn't destroy relationships. As Allyson taught Kate, we have more power over how we process and express our envy than we realize. "If envy brings the pain of knowing what we lack," wrote the psychiatrist Robert Coles, "envy can also lead us to reflection. Envious, we find ourselves asking the most important questions: who we really are, and what we really want out of life."

> **When I asked the students of my survey what they would have liked their parents to have known about their high school years, they wrote:**
>
> - "The fact that I was constantly feeling compared to other students often makes me feel like my work will never be enough, that I will always be miles behind my peers in terms of academic success."
>
> - "It took a toll on me having a best friend who was in the top 1 percent for high school."
>
> - "There was a lot of [friend] drama and I wish my parents could've taken the time to help me navigate it."
>
> - "I was severely depressed in high school and most of the time was barely keeping it together, partly as a result of the toxic culture around grades and achievements in my high school and within my group of friends."

Marginal Mattering

When Vaughan transferred to Archer, her family couldn't have been more thrilled. "We knew pretty quickly while touring schools that this was the right place for Vaughan," her mother, Tiffany, told me. Tiffany is a native of Los Angeles, an executive vice president at Paramount, and now sits on the Archer school board. It was a family priority that the school's student body be diverse—47 percent of

Archer's kids are students of color—and that the school have a strong academic focus.

Vaughan fit right in, falling in with a nice group of friends and developing a fondness for her teachers. In junior year, when Vaughan, who is half Samoan, half Black, was recruited by Georgetown to play volleyball, the school celebrated by holding a formal signing event. As the news spread, she was met with a few questions from peers that caught her off guard, like "Are you a diversity candidate?" or "Are you the first in your family to go to college?" She was told how "lucky" she was to get into Georgetown. Vaughan felt these questions diminished the incredible amount of work—getting top grades and ACT scores, working for the newspaper, and playing her sport at a competitive level—that had earned her admission to Georgetown.

Vaughan wrote about her experience for *The Oracle*. "I can only imagine what it must feel like to be admitted into your [college] of choice and ultimately feel as though you belong," she wrote. Instead, she felt like she had to constantly prove herself worthy of being admitted to a place like Georgetown.

In my national student survey, I asked students if they'd ever felt discriminated against. Many of their responses emphasized that these competitive environments can be especially toxic for students who fall outside whatever is considered the institution's "norm"— whether in terms of class, race, ethnicity, sexual orientation, or gender identity. One young woman of Mexican descent wrote about a conversation with a classmate who asked her how she, as a Mexican, could be "so smart." Another student, whose parents came from the Middle East, recalled an incident that occurred the day after Osama bin Laden was killed: "Two eighth-grade boys asked if I was happy my uncle died and that I should go to hell with him just because I looked like I was Muslim."

Several Asian American students in the survey described having to endure the harmful "model minority" stereotype—that all Asians are "performance machines" and "good at math." Students talked about how this stereotype made them feel "invisible in the classroom," like they didn't quite belong, and added to the pressure they felt to consistently perform at the highest level. Some Asian American students also talked about feeling discriminated against during college admission; they felt they needed to achieve higher test scores and GPAs than their non-Asian peers just to be in the running. One student told me about how her high school college counselor had advised her to make herself look "less Asian" on her college application so she would "have a better shot at admission." The counselor suggested she write in her essay that she was looking forward to being a part of Greek life on campus, even though she didn't intend to join a sorority.

One New York student attending private school on a scholarship described never being able to have friends over because other kids' parents were concerned about the danger of hanging out in her part of the city. A student who transitioned during high school described being treated as "an anomaly" and as a "spokesperson" in class when any queer-related topics came up. One Black student I interviewed talked about the added stress of being the only Black person on the advanced track in his overwhelmingly white school; he felt all the usual pressure to succeed for himself and also felt a burden to work extra hard so that he wouldn't, as he put it, "confirm the negative stereotypes about Black students." Another Black student at a private school in New York City described the exhaustion that came with feeling like she didn't quite belong. Sometimes, she was called by the name of another Black student in her grade: "I used to correct people, but now I don't even bother."

These experiences cut feelings of mattering at the core. Microaggressions and discrimination send a powerful message that some people in the community are more valued than others, said Blessing Uchendu, a consultant with high-performing schools and a private-practice therapist in New York City. "The more you identify yourself as living in the margins of these generally white, affluent schools, and the further away you are from the idealized norms in these communities, the more you can be made to feel like you don't measure up, that you're not enough," said Uchendu. These highly competitive environments can be particularly isolating for marginalized students, who may feel they have to work even harder to prove themselves as worthy, she said. But, unlike Vaughan, many students have no one to open up to about the experience, perpetuating a sense of isolation even more.

The more competitive students are encouraged to be, the more likely they are to experience scarcity and envy, which can fuel dehumanizing attitudes and stereotypes, explained school consultant Rachel Henes. At his competitive school in New York City, Rainier Harris, the son of Jamaican immigrants, said students had to essentially prove their worth "just to get basic respect." The competition in school turned particularly ugly during the college admissions process, when Rainier overheard hurtful comments by his classmates about how affirmative action disadvantages white applicants at top colleges. When I first spoke with Rainier, he had just started his freshman year at Columbia University. "When I got into Columbia, people weren't very friendly because they didn't think I deserved it," Rainier said. "It was as if they were blaming me or other Black students for why they might get rejected from a place like Yale." I asked Rainier if his classmates gave equal airtime to the fact that legacy kids get a leg up in the admissions process. Rainier laughed and said, "No, absolutely not."

In an effort to study how Black boys experience mattering at school, the University of Delaware researcher Roderick L. Carey and his team conducted in-depth interviews with seventeen Black adolescents at a high school in Delaware. Two main themes emerged in the interviews: One, that Black boys experience "marginal mattering," in which peers and educators use biased language that keeps Black boys on the margins of their communities—like students asking Vaughan if she's a diversity candidate or peers blaming Rainier for their own college rejections. And two, that Black boys may experience "partial mattering," where educators cultivate and celebrate only some of a Black student's skills and abilities at school. Carey, who is himself Black, gave an example from his own life. "When I tell white folks that I went to Boston College," he told me, "they sometimes would ask, 'Oh, did you play football? They assume that the only way I'd get into Boston College was sports, not my intellect."

What Black students need is what Carey calls "comprehensive mattering": they need to be valued and recognized for the full people they are. Vaughan described feeling this comprehensive mattering with her Archer teachers. She detailed one moment in particular when her English teacher at the time surprised her by saying in front of the class, "Vaughan, I didn't know you played volleyball. That's amazing." It was an experience she would never forget, she told me, as a wide smile came over her face. I asked why that moment made such an impression on her. Vaughan explained that often, especially for athletes of color, you're seen only as your sport, as if you don't have any other talents. To be known as a good student who also happened to be a volleyball player made her feel seen and that *all* of her belonged.

Healthy Competition

In the spring of her junior year, Vaughan worked on her application for editor in chief of *The Oracle*. The application began as she had expected, asking how she might handle imagined scenarios, like a student who was constantly missing deadlines. But she was struck by the final question. At the end of the long application, Ms. Taylor had written one pointed question: What will you do if you don't get the position on the paper that you want?

Ms. Taylor explained her reasoning to me: "I've been teaching a long time, and one of the most important lessons I've learned as a teacher is, don't let stuff simmer under the surface." In fact, as soon as she received the applications from Vaughan, Chloe, and Thea, she reached out to her students over email. "I'm so excited that I have three such incredibly talented and skilled people applying for this job," she wrote. "But as you know, I'm only able to pick one. I wanted to put it out there: How are you all feeling about this? Have you talked with each other about it?"

Vaughan had not discussed it directly with Thea ("In our friendship, a lot of things go without saying, so we don't have to be overt," Vaughan told me). But Chloe had brought it up, and she and Vaughan talked it through. "It was a goal that we both established for ourselves sophomore year, and I'm just telling myself that I'm putting myself out there, I am being vulnerable, and I am applying and that's already a win in and of itself," Chloe said. Chloe was focused on her own game, her own personal best. She intended to compare herself against her past self, not against her friend.

Of course, Chloe and Vaughan both knew they would be disappointed if they didn't get the position. But they were still intending to be enthusiastic members of the newspaper, leading another section of the paper and supporting their friend in the top position. Talking through the situation with Chloe was helpful, Vaughan said. It broke any tension between them.

Before researching this book, I used to believe that competition was bad for kids. A few years ago, when my son James received an email from a well-meaning coach about an "intense" basketball class where players would be "challenged physically and mentally," the kicker got my attention: "If you are not afraid to push yourself and want to surpass your peers, this is the program for you." I did a double take. "*Surpass* your peers?" My distaste was instantaneous. In high school and college, I'd seen competition drive friendships apart.

Whenever I brought up the topic of competition in my interviews, other parents were quick to draw a line in the sand, too. Some agreed with me and talked about shielding their kids from the stress of ever-rising competition. Others felt the opposite—that society is getting too soft, and that kids today are "coddled" or not "tough enough."

Ms. Taylor offered a different view. Competition isn't inherently bad, she said. Rather, how we *think* about competition is often unhealthy. When we inevitably compare ourselves to another and feel inadequate—and envy starts to bubble up—our brains attempt to dissipate the discomfort by urging us to close the gap between ourselves and our competitor. But there are two ways to close that gap: we can use our envy as a motivator and try to raise ourselves up to the other person's level—what's called "benign envy"—or we can use our envy to undermine our perceived rival, and cut them down, a posture known as "malicious envy." Whether competition becomes helpful or destructive depends on how we wield our envy. Like Ms. Taylor in her class, we can help train our kids to choose benign envy over malicious envy.

While malicious envy sees rivalry as zero-sum—your win is my loss—benign envy sees rivalry as mutually beneficial. It acknowledges that you need others, and they need you, to fulfill your and their potential. In this way, benign envy reinforces, rather than diminishes, mattering. When you reframe competition in this way—that it's not about what you are acquiring or achieving, but about the person you are *becoming*—it also emphasizes the power of relationships.

Data bears this out. In a study that examined competitive motives among more than one thousand adolescents in Italy, those who expressed a zero-sum outlook—such as "I compete with others even when they are not competing with me"—were more likely to suffer in their relationships. In another study, of 615 Canadian adolescents, the researchers Tamara Humphrey and Tracy Vaillancourt found that kids who displayed hypercompetitiveness in the early years of high school went on to display more direct and indirect aggression in twelfth grade—a finding that suggests that they grew more aggressive, and more isolated, over time. Other research has shown that hypercompetitive people are more likely to suffer from depression, anxiety, stress, and self-harm. Always needing to win makes life more challenging, Vaillancourt told me, because winning isn't always possible. By contrast, students in the same study who viewed their peers not "as competitors that hinder the winner, but rather as possible helpers" who can facilitate personal discovery had healthier relationships. This "adaptive competitive style," as it's known, is associated with high self-esteem; these adolescents also tend to be more concerned about the well-being of others.

So how exactly do we help our kids reframe competition as constructive rather than destructive? How do we help them see themselves as part of a larger whole, not as isolated individuals in a dog-eat-dog environment? The answer isn't a blithe "everyone else makes you better" pep talk—that sort of amorphous pronouncement isn't helpful in a cutthroat environment. Just as we can be explicit about envy, we can support a shift in our kids' mindset around competition. Too often, we aggravate the sense of rivalry: *Where is so-and-so applying to college? How did so-and-so play in the game today?* Instead, we can support connection when we ask about, and teach our kids to look for, what is *worthy* about their competitors. What are their competitors' strengths? What do they do well? What can we appreciate about these opponents? In what ways are they working *with us*—on a project, on a shared goal, on navigating the same incredible achievement pressure?

Competition can be mutually beneficial if you acknowledge that you need others and they need you to become who you are each meant to be. A "worthy rival," a term coined by the author Simon Sinek in *The Infinite Game*, is someone who is better than you in certain areas, and who can inspire you to get better at what you value. In the popular classic *The Inner Game of Tennis*, W. Timothy Gallwey uses the analogy of a surfer waiting for a big wave. The goal of any surfer is to ride the wave to the shore. So, why do they wait for the big one? Wouldn't an easier, smaller wave ensure success? The surfer waits for the big wave, wrote Gallwey, because he values the challenge it represents. The surfer is not necessarily out to prove himself or to bolster his own self-worth. Really, he's there to explore his capacities. Gallwey explained, "It is only against the big waves that he is required to use all his strength, all his courage and concentration to overcome; only then can he realize the true limits of his capacities." Like the big wave, Gallwey wrote, your exceptional rival isn't your enemy; he's your ally, your assistant: he creates the obstacles that allow you to bring out your best.

A worthy rival also benefits from what *we* bring to the table—our ideas, our talents, our successes. This is just as important to help our kids articulate: What strengths do *they* have that their rivals can learn or grow from? This idea—that your rivals need your strengths—is especially important for girls, who tend to struggle more than boys do with competition's impact on their social relationships. While boys are conditioned to act competitively, even among close friends, girls are socialized to be collaborative and to work together to reach their goals, which can feel at odds with competition.

One study of nearly sixty girls in grades six to twelve at a competitive school found that they felt pressure not to acknowledge their aspirations openly, which only added to their stress. In her years at Archer, Ms. Taylor has witnessed this dynamic play out. She told me about a group of girlfriends who seemed to curtail their ambition, applying only for certain editorial positions because they didn't want to compete with a friend. When she raised this concern with the girls, they denied it, so she let it go.

While boys are often taught that competition can push them to new heights, cultural stereotypes of competition among girls can be a lot more venomous—cat fights, "queen bees and wannabes," as the author Rosalind Wiseman so vividly captured in her book by the same title. For this reason, girls especially need help internalizing the message that competition and friendship don't have to be at odds with one another, said Lisa Damour, and instead can be felt "one right after the other." Damour suggested that parents model healthy competitive behavior themselves. When playing games with your children, instead of letting them win, which sends the signal that beating them is unkind, teach the benefits of being a worthy rival, playing to win while also encouraging and celebrating their efforts whenever they make a smart move.

When Damour is watching the Olympics with her daughters, she points out how the female athletes push one another when they're competing but congratulate and hug one another as soon as they cross the finish line. Damour and I talked about the example of two US champion runners, Dalilah Muhammad and Sydney McLaughlin, who have been public about relying on each other to become great athletes. The four times they have competed against each other in major events, they have broken records. As McLaughlin has explained, she knew that if she wanted to win against Muhammad, she would have to change her running style. Instead of taking fifteen strides between hurdles, she trained to take fourteen, shaving off critical time. "I just say iron sharpens iron. It's two people pushing each other to be their best," McLaughlin has said.

Consider how countercultural and profound it is for kids to learn that envy doesn't have to be shameful, and that competition can be healthy with the right mindset. "There's nothing wrong with being competitive; I'm extremely competitive," Vaughan said. But, she continued, you must draw the line somewhere. "I came to realize that everyone has a different journey. I think the only thing that I want to try to compete with is myself, how I'm progressing and continuing to improve each day to be better than I was yesterday. My friends help me do that." Vaughan told me, "I came to recognize that supporting someone else's success will never hinder or diminish my own."

Her Success Is My Success

Once the editor in chief applications were in, the wait felt torturous, but the three girls turned to one another for support. Vaughan and Chloe were in practically every class together, and they'd talk on the phone five times a day, working through projects and assignments. Inevitably, the stress of waiting for the announcement would weave itself into the conversation: *When do you think we're going to hear? Will they announce it over spring break? During class time?* "We thought and talked about it a lot," Vaughan said. Unlike in the hypercompetitive atmosphere of club volleyball, where players competing for playing time barely spoke to one another, Chloe and Vaughan leaned on each other.

Late one night, after several long weeks of waiting, Vaughan was crawling into bed after finishing her homework, ready to decompress with a little TV, when an email notification popped up on her phone from the current editor in chief: "Confidential," it read.

Vaughan took in the news. She had been awarded the coveted editor in chief position. Excited, she ran downstairs and told her parents. But she held back from reaching out to her friends; she wanted to give them the time to process the news on their own. Her accomplishment felt bittersweet. Within ten minutes, though, congratulatory texts started pouring in from Thea and Chloe. The long messages were incredibly supportive, emphasizing how deserving Vaughan was without a hint of jealousy: "I can't tell you how happy I am," "You're amazing," "We have such a good team for next year."

"It was hard not to get it, of course," recalled Chloe, who was named editor of the opinion section. Thea was named features editor. With Ms. Taylor's intentional lessons and the broader culture of Archer as a net of support, the girls understood that they were part of something bigger than themselves, that the sum of their community was greater than its individual parts. Internalizing these messages helped them manage their disappointment. They knew Vaughan was going to be a great editor in chief, that Chloe would be an excellent opinion editor, and Thea a strong features editor. They would all benefit from one another's unique strengths and, together, would make the paper the best it could be.

"So never in my heart was I like, well, why didn't I get it?" Chloe added with utter sincerity and conviction. "Her success is my success."

7

Greater Expectations

Adding Value to the
World Protects Them

dam looked at his watch. It was 1:00 p.m. He should have been heading to English class. But instead, here he was, at the top of Snoqualmie Falls, one of the largest waterfalls in Washington State, on this cold, damp, gloomy day. Adam looked up at the huge evergreens towering over him, then stepped out onto the overhang and peered down at the over-two-hundred-foot drop below. Despite the heavy mist blocking his view, one thing was very clear: he was well outside of his comfort zone.

Even with the waterfall roaring in his ears, sixteen-year-old Adam couldn't quite believe he was finally on his first mission. He'd been pulled out of class earlier that day to join the search and rescue. His teacher hadn't looked pleased when his phone had gone off in the middle of class and Adam had gathered up his books. But due to a local law, Adam was allowed to leave school for emergencies like this one. He raced down the hall and out to the parking lot. His go bag, the one he'd been told to always have on hand, was waiting for him in the trunk of his car. It was filled with supplies he might need for the mission: first aid kit, flashlight, water bottle, energy bars, a tarp, sleeping bag, rain gear, and hiking boots.

When Adam arrived at the scene, sheriff's deputies explained to him and his eight-person crew that a boy had gone missing, and his distraught mother had found a suicide note. Adam knew nothing else about him, except that he and the boy were the same age and that the boy was somewhere near the waterfall.

As part of the King County ground search and rescue unit, supervised by the sheriff's office, Adam was one of dozens of volunteers who dedicated their time to finding lost or injured hikers, hunters, and children. Search and rescue calls came every two to three days, totaling roughly two hundred each year. Volunteers were also expected to assist in natural disasters like flooding, windstorms, and earthquakes and were even sent to locate downed aircrafts. The people in Adam's unit hailed from all walks of life: Microsoft executives, stay-at-home parents, young adults. They had all become experts in wilderness navigation, survival skills, and first aid. Adam was an outlier, the youngest person by many years.

Like several students I interviewed, Adam attended a competitive public school, but his academic experience was markedly different from theirs. In elementary school, he struggled in every subject. "I was in the lowest group," he told me, "and in the bottom twenty percent of that lowest group." In third grade, his teacher suggested to his mother that she get him tested for a learning disability, and he was eventually diagnosed with a severe form of dyslexia. His parents enrolled him in a special education school to help with remediation; he was held back a year and then, in his freshman year, mainstreamed into the local high school, where he knew no one. "My parents pushed me to join the tennis team so I'd meet people," he said. It wasn't an easy transition; lunchtime was particularly hard. Sometimes Adam would spot a couple of tennis players eating lunch together and would quietly join their table. So as not to bother them, he tried to make himself invisible, avoiding eye contact and eating as quickly as possible with his head down.

At home, Adam spent his spare time watching TV. And he had a lot of time. At the advice of his guidance counselor, Adam took an easy course load as he entered high school—no honors or advanced classes. With very little effort, Adam achieved good grades, but he wasn't focused or motivated. He was just going through the motions as he put it: lonely, unmotivated, and disengaged. He felt adrift, cynical even, about what he was learning, wondering what it was all for.

But then, while working as a Boy Scout camp counselor, he'd been introduced to the search and rescue unit. The idea of finding hikers lost in the county's sometimes dangerous terrain and reuniting them with their families attracted Adam, and he decided to join. Training is essential, and Adam's would take six long months. It started in the classroom, where volunteers learned the basics: how to best locate and rescue someone, how to read different types of maps, and how to find the coordinates for a given location without a GPS. Once volunteers passed this level, they began training in the field, for moments just like this.

Within a half hour of the search and rescue unit's arrival on the scene, the boy was found, but not the way everyone had hoped. His body lay shattered on the rocks below. The search turned into a recovery. It became the team's mission to bring up the boy's body so that his mother could say a final goodbye. For three hours, Adam and the crew carefully raised the body with a pulley system, inch by inch, over two hundred feet from the rocks to the top of the cliff.

When Adam and the other volunteers placed the boy on a gurney for his mother to identify, she let out a piercing scream and broke down crying. Adam stood in the parking lot, looking at the ground, to afford her some privacy. He felt utterly helpless. It was a very intense experience, Adam said, one that still gives him a physical reaction, a shudder, when he thinks back on it.

Driving his mother's minivan home that night, with the day's dirt caked all over his shoes, all Adam could think was *What am I doing with my life?* Up to this point, the purpose of childhood was straightforward: do well in school, go to a good college, have a successful career. Then think about how to contribute to society. Adam was just a teenager—he had never thought that he could make much of an impact, even a small dent, in the lives of others. But the tragedy of the young man's suicide shifted something in him. That night, he filled out an application to become a volunteer with a teen crisis hotline. No doubt there were others out there contemplating ending their lives. Maybe he could help them avoid a similar fate.

Zooming Out

In affluent communities, kids often come to feel anything but helpful. The unintended consequence of intensive parenting is that it promotes in our kids a narrow self-focus. When we groom our children from birth to focus on developing their exceptional selves by, say, taking extra Mandarin classes, we crowd out other activities that were once marked important by society, such as being a contributing member of their community. And we are already seeing the consequences of this extreme self-focus. According to data collected from nationally representative samples of high school and college students, young people today are shifting away from more social values, like caring about community, and moving toward more self-enhancing ones, like pursuing money, fame, and image. One study conducted by researchers at the University of Michigan analyzed data from almost fourteen thousand college students. What they found was alarming: empathy has been decreasing over the past thirty years, so much so that the college kids in their study measured 40 percent lower in empathy on tests of the trait than their counterparts just a few decades ago. The drop is so startling some researchers have even declared a "narcissism epidemic."

What's causing this decline? Researchers have a hypothesis: In a hypercompetitive, individualistic society, you must be narrowly focused on your own goals just to make it. If you're worried about your own economic future, you have less bandwidth to be concerned about others. This toxic culture promotes radical individualism and self-reliance not just in adults but in our kids, too, and can encourage a kind of mandate to think about yourself first.

And some parents have embraced it. "This is their time to be selfish," one mother told me when I asked if her teens volunteered. Once they're done with college, then they can start to give back, she said. Their voices and opinions are not needed, not yet. Their path is already set for them, laid out with specific directions to keep them in line along the way—buffers in place so they don't veer off course.

This highly curated, self-serving life can breed a cynicism in teens. Even if they are contributing outwardly, they often shrug it off as padding for their résumé. One student talked about his summer service trip to help build houses in South America. But the trip did little to improve the conditions of the communities, he admitted with a bit of shame: "It was just a bunch of rich white kids who had no idea how to use a hammer and nail." Another student taught me a word I'd never heard before: "slacktivism." Slacktivists promote causes on social media to show their followers that they are caring, empathetic people—but they rarely follow through with real action. It's easy to put up a message to highlight a cause, but how many of us are taking time away from sports and studying to do something that makes a difference? one student asked me rhetorically.

When I first met Adam, I was struck not only by the clarity with which he saw his life, but also by his unusual cheerfulness. His ambition seemed infused with a certain joy. His worldview was so different from the listless or, at the other extreme, burned-out kids I'd met. I thought of Molly on the track, running in circles with her eyes closed. I thought of the student from Brooklyn who talked about needing to "fake passions" to attract the attention of top colleges. I thought of Nate, who was "tormented" by a few Bs on his transcript.

Despite our best efforts, and our best intentions, the obsessive curation of our kids' lives is not helping them fly. Many of our kids—our good, obedient, wanting-to-please-us kids—are doing what they're told. They're doing their hours of homework, taking those cello lessons, waking up early to swim laps before school, checking the boxes of community service. They're following the ultra-directed path they've been placed on, but it's not giving them the meaning they seek. Ironically, our extreme focus on their "growth" and "fulfillment" and "happiness" is stunting them.

Yes, you may be thinking, it's developmentally appropriate for teenagers to be self-centered. But when we let them overindulge in self-focus, when we don't challenge them to appreciate and empathize with others, when we don't point out the ways they can help and hammer home their responsibility to do so, we actually *hurt* them, experts say. We undermine the very growth we are trying to foster. William Damon, a Stanford University professor and expert in human development, told me that young people today are stressed and anxious not necessarily because we're overworking them but because they don't know what all their efforts are for. They are given this road map to follow, a series of hoops and tests, but without a larger sense of why they're doing it.

Children need adults to help them zoom out and see the bigger world and their role in it. In other words, it's not about landing that leadership position in the school club to improve their résumé. It's about helping them see the broader implications of their involvement: Where can they be of greater help to their classmates and communities? Where can they step up, take the lead, and do more?

We all want our kids to grow in healthy ways, to become high-functioning, happy adults. But growth isn't necessarily found in building the perfect college applicant, raising ACT scores or batting averages, or perfecting their unique, special selves. It is in helping our children take interest in the world outside their bedrooms and classrooms, to widen their reach and their circles of concern and caring—to discover, like Adam did, that they're a part of something bigger, a larger community. In other words, that their actions do matter, and that they have a responsibility to others.

When we invest too much energy in our children's self-fulfillment and self-betterment, we can fail to connect a kid to a purpose that's greater than landing a spot at Colgate or Colby—a *why* for their role in the world, a knowledge of how they bring value to others. "The biggest problem growing up today is not actually stress," notes Damon, "it's meaninglessness."

Value to Add

Amy, the twenty-year-old with a wide smile and a gentle demeanor who appeared earlier in the book, was in the middle of her junior year at Yale when I met her. In every conversation we had, Amy was intentional and thoughtful about the words she chose. So it didn't surprise me when she told me that from the moment she entered high school, she was painstakingly deliberate and singularly focused on getting admitted to Yale, her father's alma mater.

Amy grew up in a small, rural farming community of three thousand people about thirty minutes from Madison, Wisconsin. "I had bigger dreams than many people in the community and put a lot of pressure on myself to get straight As and excel athletically," she told me. For high school, she attended a nearby, small private school—so small that there were only twenty-three people in her graduating class. The first things that greeted her every morning when she walked into school were pennants from top universities: Yale, Harvard, UPenn, Columbia. Walking in that first day, she said, "I immediately felt that the bar was raised." Even though it wasn't a pressure cooker of a school, Amy struggled to maintain a flawless academic performance, feeling like she had to give 110 percent on every single assignment. She had a hard time figuring out when she had done enough.

At home, she faced different demands. Family chores were non-negotiable: the chickens needed to be fed, and the wood needed to be chopped for the fireplace, even if she'd been up late studying. Hours of the family's weekends would be spent keeping up their ten acres of land: mowing the lawn, clearing the brush, shoveling the endless Wisconsin snow off the driveway, weeding the garden, or tending to the honeybees.

Amy would protest every weekend, arguing that she had way too much on her plate, but every weekend her parents insisted she and her sisters keep up with their chores regardless. In the eyes of society, she was a great kid: she got straight As, was a top athlete, didn't drink. "I checked all the boxes," she said. But her parents pushed back: *Amy, these are your boxes, ones you've chosen and checked for yourself.* Amy joked that she should have been born to a family on the Upper East Side, where "my grades and sports medals would have been enough to satisfy my parents."

Looking back on these years, she said, the truth was that she was very absorbed in her own life and her own successes. That self-focus fed her perfectionism. Even though she protested, getting out into the woods, weeding, and chopping helped her get out of her own head. Grades and academics were important to her parents, but they were not the top priority. Their top priority was explicit: our family needs your help, and you're capable of contributing to the family in meaningful ways. Amy's parents were teaching her how to turn her inwardly focused lens outward, and they were show-ing her how to be a functioning, contributing member of society.

They were encouraging her to be humble—not to think less of herself, but to think about herself less. Humble people take an active interest in other people's lives instead of being overly consumed with their own. Humility helps with our psychological health, act-ing as an antidote to unhealthy self-involvement. It keeps things in proper perspective and buffers against the unrealistic demands we can place on ourselves.

Like Amy, I grew up with a weekly chore I dreaded: mowing the lawn of our suburban home. And like Amy, I tried desperately to get out of doing it. The back-and-forth of me resisting and my dad gently nudging me to do it—I don't know how my dad remained so patient—would always end with me mowing the lawn on Sunday night after dinner, as it was getting dark, just under my weekend deadline.

I was talking about chores with one mother of three young adults in California, and she said that when she was growing up, everyone she knew had real responsibilities, like childcare, household help, or a job, even in families with resources. They weren't "made-up" responsibilities, so there was no need for nagging or chore charts, she said. Her mother went to school and then worked, and it was just understood that she had to care for her youngest brother. "She didn't nag me, she just walked out the door to work," this mother said. There was never any sense that helping was optional.

But in many communities, today's demand for childhood suc-cess has crowded out household chores from kids' to-do lists. It's true in my house, too. Frankly, nagging my children to do their chores, as my dad did with me, became too much of a chore for me.

It was faster and easier for me to load and unload the dishwasher myself, to take out the trash, to put away their laundry. I'm not alone: in one national phone poll of 1,001 US adults, while 82 percent of adults reported having done chores growing up, only 28 percent had their kids doing chores. As one mother bluntly put it to me, "I'd rather my daughter know Mandarin than how to make her bed."

Yet what I have learned in my research is that when we let kids skip out on chores or family events so they can study or practice for their soccer games, we support an overly self-focused outlook in them. It doesn't just make them selfish and self-involved and a little hard to live with. Too much self-focus is unhealthy for them. It's associated with clinical depression, personality disorders, and anxiety.

Marty Rossmann, a professor emeritus at the University of Minnesota, has studied the benefits of chores for decades. In one study, Rossmann analyzed data that followed eighty-four children across twenty years, checking in on them at four time periods of their lives—in preschool, in early adolescence, around age fifteen, and finally in their mid-twenties. What she discovered was that the young adults who had chores in preschool were more likely to achieve in school, to have early career success, and to be self-sufficient, and were less likely to use drugs and alcohol in adulthood, as compared to those who didn't have chores or who started chores as teens. The benefits of chores endured through the years.

In the world's longest scientific study of happiness, researchers at Harvard University have followed hundreds of teenage boys over the course of their lives to see how early-life experiences affected health and aging. One interesting finding was that a strong work ethic in the teen years, such as one developed by chores, was an important predictor of midlife happiness. The psychiatrist George Vaillant, the study's former lead researcher, found that hardworking teens went on to have warmer marriages and stronger friendships, greater job satisfaction, and overall happier lives than their peers. Vaillant told me in a phone interview years ago, for an article I was writing, that "it makes sense"—these men valued hard work, the same ingredient that goes into building successful marriages, careers, families, and friendships.

Chores aren't just a way to teach responsibility and work ethic. Nor are they simply a way for parents to avoid taking out the trash. Chores cement our place in our immediate community, our family—and equip us to add value to those around us. They can be used as a tool to communicate to our children that they have a place in a world that needs them, and that their contribution can have an impact. Chores make children feel depended on. In other words, chores bolster a child's sense of mattering. While caring for others benefits us, it's just as important to care for others because it's simply the right thing to do.

Marjie Longshore, a parent educator, founder of the Family Leadership Center, and single mother of two teenagers in Yarmouth, Maine, took family contribution one step further: she made it a part of her family's identity. "We didn't really talk about it as chores," Marjie told me. "It was more like, how am I going to choose to contribute to the family today and make our home a little happier?"

While I was sitting with Marjie in her kitchen one summer afternoon, she recalled a particularly fraught night when her daughter was struggling with a writing assignment, but it was her turn to make the family dinner. She wasn't happy to have to stop working, to put it mildly. "Homework is a privilege in our house," Marjie reminded her daughter, as she helped her close her laptop. "You're the only person in this town that thinks homework is a privilege," her daughter snapped back. Marjie remembered telling her, "You can choose your feelings, but you still have to contribute."

Slowly, her daughter slouched toward the kitchen and made a racket, clanging the pots and pans in protest. Marjie chuckled a little thinking back on it: "It was a lot of noise to just heat up pasta and warm the tomato sauce that was coming from a jar." After a few minutes, though, the noise started to subside, and her daughter peeked her head around the corner of the kitchen. "Mom, is this one of your parenting tricks?" she muttered. "Well, it's working." Once at the table, Marjie complimented her daughter for cooking the pasta just right. You could see a bit of pride flash across her face for feeding her people, Marjie said. There's a power in feeling useful. Kids thrive when they're adding value to others because it makes them feel valuable themselves.

Age-Appropriate Chores

2–3	Pick up a few toys	Throw away trash	Help prepare meals
3–4	Set the table	Clear dirty dishes	Empty wastebaskets
4–5	Put dishes in dishwasher	Plan a family meal	Dust living room
5–7	Care for pets and/or plants	Empty dishwasher	Take out the trash
7–10	Make a grocery list	Family laundry	Recycle
10–13	Help neighbors with shoveling	Shop for family groceries	Lawn care
13–18	Cook family meals	Care for siblings	Run errands

Based on "Ages When Household Tasks May Begin to Be Performed by Children" by Marty Rossmann.

You Have Impact

Most of the calls Adam took at the teen crisis hotline dealt with small-scale issues. Someone was having a stressful day because of school or friends but had no one to talk to about it. Some recurring callers would call just to connect with someone. Teens are ideal for the role because those calling the crisis line generally feel more connected to a fellow teenager than they do an adult. But a few calls Adam picked up were more dire. In those calls where someone was considering suicide, if someone needed to go to the hospital or was actively harming themselves, he would call 911.

"I'd help them in that critical moment, but I really didn't like the lack of follow-up," Adam told me. "You talk to someone, you have this very intimate conversation with them, and then you hang up—who knows where on Earth they went. Those calls would stay with me." That sense of unease was enough to convince Adam that one-time contact wasn't always enough to protect somebody's mental and physical health. He wanted to find a way to establish ongoing relationships, relationships that could grow and, over time, offer reliable support. After all, having once been "the new kid" at school, he had firsthand experience with the pain of isolation.

With this in mind, and two years of crisis counseling under his belt, in his junior year, Adam founded a student support group. It connected students in the upper classes to younger students in the high school. This co-ed group, perhaps because it was founded by a boy, helped to destigmatize mental health struggles with some of his male classmates. "Boys would send me Snapchat photos of themselves crying, and I'd text them back," he said. Texting felt safer to the boys than speaking in person. In fact, when Adam would try to talk to them in person, they would never admit that they were struggling. But through this support group, Adam's classmates could really address the anxiety and depression they were feeling. They could talk about grades, about questioning their sexual identity, about social pressures, about loneliness.

As Adam talked about his work at school, I could hear in his voice the deep sense of responsibility he felt toward his classmates. Adam said the way he just listened to his classmates' stories, uninterrupted, made them feel understood, finally seen and heard. Like the search and rescue team, this school group added another layer to Adam's mattering, a deeper sense of being significant and feeling needed. He mentored the upper classes, teaching them how to be supportive, active listeners and how to normalize conversations about mental health. To matter, we need to feel competent. And after years of struggling with dyslexia, Adam was finally fully feeling competent, feeling like he had value to add.

Not every child comes to this role of adding value as organically as Adam did, but all of us are born predisposed to want to add value to the world. These impulses will grow if they're encouraged, but too much self-focus can cause these impulses to atrophy. Like our bodies, our empathy muscle needs to be exercised on a regular basis, too. And just like parents who have rules about their kids being active in a sport every season, several parents told me they take a similar approach to volunteering.

One mother in the San Francisco Bay area described a nonnegotiable volunteer mandate she created for her kids. Every week, her kids had to devote five hours to volunteer work of their choosing, and over the summer, that expectation doubled. She enforced the rule by modeling the very behavior she wanted to see in her kids. She would go with them to the local food bank, stocking donations on the shelves. "Whenever I loosened this rule, gave them a pass because their schedules were busy, I always noticed a dip in their well-being," she told me. "I've learned over the years that I have to literally schedule it into their week, just like sports practice is scheduled." She added, "They used to fight me constantly on having to go and volunteer, but now they say they look forward to it."

Now in her twenties, Sidney Montague was raised in a family that made service mandatory. While she initially found the demand frustrating, she grew to appreciate it. Sidney enjoyed volunteering the most when she could directly connect with the people she was helping, like volunteering with after-school tutoring. Knowing the young people she was helping made her feel that her actions made a difference. A deep sense of mattering takes root in our interactions with others—that's where we learn our value and grow as people. Sidney saw the appreciation in the faces of the students she was tutoring when the light bulb in their heads went on and they could solve whatever math problem they were struggling with. In fact, Sidney says, it was because of summer tutoring that she decided to major in education at NYU and pursue a career as a teacher. "I should be thanking my mom for making those volunteering hours mandatory, or I may never have found my purpose in life," Sidney told me.

■ ■ ■

For three years, Tara Christie Kinsey served as associate dean at Princeton University, where she said too many students would come to her office hours depressed, anxious, and feeling like their lives had no meaning. "It's not the students' fault," Kinsey said. "It's the fault of the system, which has produced these amazing, hardworking kids who are just maniacally jumping through the hoops, but they don't feel a sense of meaning, a sense that what they do matters or adds any real value." They're doing exactly what the system told them would get them to Princeton, and they believed in the promise that external success would deliver them a happy life. Of course, we know from decades of research that meaningless achievement doesn't give the payoff we think it will, she said.

"I could see what was working and what wasn't working," said Kinsey. So she started shifting her attention upstream: *How could we reverse engineer a K–12 education for the outcomes we actually want?* To do just that, Kinsey left Princeton to become head of the Hewitt School, a private all-girls school in New York City, where she and her colleagues are in the process of redesigning the curriculum to address "thorny real-world challenges."

Research is clear that student outcomes are stronger when they are genuinely engaged with what they are learning, so Hewitt is teaming up with nonprofits and other institutions around New York City to give their students a chance not just to learn about social issues, but to make a meaningful impact. After learning about disability rights, first graders at Hewitt visited Central Park to investigate how accessible the local playgrounds were. Drawing upon engineering principles they had studied, the students came up with suggestions for wheelchair-accessible slides and larger swings that would allow room for caregivers. The students synthesized their research into a letter to the Central Park Conservancy, advocating for new equipment. They were thrilled when they received a thoughtful reply. Hewitt students come to school knowing they are working on projects that truly matter to their world, Kinsey explained, and that connection to a greater good brings them joy.

William Damon offers these prompts for sparking meaningful conversations with children about their "why": *Why do you think it's important to know math and to know how to read and write? What does it mean to you to have a good life? To be a good person? Who do you admire?* For an older teen, you might go even further: *If you were looking back on your life, how would you want to be remembered? What would you want to be remembered for? Why? What qualities do you have that can help you achieve these goals?*

As the mother of two adolescents, Kinsey is intentional about what modeling a life of purpose looks like to her kids. When she sometimes leaves her family to go to the office on a Sunday afternoon, her kids will say, "Oh, Mom, we feel so bad for you. You work so hard." Kinsey is deliberate about how she responds: "There's nothing that beats being with you. I love being with you *and* I have this important thing that I have to do, to change how we teach girls in this city." She tells them she's excited about what she does and that she hopes they will find work like this too someday.

Kinsey is noticing the sparks that can lead to purpose in her own children now. Her daughter Charlotte, for example, is taking a class on climate change at school, and she comes home every day excited to share what she's learning. "She got so excited about this University of Colorado greenhouse gas emissions simulator that she took her computer out in the living room to show us," Kinsey said. She and her husband noticed the spark: "We said, okay, how do we turn this into a full-blown flame?" At dinner that night, they encouraged Charlotte to talk with her teacher about how they might take action at school against climate change.

Often the assumption is that the adults, the people who are "in charge," are going to fix the problems of the world because we're the ones setting up carpools and soccer practices and enrichment courses, said Kinsey. But that's not going to help the next generation figure out what they care about or how to organize and put their ideas into action. It reminded Kinsey of a famous Lily Tomlin quote: "I always wondered why somebody doesn't do something about that. Then I realized I was somebody." How do we encourage that kind of thinking in our own kids? *Yes, that's a problem, so what are you going to do about it? And how can I help you?* The agency must be theirs, Kinsey says, or else it'll just be us swooping in all the time. That approach—seeing a spark in her daughter and encouraging her to act—worked. Charlotte and her classmate explained to the school in a kind of TED Talk presentation that the consumption of meat is contributing to greenhouse gas emissions. So now every week the school has Meatless Mondays, when vegetarian meals are served. The girls are quantifying Hewitt's reduction of greenhouse gas emissions so they can see the difference one school is making.

Living purposeful lives doesn't just involve big societal causes; it can also take place in small, everyday actions, like being a good neighbor—especially when it might be easier to turn the other way. Marjie in Maine told me about one of her neighbors, an elderly bachelor whom they have adopted into their family. "He was clearly very lonely," she said. Every night after dinner, he'd ring the bell to say hello and bring by a carton of donuts that he picked up from the sale shelf at the gas station. He came from a good place, she told me, though his approach was a little odd. He wasn't socially skillful, but he was part of their community, looking for companionship, and so she said to her kids, *We have a responsibility to help him.* Marjie worked with her son, Barrett, who was twelve at the time, to push through the awkwardness of talking to the neighbor by practicing saying hello and asking the neighbor questions, like where he grew up and how he liked to spend his weekends. Over time, Barrett would occasionally stop by the neighbor's house to tinker with his power tools. When the man went away to his other house in Florida, Barrett would mow his lawn. When the weather got cold, Barrett would cover the neighbor's boat. In turn, the neighbor sent Barrett and the family postcards, telling them how much he appreciated their kindness and friendship. Marjie says that Barrett has seen, in very concrete ways, just how much he's adding value to the man's life.

Not Better *than* Others, but Better *for* Others

Other adults in our children's lives can help foster this caring mindset, too. I saw this in action when I visited Saint Ignatius High School, an all-boys Jesuit school in Cleveland. I'd been told by a local psychologist that there was something special about this school, and she challenged me to figured out the "secret sauce": how year after year they develop high-performing scholars who enjoy very low rates of mental health issues, as shown by surveys taken by the educational nonprofit Challenge Success. In one of my many interviews at the school, I spoke with the longtime teacher and award-winning soccer coach Mike McLaughlin, who graduated from Saint Ignatius himself, as did his father and grandfather. It struck me that there was an extraordinary number of school administrators and teachers I met who had also attended the school. What was it that kept them all coming back?

Coach Mike said people are drawn to the school's values and mission: to form leaders, scholars, and *men for others*. Over the course of four years, students are taught how to balance their own personal needs and goals with a responsibility to help others meet *their* needs and reach *their* goals, too. In other words, the school is deliberate about instilling an other-oriented mindset. It's a daily practice. Each day, the entire school community pauses for a five-minute daily reflection. I saw this in action during my visit. At 2:00 p.m., classes stop, the lights go off, and every student rests his head on his desk, closes his eyes, and listens as someone from the administration, faculty, staff, or student body talks over the PA about a need in the world. One day the students might hear about the effects of climate change on families living in poverty or how inflation is disproportionately affecting low-income families. These reflections widen the students' world and instill compassion. They expose students to the many ways other people need their help. Like the faculty and administrators at Saint Ignatius, we are all trying to raise kids to be the best versions of themselves—and as Coach Mike tells his students, *you are your best when your view is wider than you.*

Students get a deep dive into this "for-others" mindset during sophomore year, when every student takes a mandatory service class taught by Coach Mike. There, they learn about the responsibility of service in the community. During my visit, I sat in on this class and listened to Coach Mike lead a master class on service: how to take another person's perspective, how to actively practice empathy and compassion, how to give back. "All the other classes are going to look into your brain. You need your brain, but the world also needs hearts—and this is a class that's going to look into your heart." I sat up straight, looked around, and saw that I wasn't the only one taking his words in. He had captured every boy's attention.

Coach Mike engaged the boys in a simple exercise. First he asked them to write down everything they'd done, totally independently, without any help, to contribute to their own success. Then he asked them to make a second list of all the things others had done to support them over the past twenty-four hours. He asked the kids to put a percentage comparing the two. "It's always fun, because a kid will say, 'Uh, it's about fifty-fifty,'" he told me. "And I press them: 'Tell me really, what have *you* done?' And then they're like, 'Huh, I guess I've been driven and clothed and sheltered and fed and loved and financially supported. Maybe it's more like five to ninety-five percent.' The point is to plant this idea that they really need people—and that there are people in the world who are going to need them." There was something that felt truly countercultural in what he was teaching, especially in an all-boys setting in a world dominated by "me culture."

Students then take what they've learned and go into the community to make an impact. At first many kids are nervous about serving others in such an intimate way, Coach Mike said. He encourages them to shift their focus away from their own awkwardness and turn that focus instead to the people who need their help.

"One of the most important things people need is for you to care," he tells them.

A lot of service opportunities aimed at teens are rote: you plug in for an hour and then you never go back or see those people. Deep service, though, is about connecting with another human being and making their life better. It's about recognizing our shared humanity, doing what we can to alleviate suffering and honoring the responsibility we have to each other. It doesn't often happen in a minute. It takes time to build that kind of connection. "But you don't have to fly to Haiti and build a shelter to do meaningful volunteer work," Coach Mike told me. At Saint Ignatius, some students go to visit patients being treated for cancer, some work with refugees, some tutor young students. All their projects are relational and require them to connect with another human being. When they go out on Sunday nights to feed the homeless, they must shake hands, look people in the eye, and say, "Hi, I'm Timmy, what's your name?"

Part of the magic of the service class is that the time for volunteering is already baked in once a week for three hours during the school day. Most schools have a service requirement, and usually students must find time after school or on the weekends to meet it. But about fifty years ago, the priests of the school decided to make volunteering an essential part of the school day, as important as chemistry. What these priests undoubtedly knew, and what research shows us, is that living a life according to a value system that balances others' needs with our own boosts our well-being. In fact, part of the reason religion has been found to enhance mental health is because it reduces self-centeredness and creates a sense of belonging to a larger whole. "Serving others shapes the world, and it shapes you," Coach Mike likes to tell the boys.

Having an other-oriented mindset can be incorporated into all areas of our kids' lives beyond service hours. At home, I found myself using the language I'd picked up at Saint Ignatius when my kids were starting their summer jobs. Their first summer jobs, at age fourteen, were as camp counselors, and their why, their purpose, as they saw it, was to make sure the campers had fun, stayed safe, and learned how to make new friends. It was less easy to find their why in their next summer job: serving frozen yogurt for eight hours a day. So I channeled my inner Coach Mike. I explained that while yes, they were paid to serve yogurt and keep the shop clean, more than that, they were there to help kids and their families make fond summer memories. We talked about the ways they could make these memories sweeter, like making a point to welcome people and make them feel like they belonged there, not just another customer in line. Living life "for others," my kids started to understand, could be found in small, everyday moments, too.

In his book *The Path to Purpose*, William Damon offers this guidance for helping adolescents find their purpose:

- Listen for sparks, then fan the flames

- Ask guiding questions

- Be open to interests

- Encourage a feeling of agency, linked to responsibility

- Ask your children to contribute some minor service to the family on a regular basis and acknowledge those efforts with appreciation

- Talk about your relationships, your work, your purpose

- Introduce your children to potential mentors

Encourage Deep Connection

Helping others is about building connection, but we can also make these deep connections with people we are volunteering *with*. Sarah grew up in an affluent community and attended, as she put it, "an extremely cutthroat, competitive public high school." Sarah said that looking back, she was depressed, but she had no idea how much the competition around her was affecting her mental health. That is, until she went on a weeklong volunteer retreat with her church youth group to DC. For the first time in her life, she said, she met people who cared and talked about things other than their grades and themselves. "They were doing something I cared about, helping homeless people, and we bonded over that," she said. "In that one week, I had finally found my tribe." They showed her that relationships should be reciprocal, not transactional. The trip was a turning point in her life. "My values completely shifted," she said.

After that trip, Sarah sought out things to care about outside school. "I had been running track, but if you weren't a good runner, the coaches dismissed you," she told me. "If you're the star, they paid attention. If not, then you're a spare." So Sarah quit track and started

to spend her afternoons doing volunteer work. She found that helping others, having an outer focus, helped to reduce her stress, too.
With her new friends on the retreat, she could talk about deep, meaningful things. It made her old friendships at school feel shallow. "I
had no idea how warm and comforting it was to find people that
you could have real conversations about things you were struggling
with, without judgment." Sarah told me that she is now the kind of
friend who feels a responsibility to be there for others. "I will text
friends who are depressed and ask point-blank, 'How's your medication working? Let's talk about it.' They know I've been there too."

Building Capacity for Setbacks and Failure

At the start of his senior year, inspired by his work on the search
and rescue unit, the crisis hotline, and the school mental health
group, Adam began to consider a career in medicine. Emergency
room medicine—being there to help people in their moments of
crisis—was what interested him most. As soon as he turned eighteen, he became eligible to shadow doctors in the ER, sitting in on
trauma surgeries and even a heart transplant. "Having a firsthand
look at the relationship between a patient and the doctor and thinking about the potential impact of not getting support, that was really
a big driver for me," Adam said. "I don't love chemistry or biology,
but I understand the importance of having a strong scientific back-
ground for my future career. And having this end goal—this 'wow,
I can have this huge impact if I'm willing to put in that work'—has
been a big motivation for me."

Part of the motivation, Adam explained, was that his parents
didn't take over the process. They let him lead the way, which made

a huge difference in helping him define his purpose. They gave him the freedom to explore the activities and volunteer opportunities that interested him and supported him by driving him places and paying for things like Boy Scout fees. Being able to try new things and get hands-on experience, he said, helped move him beyond the fixed mindset that there's one straight path to a good life: getting into a good college so you can land a high-paying job. Instead, he realized, success is finding meaning in your life. When you make this shift in thinking, Adam said, you realize that you can go to community college or Harvard and still live a life that has impact.

Funnily enough, this fresh perspective didn't cause him to rest on his laurels. It did the opposite. It motivated him to reach higher, to work harder. With these goals in mind, he didn't want to skate by on easy classes; he wanted to challenge himself and see what he was capable of. "I knew that I needed to focus and not waste all this time doing things that weren't important," he said. He petitioned the school to move him into honors math. A month into the class, on his first test, he scored an F. "My dyslexia and math don't really go together," he explained. But instead of dropping back down to the regular track, Adam's newfound ambition encouraged him to stick with it. "I now had this feeling that I was doing something beyond myself," he said. His math teacher offered to tutor him every day after school, and Adam took him up on it. Adam climbed back up from an F to a final grade of a B+. "There are a lot of innately intelligent people in this world, and I'm not one of them, but I can work hard and still achieve what I want to," he told me. But being smart takes multiple forms, of course, and Adam is undoubtedly very smart.

Adam and I spoke as he was awaiting college decisions in the winter of his senior year. No longer adrift, as he'd felt freshman year, he was laser focused in what he needed to do. When I asked how he found the time and energy to take a full honors and AP course load, apply for colleges, *and* volunteer in so many capacities, he laughed it off humbly. "I have a lot of energy," he said. As a way to explore emergency medicine, he had begun training to be an EMT. School ended at 3:00 p.m., and his EMT classes were from 4:00 p.m. to 8:00 p.m., so every day he had to carefully budget his time. "I definitely put a lot of pressure on myself to be successful and to work hard, but it isn't about me," he said. "I need to work hard so I can have the knowledge and experience to help other people."

Knowing your why does more than energize; it also improves your resilience and your capacity for failure. We may not always feel understood or appreciated by others, but when we add value to something beyond ourselves, we can see firsthand that we are valuable. In this way, purpose can serve as a healthy fuel that not only protects against mental health struggles but also provides a pathway out of them. A sense of something greater than yourself can alleviate the stress, anxiety, depression, and burnout that so many of our young people today are feeling. In young people, this outlook has been shown to curb self-destructive impulses. Adam has certainly found this to be true. His why has sustained him and helped him overcome the challenges of dyslexia. Adam told me that if he didn't get into his top choice schools, he'd go to a community college and still make his way to medical school. He had found his purpose, and nothing was going to get in the way.

When we teach our kids how to live a life of purpose, how to contribute meaningfully to others, their drive becomes self-sustaining. Purpose energizes, motivates, and keeps them on track, even when challenges or setbacks inevitably occur. It curbs perfectionistic tendencies and reminds them that they're much more than any one failure. Setbacks don't become all-encompassing reflections on a person's inherent worth. When we have a sense of outward mission, we gain a long-term perspective: We see that we're not just rising and falling on our achievements and that our failures aren't as consequential as they may initially seem. This larger purpose shifts our mindset from one of scarcity and fear to one of abundance, where we see our place in the world as part of a bigger whole. In fact, practicing generosity both requires and reinforces the perception of living in a world of abundance, which then increases happiness and health.

When Adam and I next met up, it was the spring of his freshman year at UCLA, where he was on a premed track. Wandering through a blooming campus in early spring with iced teas in our hands, we passed rows of students playing frisbee on the expansive lawns. I asked him how a boy who had no interest in academics his freshman year of high school, who was just phoning it in, had gone on to be accepted into one of the most competitive schools in the country.

Adam blushed and looked down. "Honestly, I'm just an ordinary kid," he replied. Yet though he didn't use the word, Adam is extraordinary. He has learned how to embrace his strengths to overcome his weaknesses. Memorizing street and building names is extremely hard for a dyslexic person, he told me, but that knowledge is crucial for someone driving an ambulance through the UCLA campus, as he was now doing. When it comes to saving someone's life, there's little room for error and certainly no time to keep checking a map. "I can't get a call and not know where I'm going—minutes and seconds count." So he'd leaned into his strengths—persistence, empathy, work ethic—and spent weeks memorizing all the buildings, little lanes, and access points on campus. He even had his friends quiz him on their way to dinner on Friday nights.

"As I got more experience working with search and rescue, volunteering on the crisis line, shadowing doctors in an emergency room, my confidence in my abilities grew," he said, which then motivated him to take on bigger challenges. "It's really hard to sit in a high school class and say, 'This is what I believe in the world,' when all you've done is read about the world but never experienced it." Foreign languages for students with dyslexia can be quite challenging, Adam told me, but Spanish is an important skill for an emergency room doctor. During the COVID-19 pandemic, when college was online, Adam traveled to Latin America to improve his Spanish. He volunteered with a first-responder team and the Red Cross in El Salvador.

"My current big interest is looking at emergency medical services and seeing how we respond to behavioral health crises," he said. Adam explained that the EMT arrives first on the scene but receives only about thirty minutes of training on how to handle a mental health crisis. "We've never learned how to de-escalate a patient," he said. "We learn how to put on restraints, but that's about it." Adam was now helping a committee for the city of Los Angeles that was looking to train EMS workers to be first responders to patients who are suffering from mental health issues.

EMS can be a very difficult job—life isn't fair, and bad things happen, Adam told me. "But the way I think about it is, my goal is to help in whatever is going on: if I can't help the patient, then I help the family, or help the bystanders—anything to make things better." When he can't even do that, he thinks about what he can learn from the experience that will help him help someone else one day.

When I asked how classes were going, he told me they had been tough. His chemistry professor was notorious for curving the class average down. So ultimately, no matter how hard Adam studied, his score was not entirely in his hands, he said. But he knew he'd be okay—he was part of something bigger. "I've tried to transition that pressure from getting good grades to just working hard and doing my best, and from there, it is what it is," he said. Still, I found myself worrying about what this class might do to his medical school application, but when I asked him about it, he said, "When you have a purpose beyond yourself, you realize that there are infinite paths to get there."

My conversations with Adam have shifted how I spend my parental energy. If we believe our role as parents is to raise kids who will contribute to society by getting high-salary jobs and paying taxes, then perhaps it makes sense to focus narrowly on academic achievement. But if our job as parents is to show our kids their value beyond their economic contribution to society, if our job is to raise caring citizens who contribute to the common good, then it is important to exercise *those* skills just as much. Now, at the dinner table, my husband and I make a point to discuss the news and tell stories about people or issues that need our help, even if only in small ways. I guard time in our kids' schedules so they can add value at home and in their larger community. What I've come to realize is that the antidote for burnout isn't necessarily powering off, but rather reengaging to improve the world around us. That's what energizes us.

Instead of allowing our kids to drift meaninglessly for years—

wondering why they should achieve, what it's all for—we can let our kids in on the secret to living a meaningful life: "other people matter," as renowned psychologist Christopher Peterson put it. What Adam showed me over the three years we've kept in touch, what I learned from Marjie, Rick, and Coach Mike, is that your life becomes more meaningful when you know the value you can bring to others. And the more you are able to add value to others, the more meaningful your life becomes.

8

––––––––––

The Ripple Effect

Unlocking Mattering All Around You

When people asked me how I felt about turning fifty, I said: grateful. I've had very close friends who didn't get that opportunity. Getting older is a gift I never want to take for granted, so I was going to celebrate it, even if COVID-19 concerns kept the guest list on the shorter side. After two years of lockdowns, my friends commented that my birthday party felt like a coming-out party for all of us. My parents were there. My in-laws were there. A few close friends surprised me by flying in. I was also in for the surprise of my life. A couple of weeks earlier, unbeknownst to me, Caroline had secretly emailed my friends explaining our family tradition of saying one thing you love about the birthday person.

She asked them to join in by sending her something funny or heart-felt or both, describing what "you uniquely like about her or value about your friendship."

Just before dinner was served, I heard Peter ask for everyone's attention, followed by a ripple of shushing through the room. Realizing what was about to happen—there were toasts!—I quickly parked myself against a wall where I could see all three of my kids standing with my husband at the front of the room.

To my shock, they started talking about *mattering*, describing the idea to our friends. My family had gathered the emailed responses and arranged them by themes—"loyal friend," "advice giver," "celebrator of others' accomplishments," and "volunteer"—into a toast about why I *mattered* to my friends and community. It's one thing to study and write about mattering, but it's another to experience it in such a personal and profound way.

These toasts about being a valued friend came at a time when I was working through the last draft of this book and spending much less time on my relationships than I would have preferred. I was seeing friends so little that occasionally one friend would send me a text to make sure I was still alive: "JBW, are you OK?" Hearing these toasts offered an important reminder of how much these relationships meant to me. Perhaps most striking were the words from my own kids. After three years of talking about mattering, I've noticed some eye rolling when the topic comes up, or as James says, "Here she goes again."

But it turns out they were processing what I was saying. After reading the toasts, my children talked about how I made *them* feel liked they mattered. William spoke about how I always treated him respectfully, "as an equal," and how I offer a helpful perspective on anything he's struggling to solve. James looked me directly in the eye and talked about how he's learned from me that making a mistake isn't a bad thing, that I never make him feel bad or that he's any less lovable. Caroline said, "You are a wonderful role model to us, always teaching us that to feel valued, you need to add value to the world." I just stood there, against the wall, taking it all in.

The next day, I woke up trying to unpack what exactly was so profound about that evening. I think this was it: my kids had internalized mattering for themselves, and they were practicing it, and passing it on—this way of seeing the world and their place in it. What I have seen in my reporting is that knowing that you are inherently valuable, and that you add value to the world, spreads like a ripple effect. As one friend texted, "I'm no longer going to wait until a big birthday to tell a friend why they matter to me. Thanks for the reminder to tell the people we love why we love them."

Not Scarcity but Abundance

Throughout this book, we have examined up close the messages society throws at us: scarcity, envy, hyper-competition. Beneath the illusion of scarcity, beneath the fear and anxiety and envy and status seeking, we are all striving for the same basic human needs: to feel valued, to belong, to be known and loved for who we are at our core.

Mattering, as I've come to see it, offers a powerful antidote to a scarcity mindset. Knowing that people are valuable for who they are—not for how they perform, not for what they produce, not for what they acquire—releases us from the competitive chokehold. It shifts our thinking away from what we're lacking and allows us to see all that we do have. It boosts our status in healthy ways. It connects us to the best in ourselves and the best in others. Mattering, in other words, offers a perspective of abundance, freeing us from zero-sum thinking and reminding us that there is enough for everyone to go around. Mattering shows up in how we treat ourselves and how we treat one another. Choosing mattering, even when we're feeling anxious and fearful, is a deliberate choice we can make every day.

As I interviewed kids and their parents for this book, I noticed something significant: those who felt a strong sense that they mattered—to their families, to their friends, to other adults in their lives—also seemed to have an easier time expressing how *others mattered to them.* When I asked these kids what they thought led to their success, they often spent a lot of time in our interviews talking about *other* people, and how influential their parents, their teachers, their coaches, and their classmates had been in supporting them. Jack Cook, who attended Saint Ignatius in Cleveland and recently graduated from Harvard, talked about his supportive classmates in his Advanced Placement classes who were "smarter" than he was and took the time to help him when he needed it. He talked about the teachers who pushed him to challenge himself with harder classes, who believed in him before he believed in himself. As we were ending our calls, Jack thanked me for the interview and for reminding him of all the people who have done so many things to make his life better. He told me that he was going "to spend the rest of the evening reaching out to some of my old high school teachers and coaches and other people I haven't thanked in a while."

Mattering works as a virtuous, overflowing cycle. When we *feel* valued by others, when we see *how we add* value to them, we experience a fullness that then allows us to share it with others: we are encouraged to express how they are valuable and how they add to our own lives.

In other words, mattering is additive, multiplicative. When you feel loved, nurtured, and cared-for yourself, you are much more likely to be able to revel in another's success, to feel another's joy. This idea that we can relish someone else's joy is something that gets knocked out of us in our competitive, zero-sum culture. There is a Sanskrit word that captures this feeling of pleasure that comes from delighting in another's well-being: "mudita." Mudita is an unselfish joy, the belief that there is room in this world for everyone to experience happiness and success. In other words, like I saw with Chloe and Thea at Archer, even if we lose, we can still be happy we participated and even happy for the person who won: *Her success is my success.* That's mudita.

It has been so freeing to learn about mattering, but it has also come to feel like a responsibility to me. Once you know and feel its power—and conversely the feeling of not mattering—you may, like me, come to see it as an obligation to use this knowledge for good and to spread it around. If we can start making people feel like they truly, deeply, unequivocally matter to their families, to their friends, to their communities, imagine what the world would look like, feel like, be like? Mattering motivates us to want to do something about it: How can I help someone matter, even just in this one moment?

Sources of Mattering

Years ago, the author Bruce Feiler was diagnosed with a rare form of cancer. In his best-selling book *The Council of Dads*, Feiler described his worry over who would be there to support his wife and his young daughters if he didn't make it through. He reached out to a small group of friends and asked them to be a part of what he called a "council of dads," men who would be there to support and help shape the lives of his children.

What Feiler's story highlighted for me is this notion parents sometimes have that we should be able to meet our children's needs alone. (Witness the ever-revolving stack of how-to books on my bedside table, a self-imposed syllabus on how to be my children's therapist, nutritionist, motivational coach, you name it.) This is what a scarcity mindset tells us: you have to be everything, secure everything, control everything for them. This myth that we have singular control over our children's outcomes damages our kids and our relationship with them.

But a mattering mindset tells us the opposite: that we're not meant to do this alone. Our kids do far better with input from a broader network. This isn't just because the variety exposes them to more things about the world, though that is true. It's also because sensing that you are valued by a network that's larger than your immediate family reinforces your own sense of mattering. The greater the number of caring and attentive adults our children have in their lives—who know and appreciate and take an interest in who they are—the more valuable they will feel, and the more they will be exposed to how they can add value to others. I've thought of this in terms of *How can I replace myself in my kids' lives? How can I augment what I'm doing with the help of other trusted adults?*

A larger adult network is protective. Kids who are surrounded by caring adults will exhibit less risky behavior because, in part, they don't want to disappoint the people who care about them. One mother talked about warning her son to stay out of trouble in the final weeks of high school, when the majority of the schoolwork was over, but he had not yet graduated. He said to her, "Oh, don't worry, I could never let Mr. Phillips [his headmaster] down." Part of her was deflated, she said, because he wasn't worried about letting her down. But she quickly realized how the respect of other adults in her son's life was an extremely powerful force.

Surrounding our kids with trusted adults also releases us from running ourselves into the ground by trying to be everything to them. Instead, we can actively consider—and invite—an adult network that will help preserve their mattering. Ask yourself: Who are the "elders" of your greater community who can be there for your kids? Who are the adults who make your kids feel important, who listen to what they have to say? Bea Wilson, a senior in Charleston, South Carolina, has been a dancer for thirteen years. While she was always attracted to dance, she said she didn't fall in love with it until six years ago, when, by chance, she joined a studio that made her feel valued. There, she was more than just a dancer. Her teachers took an interest in who she was as a person. When she was sick, they'd text her telling her how much they missed her but to stay home and rest.

They also gave her the opportunity to give back. One day a week, she and a few other volunteers hold a class called "The Purple Tutu" to help developmentally and physically disabled kids learn to dance. Like her instructors did with her, she greets each child by name, commenting on how special their hair or their outfit looks. She's gotten to know what each kid likes, what they don't like, and she often hears from their parents how their confidence has grown, as have their dance skills. As Bea spoke, her voice sounded wistful.

She was deeply grateful, she said, for how her instructors had made her feel important—and for how she now got to do the same for other kids.

A friend's fourteen-year-old son, George, has worked for two summers at a local deli. The owner took an interest in him, getting to know his hobbies, appreciating out loud his strong work ethic and how responsible he was. When she found out that George liked to cook at home, she encouraged him to make something special that they could sell at the store. George's Guacamole is now on the menu. Now George is passing this feeling of being significant and important to the kids he babysits on the weekend. One little boy he takes care of is an expert in making rope bracelets, so George asked if he could make a couple that he could give as presents to friends— and that he'd pay him for them. Now this young boy is feeling valued. That's the ripple effect of mattering.

For Marjie Longshore in Maine, building out her family's circle involved routine investments, like taking joint vacations with friends who have become like extended family over the years. Twenty years ago, Marjie met her best friend, Emily, at a playground when their oldest kids were just one-year-olds. The two women have been de- liberate about carving out their own, distinct relationships with each other's children, introducing them to various hobbies, taking them to sporting events, even taking them to tour college campuses. "I can't begin to say how comforting it was to know that there were other adults looking out for my kids and showing them a world that was different and bigger than the world I have to share," said Marjie.

One mother in the Palo Alto area talked about how she created a "council of moms" during the turbulent teen years. Each teen had a list of five mothers who gave the kids in the group their cell phone numbers and promised confidentiality about any topic: academic pressure, drinking, relationships. They made this group formal. If one of the kids was worried about grades, any one of these mothers would meet them for coffee to discuss. If the kids found themselves at a party without a safe ride home, they could call any of these moms at any hour, no questions asked. It wasn't just giving kids explicit information about who to call. What these women were doing was making their family seen and vulnerable, giving their network of friends a peek under the hood by allowing their teens to open up and share their troubles with trusted people outside the family.

This kind of arrangement helps the adults in their lives matter, too, because they feel trusted and like they have something to offer. "Honestly, I don't always get the appreciation I want from my own kids," said one dad who was coaching his son's little league team. "So it's motivating for me to help the kids on my team because they are open about expressing their appreciation and that makes me feel like what I do actually matters."

Dialing it Up

Heading back to school after the pandemic was a transition for all kids. Wearing masks, social distancing, and eating in silence behind plexiglass was not an ideal way to go through fifth grade, as one mother told me. When her son Steven, who normally enjoyed school, said he didn't like going anymore, this mother asked him some probing questions to get to the root of his resistance. Did he think he'd be missed if he was not there? Was there one adult at school that he'd be comfortable reaching out to and talking to about this? What this mother discovered was that the disconnect her son was feeling at school was because he didn't feel a close connection to any of his teachers—the necessary masks were leaving him feeling a little anonymous.

Next to home, school is a child's most important community, a miniature society where they can learn how to be a valued contributor. But a scarcity mindset can create a narrow view of school and create a specific tension between parents and teachers or administrators. In our anxiety over our children's futures, parents can come to believe, even if subconsciously, that the mission of the school we send our children to is to get our kids into the best college possible. As one teacher in a public high-achieving school in the Northeast put it, parents can behave as if they're paying customers—"and the customer is always right," she said. Anything a teacher or school administrator does that supposedly gets in the way of that college acceptance is looked upon as a threat.

"If our parents got a call from a teacher, our parents would say, 'What did you do?'" one mother I interviewed told me. "Now, we say: 'What did the teacher do?' And then we think about how we're going to intervene by calling the principal or our lawyer."

In Suniya Luthar's student surveys, she has found that one critical area that negatively affects a student's well-being is when they feel the fracture between their parents and school. Students who perceive that collaboration is low between the adults in their lives consistently report the highest numbers of stress. If school is really a second home, Luthar notes, then the acrimonious relationship between parents and teachers is like throwing kids into the stress of an ugly divorce. It forces kids to choose sides and adds to the pressures they already feel.

Teachers are a vital source of mattering for our kids. One student I met, a senior at UPenn named Darya Bershadskaya, explained that she survived the stressful days of high school because of the good relationship she had built with her newspaper advisor and the staff. Every morning, she and the rest of the staff would get to school extra early. Instead of just talking about what had to be done in the newspaper, they talked about books, hobbies, and life beyond the classroom. "It felt a lot like a family," she said.

In other words, she continued, their newspaper advisor saw Darya and her peers as people, not just students. In fact, inspired by her advisor's dedication to his students, after graduation Darya is participating in the two-year program of Teach For America. On campus, she's been struck by the number of peers who appear to struggle because everything in their life seems conditional: their intelligence, their relationships, their worth. She feels lucky she had the space to feel her teacher's investment in her as a person: "Being part of that group, alongside my advisor and my newspaper team, felt like unconditional acceptance that paved the way for growth."

An abundant mindset helps us choose to see our school communities as a place where not just our kids need to feel that they matter, but a place where their teachers do, too. For their own mental health and well-being, teachers need to know that they are having an impact on and adding value to their community in meaningful ways. They also want and deserve to feel valued. We may already be conditioned to buy our child's teacher a holiday present, and teacher appreciation luncheons are great. But to build connectedness also means going beyond these niceties and changing our stance: from adversarial to bridge building. Liana Montague, a mother I met on Mercer Island, told me about a tradition she did with her kids each year. She asked each of her kids to write their teachers thank-you notes saying how much they meant to them. It not only got her kids in the habit of appreciating how people contribute to their lives, but it also reinforced in the teachers how much they mattered to their students.

The payoff in building healthy parent-teacher relationships for our kids is significant, even from a performance perspective. Dana, a mother from a suburban New Jersey town, told me a story about her sixth-grade son, John, who was accused by his English teacher of plagiarism. "The teacher said that he couldn't possibly have written his personal essay, that the ideas were too adultlike," she said. "John came home in tears."

Her immediate impulse was to call the school and yell at the teacher. Instead, she called a friend and vented to her. "My friend gave me the advice to have my son try to advocate for himself first," she said. The next day, John spoke to his teacher but got nowhere. So Dana reached out to the teacher to schedule a time to talk. Before the meeting, she reminded herself that she and the teacher were on the same team in her son's life; both wanted to see him succeed. "I went into the conversation giving this person I had never met the benefit of the doubt, that we both wanted what's best for John," she said. "I calmly explained that my son prided himself on being a good writer, that it was a huge part of his identity, and that while I proofread his essay, I did little more than add in a few commas." This was her son's story completely, Dana told the teacher, gently but confidently.

After a pause, the teacher thanked her for her civil response. "That moment, treating each other with respect and civility, set us up to have a terrific year together," Dana explained. They were partners. And her son's writing got even stronger because of it. "This teacher has actually turned out to be his favorite of the year," Dana told me. Had she stormed in there demanding answers, she reflected, she would have damaged that relationship for her son. Instead, with each essay he wrote, John worked hard to impress his teacher even more. "It was amazing to see how his writing got to the next level with so much support."

What a mattering framework does is allow us to shift from competition to cooperation, from feeling isolated to a sense of connectedness. To combat Steven's reluctance to go to school, he and his mom came up with a plan: he was going to focus on showing his teachers how much *they* mattered to him. He would do this by giving them his undivided attention and engagement in class and thanking them on his way out the classroom door. This simple reframe kicked off a positive upward spiral: showing his appreciation to his teachers and their response to it has shown Steven how much he matters to them, and how much they matter to him—and he has stopped complaining about going to school.

Expressions of Mattering

Showing others how they matter to us, even in small ways, can reverberate through a community. On my visit to Mercer Island, I met up with student Meghana Kakubal. Over deli salads balanced on our laps, we talked about how she was voted by her classmates to be one of three drum majors of the school band. From my visit at the school, I knew that this was a highly coveted position, a leader of the three hundred students in the band both on the field and off. Performance-wise, the drum majors conduct on the field and lead the band during parades. Behind the scenes, they lead rehearsals, organize spirit days, coordinate events, and serve as a bridge between the directors and students.

As the daughter of Indian immigrants, Meghana told me she knew what it was like to sometimes feel invisible in a community that was predominantly white. She was going to take the honor that came with her leadership position seriously and make it her mission to help all students feel seen and important.

That was not going to be a small task. Because the band is so big, it's usually the extroverts who get recognized, who feel like they belong, Meghana said. As a self-described introvert, she told me that it sometimes left her feeling like she was less valued in the band simply because she wasn't as expressive. "So, when I ran for drum major, part of my speech was that we need to make this a place that makes sure the introverts also know that they're valued and that they don't have to be the loudest person in the band to be just as integral to the band's success."

When the previous drum majors were training her, Meghana explained, one of the guys offered her advice: "You're not going to know everyone, so when someone says something to you, just respond, 'Hey, thanks.'" Meghana didn't say anything, but this advice felt wrong. She couldn't change the past, but she could change this year's band culture. Instead of just nodding to her fellow students, she was going to memorize every single band student's name. She spent those first few weekends in her role memorizing and testing herself on the band members' names. At the end of the year, an underclassman wrote Meghana a thank-you note, saying how touched she was that Meghana always called her by her name, which she said made her feel like she mattered to the group. Making each person feel valued, especially the people who can feel overlooked, helped shift the band's culture. This shift motivated more introverted students to try for leadership positions in the band, and some students who, despite previously being ready to quit band because they didn't feel like they belonged, ended up as leaders.

Another big lesson I learned in my reporting was that people need to know they matter more than they need their privacy. I learned this from a family in Cleveland. What struck me about this family is that they had built an entire life around relationships and breaking down barriers. In that family, people came first. It was evident in the way they greeted me and talked: inviting me to join them for dinner. It was evident in the way their home was set up: seating for twenty in their living room, with extra-long couches. It was evident by how comfortable the kids were joining our conversation.

The mother told me a story about when the wife of one of her son's teachers was ill. Her son checked in with the teacher from time to time, and the family reached out to the school to offer to help. It felt somewhat unusual for a teen to take such an openly compassionate initiative. It stuck with me. When something is happening in someone's life, his mother told me, "It's not polite to ignore it. It's actually polite to acknowledge it." These are the ties that connect us, that help us see we matter to one another.

Mattering offers connection on a deeper level. After making a difference with her work at the Wilton Youth Council, Vanessa Elias, one of the Wilton women I met, started looking for ways she might create connections for others. She decided it would be her mission to "re-village" Wilton and build back community ties to combat feelings of isolation and loneliness. Since 2018, she has been organizing town-wide block parties for neighbors to gather over two weekends bookending summer, in June and September, and get neighborhood kids outside playing together. The theme "building community one block at a time" is exactly what these get-togethers accomplish. The first year, more than 1,200 residents came out to celebrate in forty separate parties. The block party initiative gives neighbors a reason to reach out to one another and break through the "silos" behind the picket fences —"and not feel awkward asking for a cup of flour," she said, with a wink.

After an impromptu girls' night out, during which Vanessa opened up to a few women about her parenting struggles, it occurred to her that, while the block parties were helpful, mothers in particular needed a no-strings-attached sort of gathering—one for fun, no agenda. At first, she was met with skepticism. "When I first talked about it to a friend," she recalled, "she asked, 'But what do you *want* from me out of this—roping me into some volunteer work?'"

Vanessa was undeterred. She posted the announcement on Facebook: She was launching a social group called Women of Wilton, or WOW, where any attendee could experience "a sounding board, a story, a frustration, a laugh, and connecting with our feelings." The group now has its own Facebook page, with more than four hundred members of mixed ages spanning from thirties to fifties. Before COVID-19 they were meeting once a month. Now that COVID-19 is waning, they've started to pick up again.

The practice of mattering pierces our image-conscious lives— the misguided notion that we don't need help. These small moments puncture the facade that supposedly protects our families but, in reality, breeds loneliness. New York, as much as I love it, can be very image conscious. But practicing mattering with my neighbors means we all get to let down that public mask we sometimes wear. When we get an unexpected snowfall and our kids' snow pants don't fit, instead of feeling like a parent who is falling down on the job, a quick text—*Help, does anyone have size-ten snow pants?*—both solves the practical problem and pushes back against the idea that we are meant to do this life all alone. Mattering strengthens our social safety nets. My kids also feel a sense of comfort knowing they have several people they can turn to whenever they need help, whether it's printing out a late-night homework assignment because our printer ran out of ink or borrowing a cup of milk mid-recipe because we miscalculated just how much we'd need. Not only do I let my neighbors see my messy life, but they're also people I count on to help me through it.

Unlocking Mattering in Others

Having a mattering mindset broadens how we think about success for our kids, and what it is they truly need. Johnny, a sophomore in a New York high school, was having a tough time at school. Something was missing socially for him. Talking to his mother, she told me he had friends and was well-liked at school, but he didn't feel a strong connection to them, no one called him to hang out. Feeling a low level of mattering held him back from reaching out himself. He was caught in a trap of loneliness.

And then, three weeks into the fall semester, something happened to change that. The school musical was short one key part, and a few of Johnny's friends reached out to him and asked if he'd be willing to join. They begged him really, explaining that they wouldn't be able to perform the play without this key character filled. Johnny was on the fence: the play would take two hours of practice nearly every day and would cut into time he could spend on school work. He asked his mother for advice.

"I *could* have said he didn't have time or that it would interfere with other things, but more study time, I knew, was not what he needed," she said. She encouraged him to do it—and in the back of her mind, she thought, *This is how he can feel connected and valued by his friends again.*

Since joining the theater, Johnny has become a valued member. Not only is he a pretty good actor, he's always the first to pat a pal on the back when he nails a performance and the one who cheers the loudest from the wings. His classmates remain grateful to him for joining, when they knew theater wasn't really his thing, and they make him feel like his presence and his spirit counted toward making the play a success. Adding value and feeling valued has energized Johnny and solidified a sense of belonging at school and reinforced the idea that he did indeed matter to his friends.

Mattering now colors everything about how I parent. When things aren't going smoothly at home, when my kids are feeling lonely or stressed, I don't solve for their happiness. I solve for their mattering and use the framework to think about how best to help them. Are they struggling with feeling valued? Are they struggling with not seeing how they add value? I've even stopped telling my kids that I just want them to be happy. Happiness and well-being, I've come to realize, are the byproducts of living a life where we feel valued and add value to others.

It can be a challenge for young kids in high-achieving communities to find places where they truly add value, other than to themselves. One mother I interviewed spoke about the tension at home between her teens. Her younger child never wanted to help, and his older sister felt like she was the only one doing chores and helping the family. At age twelve, he was deeply consumed with himself, she said. He also lacked appreciation for others in the household who went out of their way to help him; he was entitled. "I think he thinks he matters *too much*," she said.

So we brainstormed together. I asked her if he had any chores. Were there any concrete ways he felt useful, depended on? Her eyes lit up: No, she said. He was never asked to add value to anyone but himself. We wondered if maybe his being overly consumed with himself was a way of compensating for a lack of mattering to others. She was going to do an experiment at home, to see if giving him some real responsibility—planning the weekly meals and grocery shopping with their babysitter—would help.

Two weeks later, she emailed me. Not only was her son helping the sitter with the grocery shopping, but he had also learned how to cook a "signature" meal himself: yogurt-marinated chicken. At dinner that first night, his sister told him that it was the best chicken she had ever had. Now her son sometimes spends time before bed reading cookbooks and looking for ways to surprise his family with other delicious meals. The mother swears that he is less focused on himself. She still has to nudge him to help out, but applying the mattering lens within her family opened up a pathway for him to feel valued and to focus more on others.

Another mother, Stacy, talked about her high-school-age son and his two best friends. Within the first two weeks of sophomore year, both of her son's friends got serious girlfriends. Instead of being one of the Three Musketeers, he was now the fifth wheel. When he'd ask them to go to a movie or play a video game, they were always too busy. Rarely did they sit together now at lunch; the other boys were often walking around campus with their girlfriends instead. He no longer felt like he mattered to them.

Stacy grew concerned as she watched her happy-go-lucky teen become sullen and withdrawn. As the summer going into his senior year approached, instead of encouraging her son to get an internship that would look good on his résumé, his mother suggested he go back to his summer camp as a counselor. What she knew was that summer camp was a place where he felt like he really mattered. Within a week of returning to camp, his low mood lifted. When he called her to check in, there was an energy and excitement to his voice again. He was remembering how much he was valued.

Stacy described a ripple effect. Her son passed forward a sense of mattering to the little campers he supervised. When one of them felt left out, he found another way for them to feel important by, say, assigning them the important task of pulling out the sailboats from the boat house. The thanks that little camper received made him feel like he was contributing, reminding him that he was a valued part of their little community.

We cannot matter alone. We matter in relationship with others. It's hard to insist on our own value to ourselves—it's so easy to lose sight of it. No amount of mindfulness or emotional regulation can do it for us. We need social proof, other people to tell us, to insist on it, to remind us of how we are inherently valuable and that our presence adds something to the world. And other people need us to remind them of their mattering. Lisa Heffernan, a cofounder of the popular parenting community Grown & Flown, has seen how her committed group of thousands comes together quickly to empathize and share advice when a struggling parent reaches out to the group for guidance: "When you post something and people pour in with helpful comments and support, what they are really saying to this struggling parent is: you matter."

Too many people today don't have a firm sense of mattering. They question their importance, their significance, their value, and this comes out in their actions as hyper-competition, a lack of civility, or anger. Imagine what the world would look like if every person on this earth knew, unequivocally, that they mattered. Christopher Emdin, a professor at the University of Southern California, once tweeted an invitation to what feels like mattering to me: "If you see beauty & magic in someone, tell them. They may not see it yet and your words may be what unlocks their vision of themselves. Just walk around unlocking magic." That's it—be the person who unlocks the magic of mattering in the people all around you. You alone can create that ripple effect.

After my birthday party, one friend wrote to me about how profound the mattering concept was and how she couldn't stop seeing it in her interactions with people now: at the supermarket checkout, at the gym, in her office. Another friend wrote to say how much she enjoyed Caroline's exercise of putting into words why someone matters to us. "We know in our hearts how much our friends mean to us, but rarely do we put it into words," she told me. "I'm going to make this a regular practice now to tell my friends *why* they mean so much to me." As one friend texted on her way home from the party: "Mattering is powerful. What a wonderful way of going through life, feeling like you matter and making others feel like they matter, too."

···

Forever I will be grateful to those who let me into their homes and into their lives, and who, in each of their own ways, added to my own sense of mattering and purpose. These conversations have stayed with me and have made me a better parent in ways I can't begin to count. When I greet my kids like the family puppy at the door, I think of Susan in Connecticut. When my kids are trying to pack too much on their plates, Jane in Mercer Island's advice that our job is to take the kettle off the heat comes to mind. When I start getting ahead of myself with worry over, say, my oldest applying to college, I think back to the wisdom of Genevieve and Vanessa in Wilton. When I'm at the end of my parenting rope, I hear Suniya Luthar's words in my head challenging me to make myself and my friendships a priority so that I can be resilient for my kids. Tim Kasser's advice to keep my goals balanced is the reminder I need when I'm too focused on my work at the expense of my friendships. When my kids seem a little off, I think of Marjie in Maine and help them shift their lens outward by focusing on others.

What I have learned through these thoughtful, intimate conversations is that under all the angst and anxiety, envy, fear, and hyper-competition, at the core we *all* really want the same thing for our kids. When we are no longer around to guide them, we want them to live a good life, to have deep, life-sustaining connections, to feel the joy of living a life of meaning, and to leave this world a little better than they found it. We want them to feel valued by those around them and to help others—in their family, in their schools, in their communities—to feel valued as well. What we want for them is to live a life that truly matters.

Acknowledgments

"A book is a dream that you hold in your hands," wrote Neil Gaiman. And I have so many people to thank for making that dream a reality.

To my wonderful agents, Christy Fletcher and Grainne Fox, thank you both for your encouragement and keen insights throughout this project. To my editor extraordinaire, Niki Papadopoulos, how lucky I am to benefit from your wisdom, clarity of vision, and uncanny ability to take in both the big picture and each and every detail. Thanks to my publisher, Adrian Zackheim, whose enthusiasm for this book at our first meeting set a fire in me that kept me on course. Kimberly Meilun, thank you for shepherding this book so thoughtfully and thoroughly throughout the process. Many thanks to Jessica Regione, Carlynn Chironna, Matthew Boezi, Meg Gerrity, Meighan Cavanaugh, Daniel Lagin, and Caitlin Noonan in production, production editorial, design, and managing editorial; interior designer Alissa Theodor; and Sarah Brody who created the eye-catching cover. And a huge thank you to my wonderful publicity and marketing team: Stefanie Rosenblum Brody, Lauren Monahan, Jacquelyn Galindo, and Lauren Lavelle.

I owe an enormous debt of thanks to the psychologists who are featured in this book, who have so generously given their time and expertise. Young people have no better advocate than Suniya Luthar, whose lifelong research is the basis of this book. Gordon Flett, thank you for your groundbreaking research on perfectionism and mattering, and for setting me on this mattering mission. It's changed my life. To Isaac Prilleltensky, your mattering framework not only helped to shape this book, it also guides my own actions daily. To Denise Pope, thank you for your guidance and the inspiring work you do to help young people, schools, and families pursue achievement in healthy ways. To Rick Weissbourd and Lisa Damour, your wisdom and sound advice permeate these pages and have deeply influenced my own parenting at home; I'm enormously grateful to you both. To Robin Stern, whose encouragement convinced me that this book needed to be written now and by me—thank you, thank you.

To the students, parents, teachers, administrators, and coaches who spoke with me so openly: Thank you for entrusting me to tell your stories. Your honesty and wisdom will undoubtedly impact lives for the better. It's already impacted mine.

When the ideas come together, when it all flows, writing really is a dream. But, other times, when the ideas won't gel, when you're in the middle of a global pandemic, that dream can feel more like a nightmare. Forever I will be grateful to the editors Kate Rodemann and Gareth Cook, who entered my life in the middle of the COVID-19 pandemic, as I was sifting through mountains of research and interviews, homeschooling my kids, and wearing hazmat suits to the grocery store. Their extraordinary editing skills, big brains, and deep insights informed this book in so many ways. I couldn't have done this without them. To the terrific Eric Torres, who helped me conduct and analyze the large-scale parenting survey. To the wonderful and wise Jeff Gassen, who assisted with both the student survey and other important research throughout the book. Thank you to the amazing Amanda Peed, who helped me in conducting pre-interviews, researching, and editing. To the ever-sharp Charlotte Goddeau, who is an incredible fact-checker, and the delightful and methodical Michaela Corning-Myers, who helped me cull together the endnotes.

Some ideas and passages of this book originated from my articles in *The Wall Street Journal* and *The Washington Post*, and I am tremendously grateful to my editors Gary Rosen, Lisa Kalis, and Amy Joyce, whose skills are a gift to writers lucky enough to work with them.

I'm so deeply grateful to my friends, who have listened to me talk on and on about this book project for years and/or who read early drafts and provided very meaningful feedback: Michelle Aielli, Jamie and Matt Bakal, Lisa Brancaccio, Lauren Smith Brody, Vicki and David Foley, Ina and Jeffrey Garten, Lisa Heffernan, Rachel Henes, Dana and Michael Jones, Frances Jones, Jenny and Matt Kabaker, Beth and Chris Kojima, Mariam Korangy, Chris Pavone, Rebecca Raphael, John and Rachel Rodin, Meredith Rollins, Pilar Queen and Andrew Ross Sorkin, and Zibby Owens. To Katie Spikes and Tira Grey, who have taught me how deep and nourishing friendship can be; there are no better cheerleaders or hand holders in the world. To the rest of my village who supports our family in so many ways, how lucky we are to get to go through life with you. To Alexandra Leon, thank you for being a role model for our children and for loving them like your own. And to my colleagues at the Mattering Movement—how grateful I am to be working side by side with you!

To my in-laws Elizabeth, Chris, Lorraine, thank you all for being such an incredible support to me over our more than two decades together and for giving me the most wonderful set of siblings. A special shout-out to my sister-in-law Catherine, whose insights informed this book.

To my parents, Carole and Pat, I'm so grateful for all you've given me—and still do—and for being wonderful role models of what parents can be. Thank you for always showing me in your words and actions how much Natalie and I matter to you. What a privilege to grow up that way. To my sister, Natalie, who has been my very best friend since day one, and to my brother-in-law, Pete—thank you both for the care you took in reading an early draft of this book and for always being there for our family day or night and in a million ways.

To William, who taught me how to be a mother with his gentle patience, empathy, and kindness—and who, more recently, earned the dubious distinction of being my full-time tech expert, sometimes even answering panicked emails in the middle of the school day. To Caroline, whose emotional intelligence I learn from each day, thank you for all your visible and invisible support throughout this project, including, among many other things, always checking that my chargers worked and were packed before a reporting trip. To James, who makes our family complete, thank you for always offering an encouraging word, "pressure point" neck massages, a laugh, or just an arm around the shoulder when needed. Your love and compassion bring out the best in people.

Finally, thank you to my Renaissance husband, Peter, whose passion and joy for life is utterly contagious and infused in everything he does: his parenting, friendships, work, travel, cooking, painting, and on and on. He is an extraordinary partner and parent (and editor!) who fills our lives with love and adventure. How grateful I am that we went on that blind date so many years ago. Words can't describe how much you matter to me.

Resources

Taking Action

At Home

The first thing parents ask me when I tell them about the book is this: How has your research changed *your* parenting? Here's a list of the changes I've made in my own house, as much for you as it is a "note to self," so I hold on to these lessons learned and continue to make them a daily practice:

Never worry alone. The research is crystal clear: the best thing we can do for our kids is take care of our own well-being and psychological health first so we can be a better resource for them. When I'm feeling overtaxed, I make a point to always reach out to my close friends for support. I model this healthy interdependence for my kids. We have a mantra now in our home: never worry alone.

Be a selfist. The psychologist Carin Rubenstein writes about how quickly she fell into the modern trap of denying herself for the sake of her children. To remedy this, she developed the idea of being a "selfist" (not to be confused with selfish), whose needs are just as important as her family's. A selfist ensures that she is well taken care of, too.

Strive to be a good enough, not perfect, parent, teacher, or coach.
Kids don't need perfect role models. In fact, perfection doesn't serve
them, and it doesn't serve the adults in their lives. Our kids need someone who is just good enough: someone who loves them and teaches them
what it means to be an imperfect but lovable human. To teach kids how
to love themselves unconditionally, they need adults in their lives modeling self-acceptance, flaws and all.

Have a "go-to" committee. If adults are to consistently offer and model
unconditional acceptance, they need to feel unconditionally accepted
themselves. Suniya Luthar suggests asking yourself which friends make
you feel unconditionally loved. Work toward having at least one or two
of these people in your life, apart from your partner. Ensure that you
regularly visit with these people, as is done in Luthar's Authentic Connections Groups.

Make home a "mattering haven." Parents can provide a child's most
significant source of mattering—or be the greatest source of contingent
mattering, feeling like they matter only when they're performing. Because
our kids are bombarded with messages on the importance of achievement, home needs to be a safe place to land, a place where their mattering is never in question.

Lead with lunch. When kids walk through the door, instead of pepper-
ing them with performance-related questions (*How'd you do on that
test?*), consider leading with "What did you have for lunch today?" This
innocuous question opens children up and sends the subtle signal that
we see them as more than a grade or performance. Don't get discouraged
if teens continue to give monosyllabic responses—push through and
keep the lines of communication going.

Schedule stressful conversations. During her son's junior year, the
psychologist Susan Bauerfeld confined stressful conversations about col-

lege to Sunday afternoons. It allowed her family to enjoy the rest of the week and focus on the other important things in their son's life.

Talk openly about values. Modeling is important, but just as important is having explicit and frequent conversations about what we genuinely value. Aim for those one hundred one-minute ongoing conversations, not just one big lecture yearly. Ask your kids if they see you as actually valuing the things that you say you value.

Take a values inventory. The psychotherapist Tina Payne Bryson offered this reflection to see if your values and your actions align: (1) look at how you spend your money when it comes to your kids; (2) look at your child's calendar; (3) pay attention to what you ask your kids about; and (4) notice what you argue with your kids about. Many parents think they're not overemphasizing achievement, but when they look at these four things, they see how their behavior is telling their kids a different story of what they value most.

Normalize difficult feelings. From time to time, everyone feels envious or compares themselves to others. Explain to kids that we don't have to judge ourselves for having these universal feelings, but we do have to hold ourselves accountable for how we act on them. Talk about the difference between healthy and unhealthy competition and give kids the tools to mine these competitive feelings, even when they are painful, for their own self-knowledge and success. Most of all, short-circuit feelings of envy by loving and accepting your child for who they are.

Be a balance keeper. Kids need to learn self-care skills. The nonprofit Challenge Success suggests the mnemonic "PDF" to remember that our kids need playtime (in older kids, "recharging" time), downtime, and family time every day.

Focus on wise striving and being energy efficient. How do you define being a "good student" in your house? For Lisa Damour, "good" doesn't mean giving everything 100 percent—that's what leads to burnout and feeds perfectionistic tendencies. Instead, it's learning to be strategic about where you spend your energy. As Damour's colleague put it: the difference between getting a 91 and a 99 is a life.

Help kids keep achievement in perspective. Parents can put "bad" grades into perspective by explaining what they truly are: a measure of their knowledge that day. A bad grade does not determine how well they'll perform in the future, how much a teacher likes them, or how much their parents value them, and our kids need to know this explicitly, notes Lisa Damour.

Tell failure stories. Live life out loud in front of your kids so they can see up close what the adults in their lives get wrong. When you make a mistake, consider modeling self-compassion out loud: *Okay, I made a mistake and here's what I learned. Now I must stop being so hard on myself. Everyone makes mistakes. I am human. I am not my mistakes.*

Teach skills of healthy *interdependence*. Instead of raising kids who think they must do it all on their own, teach them how to ask for help when they need it and model these skills yourself.

Make chores mandatory. To encourage a "we're all in this together" mindset, you might save your own household chores—paying the bills, recycling newspapers, straightening up the house—for when your kids are scheduled to do theirs. Avoid linking chores to allowances or excessive praise. Chores are what you do when you are part of a family, a contribution to the greater whole.

Widen their circle of concern and caring. Point out how other people add value to your kids' lives every day, like janitors at school who work hard to keep the school clean of germs, or teachers who sacrifice their own time to meet outside class. Broaden their circle of caring. Say thank you to the waitress and the bus driver. Children learn kindness and empathy not just by how we treat those closest to us, but also by how we treat strangers, notes Rick Weissbourd.

Make volunteering mandatory. Several families I interviewed talked about a volunteer mandate. Expose kids to lots of opportunities, let them choose their own interests, and help them find time in their schedule to manage these commitments.

Be a "mattering spotter." Point out when you see a child adding value to those around them, not with excessive praise, but simply by noticing: "I see how you helped our neighbor to bring in her groceries." Or "I noticed how you lent your notes to Sarah, who missed class this week."

Nurture parent-teacher relationships. When students feel that parents are talking negatively about their teacher, it undermines that critical relationship, akin to the acrimonious divorce of parents, notes Suniya Luthar. Students learn best from teachers they feel close to, and teachers play an essential role in buffering against achievement stress. Show respect and appreciation when you speak about or interact with their teachers. Actively build a partnership with educators so that a child can be best supported.

"Replace" yourself. Consider creating your own council of parents. Value and appreciate the adults in your children's lives. Guard that time so that they can enjoy a wider safety net of support. You might even make it formal, as some parents I interviewed did, by creating a master sheet of phone numbers and meeting together as a group.

Encourage gratitude. Help children to get into the habit of telling others explicitly why they matter. You might adopt a regular gratitude practice at home, like "the one thing I love about the birthday person." Teach kids how to think gratefully. Point out when someone goes out of their way to find a present for them, or when they do something kind that makes your child's life better. Researchers find gratitude is the glue that binds relationships together.

Taking Action

For Educators

Protecting our students from the excessive pressure to achieve will require all stakeholders—parents, teachers, coaches, and other trusted adults in the community—to work together. Below, I've gathered advice from some of the top experts in the field on how to minimize toxic achievement pressure in schools.

Employ the mattering framework. Teach everyone in the school community—teachers, faculty, students, administrators, coaches, parents—the mattering framework: how to make kids feel valued, how to help them add value, as well as how to avoid sending messages that could make them feel like they don't matter.

Prioritize community mental health. Do your teachers feel like they matter? Do your teachers feel valued? Do they have a community where they are cared for? Assess the mental health of teachers and faculty and see how you can better support them. The nonprofits Authentic Connections and Challenge Success offer support for teachers, administrators, and non-teaching staff, as well as for parents.

Get a mental health report card for your school. Schools can bring in experts to gather mental health data for their individual school. The nonprofit Challenge Success conducts in-depth, school-wide surveys involving all stakeholders, highlighting each school's unique challenges to create a more balanced and engaged student and adult experience. Authentic Connections also offers assessments of a school's climate noting each school's unique set of strengths and challenges, and actionable steps to take.

Involve all stakeholders. Challenge Success works with schools to examine their cultures from all angles. Schedules are altered to allow for more adult-student and student-student interactions. Teachers are asked to think of ways to offer students more voice, choice, and agency—and more authentic problem-solving. Students are taught the reason behind assessments for learning instead of assessments as evaluations only. They also offer workshops on increasing faculty, staff, and student well-being and belonging.

Conduct a "values" inventory. What values does your school explicitly and implicitly send its students? When you first walk in, do you see the honor roll? The sports trophies? The debate trophies? A list of major donors? Are there college pennants on the wall, and if so, which ones are represented? If a school says they prioritize kindness, caring, or mattering in their students, how do they show the student body that it's something they value as a community?

Note which students are not being seen or publicly valued. Do you recognize and celebrate "unsung heroes" in your school communities? For example, one school I visited held a weekly Hidden Talents Show. If some students are too shy to get up in front of the school, find other ways to celebrate hidden talents, like spotlighting students in the school paper or newsletter.

Ensure every student has at least one adult at school they feel they matter to. Rather than leave these connections to chance, Making Caring Common suggests employing something they call "relationship mapping." During a private meeting, teachers name students who may not have a strong relationship with an adult at school. Those students are then paired with a mentor within the school. Mentors then meet throughout the year to support one another. (More on relationship mapping can be found on Making Caring Common's website, https://mcc.gse.harvard.edu.)

Engage in meaningful diversity and inclusion work. Educate the community on ways teachers and students may be sending "anti-mattering" messages unintentionally. Examine the implicit ways as a school you may be sending a signal that certain people in the community matter more: Is your school's staff reflective of diversity? Are some of your students feeling that they only partially matter? What can you do to ensure all students feel a sense of comprehensive mattering?

Make the thinking visible. Surface the feelings that frequently come up in hypercompetitive settings. Suniya Luthar has suggested school-wide assemblies where students share their own experiences with negative social comparisons, envy, and unhealthy competition, and how they were able to get past these. Normalize these feelings and give kids the tools to manage them in healthy ways.

Find a way for everyone in the school to add value. Oprah credits her fourth-grade teacher, Mrs. Mary Duncan, with making her feel like she mattered. Mrs. Duncan did this, in part, by assigning Oprah classroom tasks. Do all the students in your school have an opportunity to add value to their school community?

Create opportunities for authentic service. Like Saint Ignatius in Cleveland, consider building lessons about service and the responsibility we have to others right into the school's curriculum. Provide students with a wide range of opportunities for meaningful multi-semester service. Consider dedicating time in the school day for service, showing how it matters just as much as math class.

Provide students with opportunities for real-life problem solving. One school I visited made adding value to others part of their school's curriculum. At the Mastery School in Cleveland, administrators partner students with members of the community to help solve a real-world problem. During my visit there, I watched students give a presentation to a Cleveland mayoral candidate on their creative ideas for encouraging greater voter turnout and more civic engagement in the community.

Rethink traditions. To minimize unhealthy competition, consider ending traditions like "sweatshirt day," where students wear apparel from the college they plan to attend, or posting college acceptances in the school paper or community newspaper.

Be mindful about using a growth mindset. Not all students need to be coached to put in more effort. In fact, some students need to be taught how to put on the brakes. As Luthar points out, it is essential that teachers know when to dial back messages like "do better."

Showcase alternative routes. Bring in speakers who didn't go to the country's top schools, but who are thriving in their chosen careers. Offer alternate narratives to the ones that focus on "traditional" narrow pathways to success.

Hold a blind college fair. Instead of a traditional college fair with banners and materials, in the blind fair college representatives list five characteristics or programs at their college on a sheet of paper. Students move from table to table without learning the names of the colleges until the end, which allows them to focus on "fit" rather than "prestige."

Consider a school-family college admissions contract. Making Caring Common's website, https://mcc.gse.harvard.edu, offers a sample contract that parents and schools can sign about mutual expectations around the college admissions process.

Hold parent workshops. Bring in experts, hold book groups, engage in community-wide, ongoing discussions around achievement pressure. Challenge Success suggests asking students to write anonymous letters to parents explaining how adults can best support them and read them aloud during parent nights.

WHAT COLLEGES AND UNIVERSITIES CAN DO

Consider lottery admissions. On Harvard's website, they note that a large percentage of their applicants are academically qualified to be admitted. In a recent admissions cycle with 2,000 seats, there were 8,000 domestic applicants with perfect GPAs. Thirty-four hundred had perfect SAT math scores, while 2,700 had perfect verbal scores. Barry Schwartz, an emeritus professor at Swarthmore College, has long championed the idea of lottery admission for highly selective institutions. The school would set criteria for students to meet, and then eligible names would simply be selected at random. A lottery, he explains, would relieve pressure on students and acknowledge the role that luck plays in college admissions. Highly qualified high schoolers would then feel freer to explore their interests rather than pad their résumé, he writes.

Actually function like nonprofits. In his book *The Meritocracy Trap*, Yale Law School professor Daniel Markovits argues that universities with nonprofit status and tax benefits should be held accountable to act charitably—in part by drawing "at least half of their students from families in the bottom two-thirds of the income distribution." Elite education has become so extravagant, writes Markovits, that colleges can afford to massively expand enrollment, particularly those with enormous endowments. Even a small increase in the number of places would help to relax the intense competition among all students.

Issue a "well-being report card." Following the example of Authentic Connections and Challenge Success, take stock of campus-wide mental health and well-being via surveys, and make the results available not just to students, faculty, and staff, but to applicants and their parents as well.

Taking Action

Community Efforts

Institute a mattering initiative in your town. Maine's 2021 Integrated Health Survey found that 51 percent of high school students and

45 percent of middle school students reported they didn't matter in the communities where they live. Kini-Ana Tinkham, director of the Maine Resilience Building Network, saw those numbers and started a state-wide initiative to change them, details of which are available on their website, https://maineresilience.org. You can build a small-scale version in your own community involving all of your community stakeholders (schools, small businesses, local government, police, social workers, non-profits).

Create a council of trusted adults. Be explicit with your kids about other adults in their lives, like neighbors, who they can turn to for support. Gather names and numbers so your children know you're serious.

Be a trusted adult for other people's children. Be dependable, really listen, treat the children with whom you come in contact with respect, expect the best, involve them in decisions, ask for their input and advice, and help connect them to people who can expose them to new ideas and experiences.

Be intentional about re-villaging your communities. Parents need support. Teachers and coaches need support. Students need a wide safety net of trusted adults. Be intentional about bringing people together and creating a safe space for people to open up. As Suniya Luthar says: Resilience rests on relationships.

Broaden conversations around "success." Instead of asking kids where they want to go to college or what they want to be when they grow up, ask them what problems in our world they want to help solve. Stop talking about "where" they want to go to college and start asking "what" they hope to do there. Recognize out loud all that goes into a "successful life" and help kids widen their definition of success beyond personal achievement.

Recommended Resources

If you're looking to dive deeper into topics raised in this book, here's a list of books and films you might want to consider.

ON ACHIEVEMENT CULTURE

BOOKS

Doing School: How We Are Creating a Generation of Stressed-Out, Materialistic, and Miseducated Students by Denise Clark Pope

The Gift of Failure: How the Best Parents Learn to Let Go So Their Children Can Succeed by Jessica Lahey

How to Raise an Adult: Break Free of the Overparenting Trap and Prepare Your Kid for Success by Julie Lythcott-Haims

Raising Kids to Thrive: Balancing Love With Expectations and Protection With Trust by Kenneth R. Ginsburg, Ilana Ginsburg, and Talia Ginsburg

Love, Money, and Parenting: How Economics Explains the Way We Raise Our Kids by Matthias Doepke and Fabrizio Zilibotti

The Meritocracy Trap: How America's Foundational Myth Feeds Inequality, Dismantles the Middle Class, and Devours the Elite by Daniel Markovits

Overloaded and Underprepared: Strategies for Stronger Schools and Healthy, Successful Kids by Denise Pope, Maureen Brown, and Sarah Miles

The Parents We Mean To Be: How Well-Intentioned Adults Undermine Children's Moral and Emotional Development by Richard Weissbourd

The Path to Purpose: *How Young People Find Their Calling in Life* by William Damon

The Price of Privilege: *How Parental Pressure and Material Advantage Are Creating a Generation of Disconnected and Unhappy Kids* by Madeline Levine, PhD

The Self-Driven Child: *The Science and Sense of Giving Your Kids More Control Over Their Lives* by William Stixrud, PhD, and Ned Johnson

The Tyranny of Merit: *What's Become of the Common Good?* by Michael J. Sandel

Under Pressure: *Confronting the Epidemic of Stress and Anxiety in Girls* by Lisa Damour, PhD

FILMS

Chasing Childhood, directed by Margaret Munzer Loeb and Eden Wurmfeld

Race to Nowhere, directed by Vicki Abeles

ON MATTERING

BOOKS

Family Matters: *The Importance of Mattering to Family in Adolescence* by Gregory C. Elliott

How People Matter: *Why It Affects Health, Happiness, Love, Work, and Society* by Isaac Prilleltensky and Ora Prilleltensky

The Psychology of Mattering: *Understanding the Human Need to be Significant* by Gordon L. Flett

ON MARGINALIZED STUDENTS

BOOKS

Biased: Uncovering the Hidden Prejudice That Shapes What We See, Think, and Do by Jennifer L. Eberhardt, PhD

Dream Hoarders: How the American Upper Middle Class Is Leaving Everyone Else in the Dust, Why That Is a Problem, and What To Do About It by Richard V. Reeves

Learning in Public: Lessons for a Racially Divided America from My Daughter's School by Courtney E. Martin

Race at the Top: Asian Americans and Whites in Pursuit of the American Dream in Suburban Schools by Natasha Warikoo

So You Want to Talk About Race by Ijeoma Oluo

Wanting What's Best: Parenting, Privilege, and Building a Just World by Sarah W. Jaffe

Why Are All the Black Kids Sitting Together in the Cafeteria?: And Other Conversations About Race by Beverly Daniel Tatum, PhD

ON SOCIAL MEDIA

BOOKS

Behind Their Screens: What Teens Are Facing (and Adults Are Missing) by Emily Weinstein and Carrie James

The Big Disconnect: Protecting Childhood and Family Relationships in the Digital Age by Catherine Steiner-Adair, EdD, with Teresa H. Barker

iGen: Why Today's Super-Connected Kids Are Growing Up Less Rebellious, More Tolerant, Less Happy—and Completely Unprepared for Adulthood by Jean M. Twenge, PhD

ON SPORTS

BOOKS

Take Back the Game: How Money and Mania Are Ruining Kids' *Sports—and Why It Matters* by Linda Flanagan

Whose Game Is It, Anyway? A Guide to Helping Your Child *Get the Most from Sports, Organized by Age and Stage* by Richard D. Ginsburg, PhD, and Stephen Durant, EdD, with Amy Baltzell, EdD

BOOK DISCUSSION QUESTIONS

1. At the start of the book, Wallace references two national reports naming kids in "high-achieving schools" an "at-risk" group for negative health outcomes. Did this surprise you? Are you seeing these negative effects of excessive pressure to achieve in your own community?

2. In chapter 1, Wallace discusses the researcher Suniya Luthar's argument that the pressure our kids feel today comes from every direction. Relationships that once protected students from stress—with parents, coaches, teachers, peers—now can feel like an added source of stress. Do you agree with Luthar? Why or why not?

3. In chapter 2, Wallace argues that adults have internalized messages in our society—scarcity, hyper-competition, rising inequality—and this can impact how we interact with the children in our lives in ways we are not always aware. Does this ring true to you? Is the scarcity parents feel in your community real or imagined? How do outside messages of the larger world impact day-to-day parenting?

4. In chapter 3, Wallace writes that outsized expectations, the fear that our kids feel that they must earn their worth, erodes their core sense of mattering, as in "I only matter when." What messages are our kids hearing at school, in the community, online, and in the larger society about who matters most in our world?

5. Decades of research find that a child's resilience rests firmly on their primary caregiver's resilience. Does this surprise you? If primary caregivers are the first responders to our kids' struggles, they need the internal resources to be there for our kids. What cultural messages might hold parents back from putting themselves first? What holds parents back from reaching out to others for support? What would it look like to put yourself first?

6. At the root of grind culture in these schools is the belief that where you go to college defines your life. In her parent survey, Wallace asked: "Parents in my community generally agree that getting into a selective college is one of the most important ingredients to later-life happiness." (73 percent of parents agreed.) Do you agree or disagree with this statement? What are some of the messages kids are hearing about what leads to a successful life? How can adults protect kids from these toxic messages?

7. In chapter 5, Wallace writes about Denise Pope's white paper that success after college is determined by "fit" over "rank"—that is, how much a student is engaged during their college years points to later life success. Were you surprised by this finding? How can we shift the conversation we're having about college?

8. In her reporting, Wallace found that the kids who thrive in competitive waters had adults in their lives who pushed back against the myths of zero-sum thinking. These adults—be they parents,

coaches, or teachers—encouraged kids to root for their classmates, to sacrifice for the greater good of the team, to help their friends and to open up enough to ask for help in return, and to confront and manage the uncomfortable feelings that arise from competing with peers. Do you think kids would benefit from learning the skills of healthy interdependence? If so, what ways can we encourage this mindset at home, in the classroom, or on the field?

9. Assigning chores can feel like a chore for parents, and because of that, many parents have opted out. When it comes to adding value to the family, what chores were you given as a child? What do your children do to help the family? What gets in the way? How can we overcome those barriers?

10. As William Damon has said, today's young people are stressed and anxious not necessarily because we're overworking them but because they don't know what they're working for. Do you agree? If so, how do you see this "lack of a why" play out at school and in their extracurricular activities?

11. In chapter 7, Wallace offers Tara Christie Kinsey's description of how deliberate she is when talking about her own sense of purpose to her kids. Where do you get your sense of purpose? Think back: Where did your spark come from and who were the people who helped you grow that spark into a flame? Do you make time to have regular conversations with your kids about what motivates you and interests you about the world, and to help them try to connect to their why?

12. A crucial part of mattering is expressing to others how much they matter to you. What are some of the barriers in our culture that stop us from telling people how much we appreciate them? What

holds us back? What are some ways we can overcome those barriers?

13. At the end of the book, Wallace makes a bold statement: "I've even stopped telling my kids that I just want them to be happy. Happiness and well-being, I've come to realize, are the byproducts of living a life where we feel valued and add value to others." Is happiness a worthy goal? Why or why not?

14. What ways can you make mattering your mission at home? What would it look like to lead with mattering in your classroom or in your neighborhood? How can you communicate to your children's friends and teachers that they matter to you? What would our world look like, feel like, be like, if each of us were on a mission to unlock mattering in everyone we meet?

Notes

INTRODUCTION: RUNNING WITH THEIR EYES CLOSED

xiv **Students attending what researchers call:** National Academies of Sciences, Engineering, and Medicine, *Vibrant and Healthy Kids: Aligning Science, Practice, and Policy to Advance Health Equity* (Washington, DC: The National Academies Press, 2019), 4–24, https://doi.org/10.17226/25466.

xiv **one in three American students:** Suniya Luthar, exchange on Sept. 24, 2022.

xvi **"alarming increases in the prevalence":** Office of the Surgeon General, "U.S. Surgeon General Issues Advisory on Youth Mental Health Crisis Further Exposed by COVID-19 Pandemic," U.S. Department of Health and Human Services, Dec. 7, 2021, https://www.hhs.gov/about/news/2021/12/07/us-surgeon-general-issues-advisory-on-youth-mental-health-crisis-further-exposed-by-covid-19-pandemic.html.

xvi **wanted to understand the pressure:** In consultation with a researcher at the Harvard Graduate School of Education, I distributed the survey to over six thousand parents nationwide during

January and February 2020. The survey was distributed online through my personal social networks and passed on via a "snowball" method, meaning that survey takers were asked to share the survey with members of their social networks. In order to adjust for imbalances in response rates (the initial sample had a high concentration of high-income parents, for example), the survey was scientifically reweighted by income, region, and residential urbanicity to better reflect national proportions. It is important in interpreting the results of the survey to keep in mind that they might not reflect how everybody in the country thinks about these issues.

xvii **Parents in my community**: My survey found that 80 percent of parents whose children go to "high-achieving schools" agreed, compared to only 60 percent of parents whose children attend less competitive schools. This large difference underscores the intensity of perceptions related to college importance.

xvii **Others think that my children's academic success**: No significant difference was found between parents whose children attend "high-achieving schools" versus less competitive schools, suggesting this is a somewhat universal feeling among modern parents.

xvii **I wish today's childhood**: Again, no significant difference was found between parents whose children attend "high-achieving schools" versus less competitive schools.

CHAPTER 1: WHY ARE OUR KIDS "AT RISK"?

5 **Luthar put together a study**: Suniya S. Luthar and Karen D' Avanzo, "Contextual Factors in Substance Use: A Study of Suburban and Inner-City Adolescents," *Development and Psychopathology* 11 (1999): 845–67.

6 **an environment of unrelenting pressure**: Terese J. Lund and Eric Dearing, "Is Growing Up Affluent Risky for Adolescents or Is the

Problem Growing Up in an Affluent Neighborhood?," *Journal of Research on Adolescence* 23, no. 2 (June 2013): 274–82.

6   **the Robert Wood Johnson Foundation:** Mary B. Geisz and Mary Nakashian, *Adolescent Wellness: Current Perspectives and Future Opportunities in Research, Policy, and Practice* (Robert Wood Johnson Foundation, 2018), https://www.rwjf.org/en/library/research /2018/06/inspiring-and-powering-the-future—a-new-view-of -adolescence.html.

6   **According to the RWJF report:** Geisz and Nakashian, *Adolescent Wellness*, 20.

7   **As one student explained:** In addition to my parenting survey, I also conducted a student survey with the help of researcher at Baylor University to better understand how achievement culture impacts today's students. We distributed the online survey to nearly five hundred students (58 percent women), ages eighteen to thirty, nationwide during April and May 2021. The survey was distributed online through my personal social networks and passed on via a "snowball" method.

7   **One survey of 43,000 students:** Jennifer Breheny Wallace, "Students in High-Achieving Schools Are Now Named an 'At-Risk' Group, Study Says," *Washington Post*, Sept. 26, 2019, https://www.washing tonpost.com/lifestyle/2019/09/26/students-high-achieving-schools -are-now-named-an-at-risk-group.

8   **students reported experiencing overwhelming anxiety:** Nance Roy, "The Rise of Mental Health on College Campuses: Protecting the Emotional Health of Our Nation's College Students," *Higher Education Today*, Dec. 17, 2018, https://www.higheredtoday.org /2018/12/17/rise-mental-health-college-campuses-protecting -emotional-health-nations-college-students.

8   **a Harvard task force found:** Nate Herpich, "Task Force Offers

8 Recommendations for Harvard as Issues Rise Nationally," *Harvard Gazette*, July 23, 2020, https://news.harvard.edu/gazette/story/2020/07/task-force-recommends-8-ways-to-improve-emotional-wellness.

8 **by age twenty-six, former students:** Suniya S. Luthar, Phillip J. Small, and Lucia Ciciolla, "Adolescents from Upper Middle Class Communities: Substance Misuse and Addiction Across Early Adulthood," Corrigendum, *Development and Psychopathology* 30, no. 2 (2018): 715–16, https://doi.org/10.1017/S0954579417001043.

10 **places like Weston, Connecticut:** Douglas Belkin, Jennifer Levitz, and Melissa Korn, "Many More Students, Especially the Affluent, Get Extra Time to Take the SAT," *Wall Street Journal*, May 21, 2019, https://www.wsj.com/articles/many-more-students-especially-the-affluent-get-extra-time-to-take-the-sat-11558450347.

10 **1.6 percent similarly diagnosed:** Belkin, Levitz, and Korn, "Many More Students."

12 **this trend has not come without:** For more, see Jay J. Coakley, *Sports In Society: Issues And Controversies* (New York: McGraw Hill, 2017).

13 **I asked these parents to rank:** This is a framework I borrowed from studies performed by Richard Weissbourd and Suniya Luthar.

14 **Even Amy Chua:** Loan Le, "Fighting the Negative 'Tiger Mom' Mentality," *Fairfield Mirror*, Mar. 8, 2012, http://fairfieldmirror.com/news/fighting-the-negative-"tiger-mom"-mentality. See also Amy Chua Official Website, https://www.amychua.com.

14 **twenty-billion-dollar competitive youth sports:** Christopher Bjork and William Hoynes, "Youth Sports Needs a Reset. Child Athletes Are Pushed to Professionalize Too Early," *USA Today*, Mar. 24, 2021, https://www.usatoday.com/story/opinion/voices/2021/03/24/youth-sports-competitive-covid-19-expensive-column/4797607001.

15 **Their requests were heartbreaking:** NJIC Web Master, "NJSIAA Student Athlete Advisory Council Pushes for More Balance," North Jersey Interscholastic Conference, Apr. 17, 2019, https://njicathlet ics.org/njsiaa-student-athlete-advisory-council-pushes-for-more -balance.

15 **In a letter to parents:** Valerie Strauss, "Kindergarten Show Canceled So Kids Can Keep Studying to Become 'College and Career Ready.' Really." *Washington Post*, Apr. 26, 2014, https://www.wash ingtonpost.com/news/answer-sheet/wp/2014/04/26/kindergarten -show-canceled-so-kids-can-keep-working-to-become-college-and -career-ready-really.

15 **the psychologist David Gleason:** David Gleason, *At What Cost: Defending Adolescent Development in Fiercely Competitive Schools* (Concord, MA: Developmental Empathy LLC, 2017), xiii.

16 **the National Elementary Honor Society:** Hilary Levey Friedman, *Playing to Win: Raising Children in a Competitive Culture* (Berkeley: University of California Press, 2013), xiv.

18 **But getting into Yale today:** Jordan Fitzgerald, "Yale Admits 2,234 Students, Acceptance Rate Shrinks to 4.46 Percent," *Yale Daily News*, Mar. 31, 2022, https://yaledailynews.com/blog/2022/03/31/yale -admits-2234-students-acceptance-rate-shrinks-to-4-46-percent.

18 **is different than getting into:** "Summary of Yale College Admissions Class of 1980 to Class of 2022," Yale University, Jan. 7, 2019, https://oir.yale.edu/sites/default/files/w033_fresh_admissions.pdf.

CHAPTER 2: NAME IT TO TAME IT

23 **Name It to Tame It:** "Name It to Tame It" is attributed to Daniel J. Siegel and Tina Payne Bryson, *The Whole-Brain Child: 12 Revolutionary Strategies to Nurture Your Child's Developing Mind* (New York: Bantam Books Trade Paperbacks, 2012).

23   **Apart from economic payoffs:** Adam Waytz, "The Psychology of Social Status," *Scientific American*, Dec. 8, 2009, https://www.scien tificamerican.com/article/the-psychology-of-social.

24   **Department of Justice announced:** Sophie Kasakove, "The College Admissions Scandal: Where Some of the Defendants Are Now," *New York Times*, Oct. 9, 2021, https://www.nytimes.com/2021/10/09 /us/varsity-blues-scandal-verdict.html.

25   **When Huffman's daughter:** Nicholas Hautman, "Felicity Huffman Details Daughter Sophia's Emotional Reaction to College Scandal: 'Why Didn't You Believe in Me?,'" *Us Weekly*, Sept. 6, 2019, https:// www.usmagazine.com/celebrity-news/news/felicity-huffman -details-daughters-reaction-to-college-scandal.

27   **an uncomfortable truth:** Cell Press, "Our Own Status Affects the Way Our Brains Respond to Others," *ScienceDaily*, Apr. 28, 2011, https://www.sciencedaily.com/releases/2011/04/110428123936.htm.

28   **we shouldn't care about status:** Loretta Graziano Breuning, *I, Mammal: How to Make Peace with the Animal Urge for Social Power* (Oakland, CA: Inner Mammal Institute, 2011), 7.

30   **the minutiae of life:** Arizona State University, "Invisible Labor Can Negatively Impact Well-Being in Mothers: Study Finds Women Who Feel Overly Responsible for Household Management and Parenting Are Less Satisfied with Their Lives and Partnerships," *ScienceDaily*, Jan. 22, 2019, https://www.sciencedaily.com/releases/2019 /01/190122092857.htm.

32   **born in 1940:** Raj Chetty et al., "The Fading American Dream: Trends in Absolute Income Mobility Since 1940," *Science* 356, no. 6336 (Apr. 2017): 398–406, https://doi.org/10.1126/science.aal4617.

32   **Millennials on average have:** Christopher Kurz, Geng Li, and Daniel J. Vine, "Are Millennials Different?," *Finance and Economics*

Discussion Series 2018-080, Board of Governors of the Federal Reserve System, 2018, https://doi.org/10.17016/FEDS.2018.080.

32 **default to a "scarcity mindset":** For more, see Sendhil Mullainathan and Eldar Shafir, *Scarcity: The New Science of Having Less and How It Defines Our Lives* (New York: Picador, 2013).

37 **starting in the 1980s:** Juliana Menasce Horowitz, Ruth Igielnik, and Rakesh Kochhar, "Trends in Income and Wealth Inequality," *Pew Research Center*, Jan. 9, 2020, https://www.pewresearch.org /social-trends/2020/01/09/trends-in-income-and-wealth-in equality.

38 **The words of Amy Chua:** Amy Chua, "Why Chinese Mothers Are Superior," *Wall Street Journal*, Jan. 8, 2011, https://www.wsj.com /articles/SB10001424052748704111504576059713528698754.

39 **Wealth can be used:** Liz Mineo, "Racial Wealth Gap May Be a Key to Other Inequities," *Harvard Gazette*, June 3, 2021, https://news .harvard.edu/gazette/story/2021/06/racial-wealth-gap-may-be-a-key -to-other-inequities.

39 **median Asian American wealth:** Dedrick Asante-Muhammad and Sally Sim, "Racial Wealth Snapshot: Asian Americans and The Racial Wealth Divide," *National Community Reinvestment Coalition*, May 14, 2020, https://ncrc.org/racial-wealth-snapshot-asian -americans-and-the-racial-wealth-divide.

40 **Black parents face:** Emily Badger, Claire Cain Miller, Adam Pearce, and Kevin Quealy, "Extensive Data Shows Punishing Reach of Racism for Black Boys," *New York Times*, Mar. 19, 2018, https:// www.nytimes.com/interactive/2018/03/19/upshot/race-class-white -and-black-men.html.

43 **left voicemail messages:** Caitlin Gibson, "When Parents Are So Desperate to Get Their Kids into College That They Sabotage

Other Students," *Washington Post*, Apr. 3, 2019, https://www.wash
ingtonpost.com/lifestyle/on-parenting/when-parents-are-so
-desperate-to-get-their-kids-into-college-that-they-sabotage
-other-students/2019/04/02/decc6b9e-5159-11e9-88a1-ed
346f0ec94f_story.html; Adam Harris, "Parents Gone Wild: High
Drama Inside D.C.'s Most Elite Private School," *The Atlantic*,
June 5, 2019, https://www.theatlantic.com/education/archive/2019/06
/sidwell-friends-college-admissions-varsity-blues/591124.

CHAPTER 3: THE POWER OF MATTERING

47 **teens have always wondered:** Jennifer Breheny Wallace, "The
Teenage Social-Media Trap," *Wall Street Journal*, May 4, 2018,
https://www.wsj.com/articles/the-teenage-social-media-trap
-1525444767.

49 **a striking 33 percent increase:** Thomas Curran and Andrew P.
Hill, "Perfectionism Is Increasing Over Time: A Meta-Analysis of
Birth Cohort Differences From 1989 to 2016," *Psychological Bulle-
tin* 145, no. 4 (2019): 410–29, https://doi.org/10.1037/bul0000138.

50 **parents' love and affection:** Konrad Piotrowski, Agnieszka Bo-
janowska, Aleksandra Nowicka, and Bartosz Janasek, "Perfectionism and Community-Identity Integration: The Mediating Role of
Shame, Guilt and Self-Esteem," *Current Psychology* (2021), https://
doi.org/10.1007/s12144-021-01499-9.

50 **legendary social psychologist Morris Rosenberg:** Morris Rosenberg and B. Claire McCullough, "Mattering: Inferred Significance
and Mental Health Among Adolescents," *Research in Community
and Mental Health* 2 (1981): 163–82, https://psycnet.apa.org/record
/1983-07744-001.

51 **Do people depend on you:** On March 31, 2017, keynote speaker
Greg Elliott spoke to Community College of Rhode Island (CCRI)

faculty and staff and asked similar questions to conjure the feelings of mattering.

51 **As long as we live:** Rebecca Newberger Goldstein, "The Mattering Instinct," *Edge*, Mar. 16, 2016, https://www.edge.org/conversation /rebecca_newberger_goldstein-the-mattering-instinct.

51 **mattering to our parents:** Isaac Prilleltensky, "What It Means to 'Matter,'" *Psychology Today*, Jan. 4, 2022, https://www.psychology today.com/us/blog/well-being/202201/what-it-means-matter.

51 **virtuous cycle of interdependence:** Isaac Prilleltensky and Ora Prilleltensky, *How People Matter: Why It Affects Health, Happiness, Love, Work, and Society* (Cambridge: Cambridge University Press, 2021), 5.

52 **the story we tell ourselves:** Mark R. Leary, "Sociometer Theory and the Pursuit of Relational Value: Getting to the Root of Self-Esteem," *European Review of Social Psychology* 16, no. 1 (Jan. 2005): 75–111, https://doi.org/10.1080/10463280540000007.

53 **Flett notes seven critical:** Gordon Flett, *The Psychology of Mattering: Understanding the Human Need to be Significant* (London: Elsevier, 2018), 32.

55 **My survey also asked students:** This question was inspired by the Challenge Success "I Wish" campaign. See "'I Wish' Campaign," Challenge Success, Resources, https://challengesuccess.org/resources /i-wish-campaign.

57 **difference between what we say:** Roy F. Baumeister, Ellen Bratslavsky, Catrin Finkenauer, and Kathleen D. Vohs, "Bad Is Stronger Than Good," *Review of General Psychology* 5, no. 4 (2001): 323–370, https://doi.org/10.1037//1089-2680.5.4.323.

57 **Criticism, research suggests:** Timothy Davis, "The Power of Positive Parenting: Gottman's Magic Ratio," *Challenging Boys*, last updated

2022, https://challengingboys.com/the-power-of-positive-parenting
-gottmans-magic-ratio.

57 **teenage negativity overperforms:** Laura L. Carstensen and Mar-
guerite DeLiema, "The Positivity Effect: A Negativity Bias in Youth
Fades with Age," *Current Opinion in Behavioral Sciences* 19, no. 1
(2018): 7–12, https://doi.org/10.1016/j.cobeha.2017.07.009.

58 *Perceived* **parental criticism:** Suniya S. Luthar and Bronwyn E.
Becker, "Privileged but Pressured? A Study of Affluent Youth," *Child
Development* 73, no. 5 (Sept. 2002): 1593–1610, https://doi.org/10.1111
/1467-8624.00492.

58 **It can set our children up:** Brené Brown, *The Gifts of Imperfection:
Let Go of Who You Think You're Supposed To Be and Embrace Who
You Are* (Minneapolis: Hazelden Information & Educational Ser-
vices, 2010).

58 **"What gets in early":** Gregory C. Elliott, *Family Matters: The
Importance of Mattering to Family in Adolescence* (Chichester, UK:
Wiley-Blackwell, 2009), 39.

59 **a false self:** Alice Miller, *The Drama of the Gifted Child: The
Search for the True Self* (New York: Basic Books, 1997). For more,
see Gabor Maté, *The Myth of Normal: Trauma, Illness, and Healing
in a Toxic Culture* (New York: Avery, 2022).

60 **"Conditional regard" is:** Ece Mendi and Jale Eldeleklioğlu, "Parental Conditional Regard, Subjective Well-Being and Self-Esteem:
The Mediating Role of Perfectionism," *Psychology* 7, no. 10 (2016):
1276–95, https://doi.org/10.4236/psych.2016.710130.

61 **parenting styles and well-being:** Avi Assor, Guy Roth, and Edward
L. Deci, "The Emotional Costs of Parents' Conditional Regard: A
Self-Determination Theory Analysis," *Journal of Personality* 72,
no. 1 (2004): 47–88, https://doi.org/10.1111/j.0022-3506.2004.00256.x.

62   **invest their self-worth:** Dorien Wuyts, Maarten Vansteenkiste, Bart Soenens, and Avi Assor, "An Examination of the Dynamics Involved in Parental Child-Invested Contingent Self-Esteem," *Parenting* 15, no. 2 (2015): 55–74, https://doi.org/10.1080/15295192.2015.1020135.

63   **Bill recalled reading:** Elliott, *Family Matters*, 187.

64   **Madeline Levine calls:** Madeline Levine, *The Price of Privilege: How Parental Pressure and Material Advantage Are Creating a Generation of Disconnected and Unhappy Kids* (New York: Harper-Collins, 2006), 133–40.

65   **deal with our disappointment:** Levine, *The Price of Privilege*, 146.

68   **Harvard's Richard Weissbourd:** Richard Weissbourd, *The Parents We Mean to Be: How Well-Intentioned Adults Undermine Children's Moral and Emotional Development* (New York: Mariner Books, 2010).

68   **becoming a "strengths spotter":** Lea Waters, *The Strength Switch: How the New Science of Strength-Based Parenting Can Help Your Child and Your Teen to Flourish* (New York: Avery, 2017).

69   **two-thirds of us don't:** Michelle McQuaid, "Don't Make a Wish—Try Hope Instead," VIA Institute on Character, Achieving Goals, Jan. 31, 2014, https://www.viacharacter.org/topics/articles/don%27t-make-a-wish-try-hope-instead.

69   **The VIA survey:** "The VIA Character Strengths Survey," VIA Institute on Character, https://www.viacharacter.org/survey/account/Register.

71   **Gordon Flett offers tips to convey:** Flett, *Psychology of Mattering*, 117.

71   **NYU professor Scott Galloway:** Scott Galloway, *The Algebra of Happiness: Notes on the Pursuit of Success, Love, and Meaning* (New York: Portfolio, 2019), 148–9.

72 **study out of Notre Dame:** "Parent Touch, Play and Support in Childhood Vital to Well-Being as an Adult," *Notre Dame News,* Dec. 21, 2015, https://news.nd.edu/news/parent-touch-play-and -support-in-childhood-vital-to-well-being-as-an-adult.

73 **having to learn about Fortnite:** Bingqing Wang, Laramie Taylor, and Qiusi Sun, "Families that Play Together Stay Together: Investigating Family Bonding through Video Games," *New Media & Society* 20, no. 11 (2018): 4074–94, https://doi.org/10.1177/1461444818767667.

73 **serves as a model for the kind:** Jennifer Breheny Wallace, "The Right Way for Parents to Question Their Teenagers," *Wall Street Journal,* Nov. 23, 2018, https://www.wsj.com/articles/the-right-way -for-parents-to-question-their-teenagers-1542982858.

CHAPTER 4: YOU FIRST

84 **Since the mid-1970s:** Anthony Cilluffo and D'Vera Cohn, "7 Demographic Trends Shaping the U.S. and the World in 2018," Pew Research Center, Apr. 25, 2018, https://www.pewresearch.org/fact -tank/2018/04/25/7-demographic-trends-shaping-the-u-s-and-the- world-in-2018.

84 **Additionally, panel studies:** See William Delgado, "Replication Data for The Education Gradient in Maternal Enjoyment of Time in Childcare," Harvard Dataverse, V1, June 14, 2020. See also Ariel Kalil, Susan E. Mayer, William Delgado, and Lisa A. Gennetian, "The Education Gradient in Maternal Enjoyment of Time in Childcare," University of Chicago, Becker Friedman Institute, June 14, 2020.

85 **sociologist Sharon Hays:** Sharon Hays, *The Cultural Contradictions of Motherhood* (New Haven: Yale University Press, 1996).

85 **While mothers in particular:** Charlotte Faircloth, "Intensive Fatherhood? The (Un)involved Dad," in Ellie Lee, Jennie Bristow,

Charlotte Faircloth, and Jan Macvarish, *Parenting Culture Studies* (London: Palgrave Macmillan, 2014): 184–99, https://doi.org/10.1057 /9781137304612_9.

85 **According to Pew Research:** Gretchen Livingston and Kim Parker, "8 Facts about American Dads," Pew Research Center, June 12, 2019, https://www.pewresearch.org/fact-tank/2019/06/12 /fathers-day-facts.

85 **The "good father effect":** Lydia Buswell, Ramon B. Zabriskie, Neil Lundberg, and Alan J. Hawkins, "The Relationship Between Father Involvement in Family Leisure and Family Functioning: The Importance of Daily Family Leisure," *Leisure Sciences* 34, no. 2 (Mar. 2012): 172–90, https://doi.org/10.1080/01490400.2012.652510.

85 **Same-sex couples can struggle:** Maaike van der Vleuten, Eva Jaspers, and Tanja van der Lippe, "Same-Sex Couples' Division of Labor from a Cross-National Perspective," *Journal of GLBT Family Studies* 17, no. 2 (Dec. 2020): 150–67, https://doi.org/10.1080/1550428X .2020.1862012.

86 **"same dynamics as heterosexuals":** Claire Cain Miller, "How Same-Sex Couples Divide Chores, and What It Reveals About Modern Parenting," *New York Times*, May 16, 2018, https://www .nytimes.com/2018/05/16/upshot/same-sex-couples-divide-chores -much-more-evenly-until-they-become-parents.html.

87 **the more empathetic a mother:** Erika M. Manczak, Anita De-Longis, and Edith Chen, "Does Empathy Have a Cost? Diverging Psychological and Physiological Effects Within Families," *Health Psychology* 35, no. 3 (Mar. 2016): 211–18, https://doi.org/10.1037 /hea0000281.

87 **Intensive parenting is also:** "Does Being an Intense Mother Make Women Unhappy?," *Springer* via *ScienceDaily*, July 5, 2012, https:// www.sciencedaily.com/releases/2012/07/120705151417.htm.

88   **"leaving center stage":** Jennifer Senior, *All Joy and No Fun: The Paradox of Modern Parenthood* (New York: Ecco, 2014), 199.

88   **mothers with middle-school-age:** Suniya S. Luthar and Lucia Ciciolla, "What It Feels Like to Be a Mother: Variations by Children's Developmental Stages," *Developmental Psychology* 52, no. 1 (2016): 143–54, https://doi.org/10.1037/dev0000062.

92   **For decades now, sociologists:** Robert D. Putnam, *Bowling Alone: The Collapse and Revival of American Community* (New York: Simon & Schuster, 2001).

95   **20 percent of Wilton students:** "Privileged and Pressured Presentation Summary," compiled by Genevieve Eason, Wilton Youth Council, https://www.wiltonyouth.org/privileged-pressured-summary.

95   **"A feeling of not mattering":** Gordon Flett, *The Psychology of Mattering: Understanding the Human Need to be Significant* (London: Academic Press, 2018), 123.

96   **as "proximal separation":** "The Most Important Thing We Can Do for Our Children Is to Learn How to Manage OUR Stress," 13D Research, Aug. 9, 2017, https://latest.13d.com/the-most-important-thing-we-can-do-for-our-children-is-learn-how-to-manage-our-stress-62f9031f55c4.

96   **"parent is psychologically present":** Flett, *The Psychology of Mattering*, 116. See also Brooke Elizabeth Whiting, "Determinants and Consequences of Mattering in the Adolescent's Social World" (PhD diss., University of Maryland College Park, 1982).

97   **Decades of resilience research:** Jennifer E. DeVoe, Amy Geller, and Yamrot Negussie, eds., *Vibrant and Healthy Kids: Aligning Science, Practice, and Policy to Advance Health Equity* (Washington, DC: The National Academies Press, 2019).

98 **Social support, research finds:** Thomas W. Kamarck, Stephen B. Manuck, and J. Richard Jennings, "Social Support Reduces Cardiovascular Reactivity to Psychological Challenge: A Laboratory Model," *Psychosomatic Medicine* 52, no. 1 (1990): 42–58, https://doi.org/10.1097/00006842-199001000-00004.

99 **two people are standing together:** Simone Schnall, Kent D. Harber, Jeanine K. Stefanucci, and Dennis R. Proffitt, "Social Support and the Perception of Geographical Slant," *Journal of Experimental Social Psychology* 44, no. 5 (Sept. 2008): 1246–55, https://doi.org/10.1016/j.jesp.2008.04.011.

99 **a twelve-week program:** Suniya S. Luthar et al., "Fostering Resilience among Mothers under Stress: 'Authentic Connections Groups' for Medical Professionals," *Women's Health Issues* 27, no. 3 (May–June 2017): 382–90, https://doi.org/10.1016/j.whi.2017.02.007.

99 **weekly one-hour meetings:** Sherry S. Chesak et al., "Authentic Connections Groups: A Pilot Test of an Intervention Aimed at Enhancing Resilience Among Nurse Leader Mothers," *Worldviews on Evidence-Based Nursing* 17, no. 1 (Feb. 2020): 39–48, https://doi.org/10.1111/wvn.12420.

99 **Subsequent studies by Luthar:** Suniya S. Luthar, Nina L. Kumar, and Renee Benoit, "Toward Fostering Resilience on a Large Scale: Connecting Communities of Caregivers," *Developmental Psychopathology* 31, no. 5 (Dec. 2019): 1813–25, https://doi.org/10.1017/S0954579419001251.

100 **they didn't have the bandwidth:** U.S. surgeon general Vivek Murthy writes about his similar experience in his book *Together: The Healing Power of Human Connection in a Sometimes Lonely World* (New York: HarperCollins, 2020), 275.

101 **may make us the happiest:** Senior, *All Joy and No Fun*, 5.

103 **anything else: never worry alone:** Edward M. Hallowell, *The Childhood Roots of Adult Happiness: Five Steps to Help Kids Create and Sustain Lifelong Joy* (New York: Ballantine Books, 2002).

CHAPTER 5: TAKING THE KETTLE OFF THE HEAT

110 **Ranked by *Money* magazine:** Julia Hess, "Mercer Island Featured as Best Place to Live in Washington," *My Mercer Island*, Jan. 29, 2018, https://mymercerisland.com/mercer-island-best-place-to-live-washington.

111 **sociologists have been documenting:** Charles Murray, "SuperZips and the Rest of America's Zip Codes," *American Enterprise Institute*, Feb. 13, 2012, https://www.aei.org/research-products/working-paper/superzips-and-the-rest-of-americas-zip-codes.

112 **650 SuperZip communities:** Carol Morello and Ted Mellnik, "Washington: A World Apart," *Washington Post*, Nov. 9, 2013, https://www.washingtonpost.com/sf/local/2013/11/09/washington-a-world-apart.

112 **Kids sense a duty:** The "encore effect" is a term coined by Gordon Flett to describe how high performers find pressure to keep repeating high performance. I think it also works well to describe the pressure on children of high earners.

113 **Wealth is concentrated:** Andy Kiersz, "MAP: Here Are The 20 'Super-Zips' Where America's Ultra-Elite Reside," *Business Insider*, Dec. 9, 2013, https://www.businessinsider.com/map-americas-super-elite-live-in-these-zip-codes-2013-12.

114 **"I would cry in the hospital":** Meghana Kakubal, Lila Shroff, and Soraya Marashi, "Pressure, Insomnia and Hospitalization: The New Normal for Students Applying to College," *KUOW RadioActive*, Apr. 3, 2019, https://www.kuow.org/stories/what-students-go-through-to-get-into-college.

116 **difference between getting a 91 and a 99:** Lisa Damour, "Why Girls Beat Boys at School and Lose to Them at the Office," *New York Times*, Feb. 7, 2019, https://www.nytimes.com/2019/02/07 /opinion/sunday/girls-school-confidence.html.

117 **students take a health survey:** Cynthia Goodwin, "Gearing Up for Summer: Findings and Recommendation on Our Youth Well-Being Student Survey," *Mercer Island Living*, June 2019.

117–118 **Luthar describes Mercer Island:** Suniya S. Luthar, Samuel H. Barkin, and Elizabeth J. Crossman, "'I Can, Therefore I Must': Fragility in the Upper-Middle Classes," *Developmental Psychopathology* 25, no. 4, pt. 2 (Nov. 2013): 1529–49, https://doi.org/10.1017 /S0954579413000758.

118 **Having the privilege of choices:** Barry Schwartz, *The Paradox of Choice: Why More is Less* (New York: HarperCollins, 2004).

118 **The growth-mindset ideology:** Carol S. Dweck, *Mindset: The New Psychology of Success* (New York: Ballantine Books, 2006).

119 **"backing off when they should":** Suniya S. Luthar, Nina L. Kumar, and Nicole Zillmer, "High-Achieving Schools Connote Risks for Adolescents: Problems Documented, Processes Implicated, and Directions for Interventions," *American Psychologist* 75, no. 7 (2020): 983–95, https://doi.org/10.1037/amp0000556.

119 **compulsive and excessive need:** Paweł A. Atroszko, Cecilie Schou Andreassen, Mark D. Griffiths, and Ståle Pallesen, "Study Addiction—A New Area of Psychological Study: Conceptualization, Assessment, and Preliminary Empirical Findings," *Journal of Behavioral Addictions* 4, no. 2 (2015): 75–84, https://doi.org/10.1556/2006 .4.2015.007.

119 **Scholars find that "study addiction":** Paweł A. Atroszko, Cecilie Schou Andreassen, Mark D. Griffiths, and Ståle Pallesen, "The Relationship Between Study Addiction and Work Addiction: A

Cross-Cultural Longitudinal Study," *Journal of Behavioral Addictions* 5, no. 4 (2016): 708–14, https://doi.org/10.1556/2006.5.2016.076.

120 **One study of college students:** Atroszko et al., "The Relationship Between Study Addiction and Work Addiction."

121 **attach to material goods:** Johann Hari, *Lost Connections: Uncovering the Real Causes of Depression—and the Unexpected Solutions* (New York: Bloomsbury, 2018), 125.

121 **people who prioritize materialistic goals:** Evan Nesterak, "Materially False: A Q&A with Tim Kasser about the Pursuit of the Good Life through Goods," *Behavioral Scientist*, Sept. 9, 2014, https://behavioralscientist.org/materially-false-qa-tim-kasser-pursuit-good-goods.

121 **Kasser and his colleagues:** Tim Kasser et al., "Changes in Materialism, Changes in Psychological Well-Being: Evidence from Three Longitudinal Studies and an Intervention Experiment," *Motivation and Emotion* 38 (2014): 1–22, https://doi.org/10.1007/s11031-013-9371-4.

126 **Paul Tough, in his book:** Paul Tough, *The Inequality Machine: How College Divides Us* (Boston: Houghton Mifflin Harcourt, 2019), 25.

126 **Denise Pope, a cofounder of Challenge Success:** "A 'Fit' Over Rankings: Why College Engagement Matters More Than Selectivity," Challenge Success, Resources, May 14, 2021. https://challengesuccess.org/resources/a-fit-over-rankings-why-college-engagement-matters-more-than-selectivity.

127 **As Malcolm Gladwell explained:** Malcolm Gladwell, "The Order of Things: What College Rankings Really Tell Us," *New Yorker*, Feb. 6, 2011, https://www.newyorker.com/magazine/2011/02/14/the-order-of-things.

127 **"The broader lesson everyone":** Anemona Hartocollis, "U.S.

News Dropped Columbia's Ranking, but Its Own Methods Are Now Questioned," *New York Times*, Sept. 12, 2022, https://www.nytimes.com/2022/09/12/us/columbia-university-us-news-ranking.html.

127 **Columbia is hardly alone:** See David Wagner, "Which Schools Aren't Lying Their Way to a Higher U.S. News Ranking?," The *Atlantic*, Feb. 6, 2013, https://www.theatlantic.com/national/archive/2013/02/which-schools-arent-lying-their-way-higher-us-news-ranking/318621. See also Max Kutner, "How to Game the College Rankings," *Boston Magazine*, Aug. 26, 2014, https://www.boston magazine.com/news/2014/08/26/how-northeastern-gamed-the-college-rankings.

127 **Pew Research conducted a study:** Anna Brown, "Public and Private College Grads Rank about Equally in Life Satisfaction," Pew Research Center, May 19, 2014, https://www.pewresearch.org/fact-tank/2014/05/19/public-and-private-college-grads-rank-about-equally-in-life-satisfaction.

135 **musicians who were:** "Why You Should Work Less: A Second Look at the 10,000 Hour Rule," The Neuroscience School, 2020, https://neuroscienceschool.com/2020/05/22/why-you-should-work-less.

136 **Like these world-class musicians:** "The Youth Risk Behavior Surveillance System (YRBSS): 2019 National, State, and Local Results," National Center for HIV/AIDS, Viral Hepatitis, STD, and TB Prevention Division of Adolescent and School Health, 2019, https://www.cdc.gov/healthyyouth/data/yrbs/pdf/2019/2019_Graphs_508.pdf.

136 **moodiness, feelings of worthlessness:** Andrew J. Fuligni, Erin H. Arruda, Jennifer L. Krull, and Nancy A. Gonzales, "Adolescent Sleep Duration, Variability, and Peak Levels of Achievement and Mental Health," *Child Development* 89, no. 2 (Mar. 2018): 18–28, https://doi.org/10.1111/cdev.12729.

140 **Adolescents who reported:** Lucia Ciciolla, Alexandria S. Curlee, Jason Karageorge, and Suniya S Luthar, "When Mothers and Fathers Are Seen as Disproportionately Valuing Achievements: Implications for Adjustment Among Upper Middle Class Youth," *Journal of Youth and Adolescence* 46, no. 5 (May 2017): 1057–75, https://doi.org/10.1007/s10964-016-0596-x.

CHAPTER 6: ENVY

142 **And local context matters:** Robert H. Frank, *Falling Behind: How Rising Inequality Harms the Middle Class* (Berkeley: University of California Press, 2007), 30.

143 **On the other hand, when too:** Prashant Loyalka, Andrey Zakharov, and Yulia Kusmina, "Catching the Big Fish in the Little Pond Effect: Evidence from 33 Countries and Regions," *Comparative Education Review* 62, no. 4 (Nov. 2018): 542–64, https://doi.org/10.1086/699672.

143 **water they swim in:** For more on this idea, see David Foster Wallace's May 21, 2005, Kenyon College commencement address, https://people.math.harvard.edu/~ctm/links/culture/dfw_kenyon_commencement.html#:~:text=The%20really%20important%20kind%20of,and%20understanding%20how%20to%20think.

144 **"This Year's College Admissions Horror Show":** Nicole LaPorte, "This Year's College Admissions Horror Show," *Town & Country*, Apr. 1, 2022, https://www.townandcountrymag.com/society/money-and-power/a39560789/college-admissions-2022-challenge-news.

146 **isolating effects of the pandemic:** Jean M. Twenge et al., "Worldwide Increases in Adolescent Loneliness," *Journal of Adolescence* 93 (Dec. 2021): 257–69, https://doi.org/10.1016/j.adolescence.2021.06.006.

146 **"dispose of them":** Isaac Lozano, "'It Literally Consumes You': A Look into Student Struggles with Mental Health at Stanford," *Stanford Daily*, Apr. 21, 2022, https://stanforddaily.com/2022/04/21/it-literally -consumes-you-a-look-into-student-struggles-with-mental -health-at-stanford.

147 **kids grow into teenagers:** Gordon Flett, *The Psychology of Mattering: Understanding the Human Need to be Significant* (London: Academic Press, 2018), 31.

147 **followed 365 students:** Julie Newman Kingery, Cynthia A. Erdley, and Katherine C. Marshall, "Peer Acceptance and Friendship as Predictors of Early Adolescents' Adjustment Across the Middle School Transition," *Merrill-Palmer Quarterly* 57, no. 3 (2011): 215–43, https://doi.org/10.1353/mpq.2011.0012.

148 **adolescents who had experienced:** Rachel K. Narr, Joseph P. Allen, Joseph S. Tan, and Emily L. Loeb, "Close Friendship Strength and Broader Peer Group Desirability as Differential Predictors of Adult Mental Health," *Child Development* 90, no. 1 (Aug. 2017): 298–313, https://doi.org/10.1111/cdev.12905.

152 **Teachers and coaches:** Gregory C. Elliott, *Family Matters: The Importance of Mattering to Family in Adolescence* (Chichester, UK: Wiley-Blackwell, 2009), 58.

160 **"envy brings the pain":** Robert E. Coles, "The Hidden Power of Envy," *Harper's Magazine*, Aug. 1995, https://harpers.org/archive /1995/08/the-hidden-power-of-envy.

164 **Microaggressions and discrimination:** Isaac Prilleltensky and Ora Prilleltensky, *How People Matter: Why it Affects Health, Happiness, Love, Work, and Society* (Cambridge: Cambridge University Press, 2021), 224–26.

165 **how Black boys experience:** Roderick L. Carey, Camila Polanco, and Horatio Blackman, "Black Adolescent Boys' Perceived School

Mattering: From Marginalization and Selective Love to Radically Affirming Relationships," *Journal of Research on Adolescence* 32, no. 1 (Dec. 2021): 151–69, https://doi.org/10.1111/jora.12706.

168 **study that examined competitive motives:** Ersilia Menesini, Fulvio Tassi, and Annalaura Nocentini, "The Competitive Attitude Scale (CAS): A Multidimensional Measure of Competitiveness in Adolescence," *Journal of Psychology & Clinical Psychiatry* 9, no. 3 (2018): 240–44, https://doi.org/10.15406/jpcpy.2018.09.00528.

168 **another study, of 615 Canadian adolescents:** Tamara Humphrey and Tracy Vaillancourt, "Longitudinal Relations Between Hyper-competitiveness, Jealousy, and Aggression Across Adolescence," *Merrill-Palmer Quarterly* 67, no. 3 (July 2021): 237–68, https://doi.org/10.13110/merrpalmquar1982.67.3.0237.

169 **Vaillancourt told me:** Jennifer Breheny Wallace, "Teaching Girls to Be Great Competitors," *Wall Street Journal*, Apr. 12, 2019, https://www.wsj.com/articles/teaching-girls-to-be-great-competitors-11555061400.

169 **a "worthy rival":** Simon Sinek, *The Infinite Game* (New York: Portfolio, 2019); and for more, Darya Sinusoid, "A Worthy Rival: Learn from the Competition," *Shortform* (blog), June 11, 2021, https://www.shortform.com/blog/worthy-rival.

169 **W. Timothy Gallwey uses:** W. Timothy Gallwey, *The Inner Game of Tennis: The Classic Guide to the Mental Side of Peak Performance* (New York: Random House, 1974).

170 **While boys are conditioned:** Jennifer Breheny Wallace, "Teaching Girls to Be Great Competitors."

170 **nearly sixty girls:** Renée Spencer, Jill Walsh, Belle Liang, Angela M. Desilva Mousseau, and Terese J. Lund, "Having It All? A Qualitative Examination of Affluent Adolescent Girls' Perceptions of Stress and Their Quests for Success," *Journal of Adolescent Research*

33, no. 1 (Sept. 2016): 3–33, https://doi.org/10.1177/07435584 16670990.

171 **For this reason, girls:** Jennifer Breheny Wallace, "Teaching Girls to Be Great Competitors."

171 **"iron sharpens iron":** Amy Tennery, "Athletics–'Iron Sharpens Iron': McLaughlin, Muhammad Hurdle to New Heights," Reuters, Aug. 4, 2021, https://www.reuters.com/lifestyle/sports/athletics-iron -sharpens-iron-mclaughlin-muhammad-hurdle-new-heights -2021-08-04.

CHAPTER 7: GREATER EXPECTATIONS

179 **shifting away from more social:** Jean M. Twenge, "How Dare You Say Narcissism Is Increasing?," *Psychology Today*, Aug. 12, 2013, https://www.psychologytoday.com/us/blog/the-narcissism -epidemic/201308/how-dare-you-say-narcissism-is-increasing.

179 **What they found was alarming:** Diane Swanbrow, "Empathy: College Students Don't Have as Much as They Used To," *Michigan Today*, June 9, 2010, https://michigantoday.umich.edu/2010/06/09 /a7777.

179 **The drop is so startling:** Jean M. Twenge and M. Keith Campbell, *The Narcissism Epidemic: Living in the Age of Entitlement* (New York: Atria, 2009).

182 **"not actually stress":** Terri Lobdell, "Driven to Succeed: How We're Depriving Teens of a Sense of Purpose," *Palo Alto Weekly*, Nov. 18, 2011, https://ed.stanford.edu/news/driven-succeed-how -were-depriving-teens-sense-purpose.

184 **encouraging her to be humble:** Rick Warren, *The Purpose Driven Life: What on Earth Am I Here For?* (Grand Rapids: Zondervan, 2002).

184 **today's demand for childhood success:** Jennifer Breheny Wallace,

"Why Children Need Chores," *Wall Street Journal*, Mar. 13, 2015, https://www.wsj.com/articles/why-children-need-chores-1426262655.

185 **It's associated with clinical depression:** Leon F. Seltzer, "Self-Absorption: The Root of All (Psychological) Evil?," *Psychology Today*, Aug. 24, 2016, https://www.psychologytoday.com/us/blog/evolution-the-self/201608/self-absorption-the-root-all-psychological-evil.

185 **researchers at Harvard University:** For more on this research, see Robert Waldinger, MD, and Marc Schulz, PhD, *The Good Life: Lessons from the World's Longest Scientific Study of Happiness* (New York: Simon & Schuster, 2023).

186 **for an article I was writing:** Jennifer Breheny Wallace, "How to Get Your Kids to Do Their Chores," *The Huffington Post*, Apr. 23, 2015, https://www.huffpost.com/entry/how-to-get-your-kids-to-do-their-chores_b_7117102.

191 **deep sense of mattering:** Isaac Prilleltensky and Ora Prilleltensky, *How People Matter: Why It Affects Health, Happiness, Love, Work, and Society* (Cambridge: Cambridge University Press, 2021), 78.

193 **William Damon offers these prompts:** William Damon, *The Path to Purpose: How Young People Find Their Calling in Life* (New York: Free Press, 2009), 183–86.

198 **religion has been found:** Samantha Boardman, *Everyday Vitality: Turning Stress into Strength* (New York: Penguin Books, 2021), 188–89.

199 ***The Path to Purpose:*** Damon, *Path to Purpose*, 183–202.

203 **curb self-destructive impulses:** William Damon, *Greater Expectations: Overcoming the Culture of Indulgence in Our Homes and Schools* (New York: Free Press Paperbacks, 1995), 31.

204 **practicing generosity both requires and reinforces:** Christian

Smith and Hilary Davidson, *The Paradox of Generosity: Giving We Receive, Grasping We Lose* (Oxford: Oxford University Press, 2014), 71.

207 **secret to living a meaningful:** Christopher Peterson, "Other People Matter: Two Examples," *Psychology Today*, June 17, 2008, https://www.psychologytoday.com/us/blog/the-good-life/200806/other-people-matter-two-examples.

CHAPTER 8: THE RIPPLE EFFECT

213 **Years ago, the author:** Bruce Feiler, *The Council of Dads: My Daughters, My Illness, and the Men Who Could Be Me* (New York: William Morrow, 2010).

214 **Kids who are surrounded:** See the National Longitudinal Study of Adolescents to Adult Health, accessible at "Social, Behavioral, and Biological Linkages Across the Life Course," Add Health, https://addhealth.cpc.unc.edu.

224 **more than 1,200 residents:** GOOD Morning Wilton Staff, "Get Ready for Wilton's 2nd Annual Big Block Party Weekend," *GOOD Morning Wilton*, May 29, 2019, https://goodmorningwilton.com/get-ready-for-wiltons-2nd-annual-big-block-party-weekend.

RESOURCES: TAKING ACTION AT HOME

237 **Never worry alone:** See Edward M. Hallowell, *The Childhood Roots of Adult Happiness: Five Steps to Help Kids Create and Sustain Lifelong Joy* (New York: Ballantine Books, 2002).

237 **The psychologist Carin Rubenstein:** Carin Rubenstein, *The Sacrificial Mother: Escaping the Trap of Self-Denial* (New York: Hachette Books, 1999).

238 **Strive to be a good enough:** "Good enough parent" is a term that

was developed by D. W. Winnicott. For more on this concept, please see his book *The Child, the Family, and the Outside World* (Harmondsworth, UK: Penguin, 1964).

240 **keep achievement in perspective:** Jennifer Breheny Wallace, "The Perils of the Child Perfectionist," *Wall Street Journal*, Aug. 31, 2018, https://www.wsj.com/articles/the-perils-of-the-young-perfectionist -1535723813.

241 **gratitude is the glue:** For more on gratitude research, see Summer Allen, "The Science of Gratitude," Greater Good Science Center, May 2018, https://happierway.org/pillars/well-being/articles/the -science-of-gratitude.

RESOURCES: TAKING ACTION FOR EDUCATORS

244 **Oprah credits her fourth-grade teacher:** Gordon Flett, *The Psychology of Mattering: Understanding the Human Need to be Significant* (London: Academic Press, 2018), 20–1.

246 **function like nonprofits:** Daniel Markovits, *The Meritocracy Trap: How America's Foundational Myth Feeds Inequality, Dismantles the Middle Class, and Devours the Elite* (New York: Penguin Press, 2019), 275–84.

Index

educators
and Black students, 165
building partnership with, 165
"taking action" resources for,
242–46
See also teachers; tutors
elementary school, 16, 18, 26, 46, 147,
158, 176–77
Elias, Vanessa, 90–91, 223–24, 230
elite colleges
admission lotteries for, 245–46
affirmative action and, 164–65
competition for, 15, 246
conversations about, 133
"faking passions" for, 180
and happiness/success, 125–31
illegal scheme for, 24–25
parents focus on, 26, 29, 42–43, 111,
124, 139
pressure to go to, 26, 29, 31
rankings and, 125–31
reject myth about, 125–31
schools prioritize, 26, 182
self-worth tied to, xviii, 53
students worked towards, 1–2, 114
Elliott, Gregory, 51, 53, 58, 63
Emdin, Christopher, 229
emotional support, 79–80, 87–90,
95–98, 103, 150, 158–61
emotions
mindfully expressed, 65–66, 71
normalize difficult ones,
239, 244
numbing them, 1, 3–4
produced by competition,
158–61, 244
share them in school, 244
empathy, xx, 87, 179–81, 190, 197,
205, 241
emptiness, xv, 5, 88
energy efficiency, 239–40
English, Elizabeth, 152
envy
benign vs. malicious, 167–68
and feeling valued, 211
materialism and, 124

negative effects of, 151–52, 164
parental guidance for, 159–60, 169,
230, 239
positive aspects of, 154, 160, 168,
171–72
and social comparison, 151,
167–68, 244
Erickson, Erik, 12
ethnicity, 7, 162
Evanston, Illinois, 34, 36
evolution, 31–33
exhaustion
of kids, 3, 5, 13, 16, 163–64, 180
and materialism, 121
of mothers, 38, 87, 90, 93–95
of parents, 65, 78–79, 84, 95, 98, 121
See also burnout
extracurricular activities
boundaries for, 109–11
cause stress, 8, 14
chauffeuring kids to, 84, 90, 100
in college, 129–30
and college admissions, 2, 38, 47, 158
competition in, xiv, 143
money spent on, 35
parents advise on, 88–89
parents manage them, 10, 30, 34,
80, 86
and scholarship dollars, 25
and status seeking, 28

Facebook, xvi, 224
factory workers, 35–36
failures, 49, 61–62, 65, 71, 203–4, 240
"false self," 58–64
families, 155
and achievement pressure, xvii, 6–7
in affluent communities, 109–14
children's needs first in, 83–88
clarify goals of, 137–39
closeness in, 72–73, 96
dinnertime and, 64, 107, 124, 206
importance of, 117
mandate volunteering, 190–91
and mattering, 146–47, 212–13, 227
people come first to, 223

everything in moderation, 139–40
and materialism/mental health,
131–34
protect children from, 115–20, 136
reject myth of top colleges, 125–31
take deliberate breaks from, 135–38
Grown & Flown, 228–29
growth mindset, 118–20, 181–82, 245
guidance counselors, 81, 177

Hallowell, Edward, 103
happiness
and affluence, 112
childhood chores and, 185–86
and feeling valued, 226
and friendships, 101–3, 148
intrinsic values lead to, 122–23
parents focus on, xvii, 13–14,
37–38, 181
scientific study of, 185–86
status and, 30, 112
success and, 9–10, 122–23, 192
and top colleges, xvii, 125–31
Harley Avenue Primary School (New
York), 15
Harris, Rainier, 164–65
Harvard Graduate School of
Education, xvi, 29
Harvard University, 8–9, 42, 68, 144,
182, 185–86, 202, 212, 245–46
Hays, Sharon, 85
Heffernan, Lisa, 228–29
help, asking for, 103–5, 148–49,
154–58, 240
Henes, Rachel, 114, 164
Hewit School (New York City), 192–94
High Price of Materialism, The
(Kasser), 121
high school
being measured at, 47
and college contract, 245
competition in, 3, 8, 48, 168–69
grade schools feed into, 26
high expectations in, 109–11
less competitive ones, 142–43,
182–83

a means to an end, 125
mental health struggles in, 189–90
not mattering in, 246–47
parents track students in, 43
workload rise in, 116
Hill, Andrew, 49, 119
Hirsch, Victoria, 41
hobbies, 16, 30, 38, 87, 216
home, the, 218
escape pressure in, 66, 88
feeling you matter in, 227, 238
isolating or unsafe in, 59, 96
kids are themselves in, 63–64, 72
modeling vulnerability in, 157–58
practice gratitude in, 241
society's expectations for, 85
supportive, 146, 150, 157
"taking action" resources for,
237–41
talk about values in, 136–37
homework, 15, 158, 180, 187
asking about, 19, 33
parents help with, 35, 84, 100
parents supervise it, 34, 66–67, 80
supplemental, 38
honors
classes, 18–19, 81–83, 110, 142–43,
202–3
rolls/societies, 15–16, 47
See also advanced classes
hormones, 8, 28, 99
Huffman, Felicity, 24–25
humility, 105, 184, 204
Humphrey, Tamara, 168
hypercompetitive culture, 211
coping with, 141–46
mental health issues and, 168–69
parents' role in, 49, 115
radical individualism of, 179
and self-worth, 229
societal norms of, 13
of sports, 172

I, Mammal (Bruening), 28–29
identity, 7, 12–13, 44, 50, 53, 73,
147, 162

income
    of college grads, 34–36, 111–12, 128
    focus on, 179, 206
    inequality in, 35, 37, 39–40, 246
    low, 7, 10, 32, 128, 196, 246
    of mothers, 83, 91
    and parenting, 32–36
    and status-driven goals, 122–23
    top percentile, xv, 7, 111–12
    and your values, 137
individualism, 103, 179–80. *See also*
    self-focus
inequality, xx, 33, 35–37, 39–40, 49
*Inequality Machine: How College
    Divides Us, The* (Tough), 126
Infinite Game, The (Sinek), 169
Inner Game of Tennis, The (Gallwey),
    169–70
Instagram, 28, 47–48, 123, 159–60
"intensive parenting," 19, 36, 83–88,
    93–95, 178–82
interdependence, 51, 149, 237, 240
internships, 4, 129–30, 228
IQ tests, 45–48
isolation, 87, 91, 142
    and being perfect, 60
    combat feelings of, xxi, 221,
        223–24
    counseling/support for, 189–90
    in the home, 96, 146
    and hypercompetitiveness, 164, 168
    of marginalized students, 164
    materialism and, 121
Italy, 168
Ivy League colleges, xx, 24, 42, 158,
    182. *See also specific colleges*

judgment
    and child's success, xvii, 19, 62, 107
    by others, 19–20, 107, 134
    of ourselves, 19, 44, 239
    places free of, 72, 106, 125, 201
    praise as form of, 67–68

Kakubal, Meghana, 221–23
Kasser, Tim, 121–24, 131–35, 230

Kimmerer, Robin Wall, 125
kindergarteners, 15, 45–48, 69
Kinsey, Tara Christie, 191–94
Kumar, Nina, 119

learning disabilities, 10, 177, 190,
    202–5
Leimone, Thea, 150, 154–55, 158, 166,
    173, 213
Levine, Madeline, xv, 64–65
life satisfaction
    childhood chores and, 186
    and living a balanced life, 137
    materialism and, 133
    and parental guidance, 130–31
    and top colleges, 127–31, 133
Lloyd, Chrishana, 40
London, England, 83–84, 92–93, 112
loneliness, 4, 7, 146
    and being perfect, 60
    community building and,
        223–24
    friendships and, 147–50, 225–26
    of high schoolers, 177, 225
    of middle schoolers, 88
    and need to feel valued, 50, 52
    social comparison and, 151
    support groups for, 190
Longshore, Marjie, 186–87, 194–95,
    207, 216, 230
Los Angeles, California, xvii, 141,
    146, 161
Loughlin, Lori, 24
love, 43
    and being perfect, 5, 12, 48–49,
        59–60, 238
    conditional, 58, 60–62, 64
    and the "false self," 58–60
    good warmth and, 64–67, 70
    parental, 49–50, 53–55, 57–61
    and parents' sacrifices, 88
    tied to achievement, 48–50, 55,
        59–62
    unconditional, 60–61, 67–68, 75,
        150, 211, 239
    and what children hear, 54–58, 67

public universities, 125–28
puppy dog principle, 70–73
Purdue University study, 128–30
purpose, a life of, 10, 13–14, 96,
    191–94, 199–207, 230

race, 7, 91, 161–66, 162
Race at the Top (Warikoo), 143–44
racial wealth disparities, 39–40
racism, xx
rankings
    of children, 16, 28, 39, 43, 47–48
    of colleges, 41, 125–31
    housing prices linked to, 15
    of schools, 15–16, 18, 79–80, 110
recharging, 15, 124, 239. *See also*
    downtime; playtime; rest/sleep
relationships
    conditional, 29, 219
    gratitude binds them, 241
    impaired by excess studying,
        119–20
    importance of, 138, 168
    invest time in, 121–23
    life-sustaining, 98–107, 169
    "relationship mapping" and, 243
    resilience rests on, 247
    that deliver mattering, 54
    transactional, 121–22, 200
    See also friendships; parent-child
        bond; spouses/partners
reliance on others, 155–58. *See also*
    self-reliance
religion, 92, 198, 200
resilience, 67, 97, 100, 105, 140, 203,
    230, 247
rest/sleep, xiv, 3, 15, 89, 110, 115, 132,
    135–38
résumés
    children judge themselves by, 44
    and college admissions, 127
    padding of, 9, 138, 180, 228, 246
    parental guidance for, 33, 181
    start them early, 41–42
rivalry, 43, 168–71. *See also*
    competition

Robert Wood Johnson Foundation
    (RWJF), 6–7
Rosenberg, Morris, 50
Rossmann, Marty, 185, 188
rule-breaking behavior, 6, 140, 214–15

Saint Ignatius High School (Cleveland),
    195–99, 212
same-sex couples, 85–86
SATs, 48, 63, 133, 138, 246
Scandinavia, 35–36
"scarcity mindset," 32–33, 40, 124, 204,
    211, 214, 218
Schneider, Matt, 85
scholarships, 25–26, 43, 47, 128, 163
school administrators, 14–16, 45–46,
    126, 145, 196, 218, 242
school bands, 221–23
school shooters, 52
self-care, 83, 98, 239
self-esteem, 50–51, 60–64, 122, 147, 169
self-focus, 179–85, 190, 197, 227
self-harm, 52, 89–90, 95, 168–69
"selfist," 237
self-reliance, 91, 149, 157, 179
self-worth, 96, 155, 204
    based on achievement, xviii–xix, 3,
        48–50, 53–58, 114
    children question it, 16, 44
    competition and, 143, 146
    conditional, 219
    and "feeling valued," 50–54, 58, 68
    friendships and, 105, 148
    and grades, 17, 56, 74–75
    linked to success, 61–62
    marginalized students and, 164
    of parents, 64, 79, 105, 229
    pride and, 133–34
    tied to materialism, 146
    undermining of, xvi, 12–13
Seligman, Martin, 69
Senior, Jennifer, 87–88
sex, 132–33, 147
sexual orientation, 162, 190
Shaker Heights, Ohio, 112
Sidwell Friends School, 43